Praise for *Life on* t

"It's a story that grabs your interest and quickly boils your blood."
—*The San Diego Union-Tribune*

"Returning to outside life after prison . . . turns out to be full of catch-22s. . . . It's frustrating and confounding. And the madder you are about it, the more you'll know this book has worked its magic on you."
—*Chicago Sun-Times*

"Every once in a while you read something in which the characters are so vivid you find yourself thinking about them even when you're not immersed in the text. *Life on the Outside: The Prison Odyssey of Elaine Bartlett* is such a book. . . . It's journalism in the powerful tradition of Michael Harrington, Jacob Riis, and Margaret Sanger."
—*New York Law Journal*

"*Life on the Outside* encompasses the sweep of black New York, from the heroin-soaked days of Claude Brown's *Manchild in the Promised Land* to the present-day vicissitudes of Rockefeller and workfare. The book is hugely compelling."
—*The Nation*

"A riveting tale of how America's prison-industrial-complex sets up people of color, churns them through the system, and spits them lifelessly back on the streets."
—*High Times*

"Compulsively readable account of a life wasted by the war on drugs but later reclaimed. . . . Elaine's story forces the reader to consider the toll exacted by the myopic and effectively racist public policies that purport to address the social conundrum of illicit drugs in a market economy. Powerful stuff, grievously well rendered."
—*Kirkus Reviews*

"This powerful testament to tenacity raises important questions about this nation's inadequately funded and poorly designed reentry system."
—*Booklist*

"Gonnerman makes an excellent argument for the ways in which the New York criminal justice system, particularly the 'tough on crime' measures imposed in the last three decades, fails poor and less educated people. She skillfully uses Bartlett, a tough, assertive woman who struggles to hold a job and keep her family together after their years of enforced separation, as an exemplar of the wide-ranging impact of incarceration on both ex-cons and the communities they leave behind, a social problem just beginning to be studied."

—*Publishers Weekly*

"*Life on the Outside: The Prison Odyssey of Elaine Bartlett,* a powerful new book by Jennifer Gonnerman, offers an unvarnished glimpse into the life of a former prisoner. It joins a growing list of literature emerging on the issue of prisoner reentry."

—*Bookpage*

"Elaine Bartlett is a real person for whom conservative and liberal nostrums are unreal. Jennifer Gonnerman's searing book will drag you into a world where an ex-con like Bartlett, a mother of four, serves a ridiculous sentence for a first drug offense, then with no confidence, no job, and few skills leaves prison and struggles to survive. Gonnerman crafts a first-rate story with universal meaning from the particulars of Bartlett's life. This luminous book gets inside your brain and doesn't escape."

—Ken Auletta, media correspondent, *The New Yorker,* and author of *Backstory: Inside the Business of News*

"Through the remarkable Elaine Bartlett, Jennifer Gonnerman deftly maps out the middle passage of what is perhaps the most pernicious social injustice of our time. She charts a seemingly impenetrable intersection of problems, fact by brutal fact. Only writing and reporting of this caliber could track the intricate ways in which our nation's prison industry is also family business, and show how harsh sentences don't end on the outside."

—Adrian Nicole LeBlanc, author of *Random Family*

"The Rockefeller Drug Laws were put into effect to show that New York State was tough on crime, but when you look at the case of Elaine Bartlett you don't think 'tough on crime' but 'human rights violation,' 'cruel and unusual punishment,' or just plain 'immoral.'"

—Charles Grodin, actor and author of *I Like It Better When You're Funny*

LIFE ON THE OUTSIDE

LIFE ON THE OUTSIDE

THE PRISON ODYSSEY
of ELAINE BARTLETT

JENNIFER GONNERMAN

PICADOR
FARRAR, STRAUS AND GIROUX
NEW YORK

www.picadorusa.com

Picador® is a U.S. registered trademark and is used by Farrar, Straus and Giroux under license from Pan Books Limited.

For information on Picador Reading Group Guides, as well as ordering, please contact the Trade Marketing department at St. Martin's Press.
Phone: 1-800-221-7945 extension 763
Fax: 212-677-7456
E-mail: trademarketing@stmartins.com

Portions of this book appeared, in different form, in *The Village Voice*.

Grateful acknowledgment is made to Warner Bros. Publications for permission to quote lyrics from "I'm Coming Out" by Nile Rodgers and Bernard Edwards, copyright © 1980 Bernard's Other Music and Tommy Jymi, Inc. All Rights o/b/o Bernard's Other Music administered by Warner-Tamerlane Publishing Corp.

Grateful acknowledgment is also made to the *Times Union* of Albany for permission to reprint an article from its November 9, 1983, edition.

Designed by Debbie Glasserman

Library of Congress Cataloging-in-Publication Data

Gonnerman, Jennifer, 1971–
    Life on the outside : the prison odyssey of Elaine Bartlett / Jennifer Gonnerman.
        p. cm.
Include bibliographical references.
    ISBN 0-312-42457-4
    EAN 978-0312-42457-2

    1. Bartlett, Elaine. 2. Women ex-convicts—United States—Biography. 3. Women prisoners—United States—Biography. 4. Women narcotics dealers—United States—Biography. 5. Bedford Hills Correctional Facility (N.Y.) I. Title.

HV9468.B28G66 2004
365'.43'092—dc22   2003017790

First published in the United States by Farrar, Straus and Giroux

For my grandmothers

Alice Hopkins Weismann

(1911–1998)

and

Elizabeth Tobey Gonnerman Erb

(1915–   )

CONTENTS

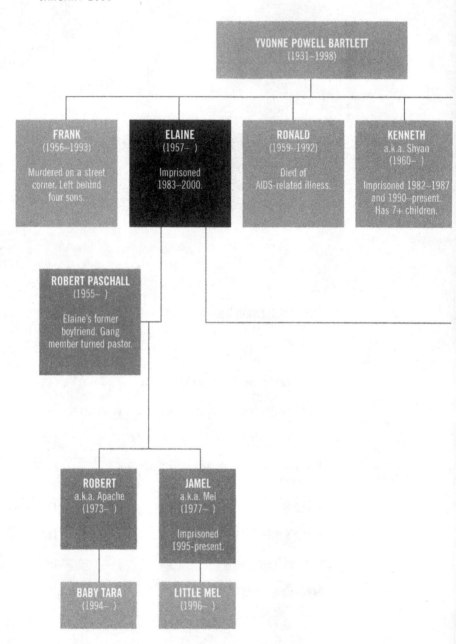

THE BARTLETT FAMILY
JANUARY 2000

YVONNE POWELL BARTLETT
(1931–1998)

FRANK
(1956–1993)

Murdered on a street corner. Left behind four sons.

ELAINE
(1957–)

Imprisoned 1983–2000.

RONALD
(1959–1992)

Died of AIDS-related illness.

KENNETH
a.k.a. Shyan
(1960–)

Imprisoned 1982–1987 and 1990–present. Has 7+ children.

ROBERT PASCHALL
(1955–)

Elaine's former boyfriend. Gang member turned pastor.

ROBERT
a.k.a. Apache
(1973–)

JAMEL
a.k.a. Mel
(1977–)

Imprisoned 1995–present.

BABY TARA
(1994–)

LITTLE MEL
(1996–)

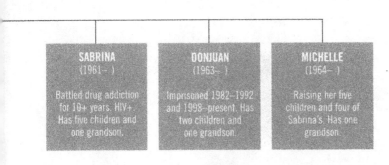

SABRINA
(1961–)

Battled drug addiction for 10+ years. HIV+. Has five children and one grandson.

DONJUAN
(1963–)

Imprisoned 1982–1992 and 1998–present. Has two children and one grandson.

MICHELLE
(1964–)

Raising her five children and four of Sabrina's. Has one grandson.

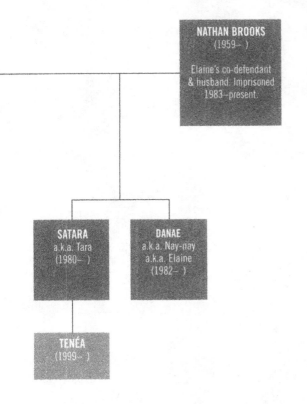

NATHAN BROOKS
(1959–)

Elaine's co-defendant & husband. Imprisoned 1983–present.

SATARA
a.k.a. Tara
(1980–)

DANAE
a.k.a. Nay-nay
a.k.a. Elaine
(1982–)

TENÉA
(1999–)

LIFE ON THE OUTSIDE

Bedford Hills Correctional Facility
Bedford Hills, New York
January 26, 2000

Elaine Bartlett strutted the last few yards to the prison's front door and stepped out into the brisk winter air. This morning, she had made every effort to look good. She wore an electric-purple pantsuit, black suede boots, and several coats of lavender glitter nail polish. Snowflakes landed on her trench coat, but she did not pause to brush them off. As quickly as her three-inch heels would permit, she marched down the icy asphalt driveway.

Once she passed through the front gate, she headed straight for a young man in a gray parka. She dropped her pocketbook on the snow, and threw her arms around him. The two embraced for nearly a minute, rocking back and forth. Nothing could distract them. Not the shrieks of friends and relatives greeting two other women. Not the prison guard standing three feet away. Not the rifle in the window of the watchtower above them.

Elaine placed her hands on her son's cheeks, kissed his lips, then raised herself on her tiptoes and hugged him once more, this time wrapping her arms around his neck. He held her tightly, too, as if to ensure they would never be separated again. Neither of them wanted to rush this reunion. After all, they had been waiting for this moment for sixteen years, two months, two weeks, and four days. By the time

they finally let go of each other, there was a smudge of cranberry lipstick on the collar of his parka.

Elaine had been twenty-six years old when she arrived at this
prison in 1984, with a 20-to-life sentence for selling cocaine. Before
her arrest, she had been living in a housing project in East Harlem
with Apache, then ten, and her three younger children, ages six,
three, and one. Now all her children were grown, and the three oldest
each had a child of their own.

At forty-two, Elaine no longer looked the same as she had when
she first came here. The prison's starchy diet had added a few pounds
to her five-seven frame. A fresh dye job hid her gray roots. Her once-
prominent cheekbones had disappeared, and her eyes were puffy. She
looked as if she hadn't had a good night's sleep in years.

Apache didn't look the same either, of course. When she left him,
he had been a skinny ten-year-old with a mop of curls. Now he was
six-foot-two and weighed 210 pounds. He had a mustache, a receding
hairline, and a silver stud in his left ear. He dressed like any other
twenty-six-year-old, but there was a heaviness about him that made
him seem much older.

As the oldest child, he had tried to fill his mother's role ever since
she had left, struggling to raise his younger brother and sisters while
still a child himself. Over the years, he had come to this maximum-
security prison in Westchester County more times than he could
remember—maybe sixty or seventy, maybe a hundred. Usually, he
brought his sisters, Satara and Danae, with him.

"Where's Tara and Nay-nay?" Elaine asked, referring to them by
their nicknames.

"Tara is asleep and Nay-nay is in school," Apache said.

Elaine's smile disappeared. She considered grilling Apache about
why they had not come, but then thought better of it. At the moment,
she did not need to be reminded of any family tensions.

Glancing across the road, she saw a row of television camera
tripods stuck in a snowbank. She knew they were here for her and the
two other women who had just been released. One month earlier,
two days before Christmas, Governor George Pataki had granted

clemency to the three of them, shaving a few years off each of their sentences so they could go home early. Of the state's seventy thousand prisoners, they were the only ones who had received clemency.

Elaine linked her fingers with Apache's and led him toward the cameras. In all their hours together in the prison visiting room, he had never allowed himself to break down in front of her. Her daughters and mother had cried often, but he never did. Elaine heard that he sometimes cried on the ride home, but she never saw his tears.

This morning, though, his eyes looked watery. Once they crossed the road, she kissed his right cheek, then pressed her face against the crook of his neck. The next time she glanced up, she saw tears starting down his cheeks. She reached up to hold his face in her palms, then used her thumbs to brush the tears away.

"Hey," she said. "It's going to be all right."

For both of them, this morning represented much more than a long-awaited reunion. It marked an enormous shift in responsibility. Now the burden of trying to hold their family together would no longer be his alone. After Elaine returned home, he would not have to play the role of parent to Satara and Danae anymore.

"Congratulations," said a WCBS-TV reporter, pointing his microphone toward Elaine. "What are your thoughts after coming out after so many years?"

"I waited for so long that I'm just thankful the governor gave me my life back," she said, draping one arm around Apache's shoulders. "Today, my life starts again."

Arriving at this prison in the back of a sheriff's van, watching the metal gate open and then close behind her, she felt as if she had died. Nobody inside the prison seemed to care that she had never been arrested before, or that she had left behind four small children. All that mattered were two numbers: the length of her sentence and the ID on her shirt, 84-G-0068.

Now, standing outside the prison's gates, licking snowflakes off her lips, feeling her son's head on her shoulder, she began to feel alive. No longer was she merely a number. Now she was Elaine Bartlett once again.

"What's the first thing you're going to do when you get home?" the reporter asked.

"I'm going to enjoy my family and hold them and just show them how much love I've carried all these years, and let them know that without them I wouldn't have made it," she said.

"Do you feel that society will let you live down your crime when you leave here? Are you worried about people judging you?"

"I'm not worried about them judging me. Even though I went through a lot of pain and suffering, I took everything good as well as bad and I'm bringing that out with me. So I can stand here and say I am very proud of the woman I am today, that I was able to keep a bond with my family despite being incarcerated and be the best mother that I could be from behind these walls."

Elaine did not reveal her ambitions to the reporters circling around, but when she was alone with Apache, she poked him under the chin. "Hold your head up," she said. "I'm very proud of you, and I'm going to make you very proud of me." As if to reinforce her point, she leaned over and kissed him on the cheek. "We're going to change the whole cycle of the Bartlett family for the next generation," she said.

She was determined to keep not only herself out of prison but everyone else in her family, too. It would not be easy. Prison, drugs, poverty, and violence had all been part of her family for as long as she could remember. At the moment, she had two brothers in the state prison system and her younger son was on Rikers Island, awaiting trial in a drug-conspiracy case.

While she was in prison, she had earned a two-year college degree. Now she wanted the same for her children and grandchildren—for them to finish high school and for at least a few of them to go to college, too. She knew that Apache would be her biggest ally in this campaign. He had never gone to prison, did not use drugs, and had never even tried marijuana. Recently, he had started working as a basketball coach at a Catholic high school in Manhattan.

The reporters packed up their equipment and headed for their cars, but Elaine was not ready to go. She slipped off her trench coat and swung it over one shoulder. Then she pranced back and forth atop the wet snow in the parking lot, showing off her new pantsuit and her high-heeled boots. Just in case anyone was watching from the prison's windows, she wanted to make sure they got a good look. Whenever anyone talked about her in the future, she wanted them to recall how she had strutted out of here with her head held high.

"Do you like my outfit?" she asked the smattering of people who were left. "I'm a free woman now. It's all good."

After collecting a few more compliments, she strode over to a van in the parking lot. Her friend Lora Tucker sat behind the steering wheel. Elaine slid into the back, next to Apache. The van lurched out of the parking lot, and a few minutes later, they were all hurtling down the Saw Mill River Parkway, heading south toward her welcome-home party.

"I cannot believe it," Elaine said. "I did not think I was going to survive this." She grabbed Apache's hand and curled her fingers around his. "It's all over," she said. "No more sleepless nights, right?" She reached over and stroked his cheek. "No more sleepless nights."

After so many years in prison, being able to touch her son felt like a luxury. She no longer had to brace herself for that dreaded moment when a guard would walk toward them and say, "Hurry up. You've got five minutes." In the backseat of the van, she kept her fingers entwined with his. Only by holding on to him could she make this moment feel real, and convince herself that freedom was no longer just a dream.

In America's cities, former prisoners are everywhere. Seated across from you on the subway. Pushing the cart next to yours in the supermarket. Standing behind you in line at the movies. It is impossible to pick out these ex-prisoners, of course. Once they are no longer required to wear cotton jumpsuits or ID cards pinned to their chests, they look just like everybody else.

The reality is inescapable: America has become a nation of ex-cons. Thirteen million people have been convicted of a felony and spent some time locked up. That's almost 7 percent of U.S. adult residents. If all of these people were placed on an island together, that island would have a population larger than many countries, including Sweden, Bolivia, Senegal, Greece, or Somalia.

In some ways, America's transformation into a nation of ex-cons is not surprising. In the 1970s and 1980s, a nationwide "war on drugs," combined with tougher sentencing policies, laid the groundwork for an unprecedented prison boom. Since 1970, the number of people in U.S. prisons has grown more than six-fold. In 2002, the nation's jail and prison population exceeded two million for the first time.

There is another side to this prison boom story that few people have wanted to talk about: Almost everybody who goes to prison eventually comes home. The same legislators who called for tough-on-crime laws rarely considered the long-term consequences of locking up so many people. And so, as America's prison population ballooned, there were few preparations made for the day when nearly all these prisoners would be set free.

Our nation's prisons now release more than 600,000 people a year. That's more than the entire population of Boston, Seattle, or Washington, D.C. And this number continues to grow, fueling an invisible exodus: men and women leaving their prisons and moving back to the places where they once lived.

Most prisoners come from urban areas, and most return to the same neighborhoods they left. Thirty thousand prisoners return to Los Angeles County every year. Twenty thousand return to New York City. Fifteen thousand go back to Chicago. Within these cities, ex-prisoners are usually concentrated in just a few neighborhoods, places like the South Side of Chicago or Manhattan's Lower East Side.

Men and women come back from prison changed people. They carry scars, visible and invisible, from their years behind bars. Some come home with HIV or Hepatitis C or tuberculosis. They have new friends, new enemies, maybe a new gang affiliation. All the frustration and rage that has built up inside them while they were locked up comes home with them, too.

In prison, they may have kicked an addiction, or they may have

picked up a drug habit they'd never had before. They may have acquired a new resolve to abandon their criminal ways and turn their
lives around. Or they may have learned from other prisoners how to
become a better criminal—a more skilled car thief or dope dealer or
gunrunner.

Most ex-prisoners have no money, few job skills, little education,
and a history of addiction. An estimated 16 percent suffer from a serious mental illness. With little or no assistance, these men and women
are expected to rebuild their lives and stay out of prison. Not surprisingly, the odds of success are slim: Forty percent of people released
from prison are back behind bars within three years because of a new
crime or a parole violation.

Eighty percent of people leaving prison are supervised by parole officers. In many ways, parole functions as a sort of invisible prison.
Parolees cannot get high, skip appointments with their officers, stay
out past curfew, socialize with other felons, or leave town without permission. Any violation of these or many other rules could earn them
a trip back to jail.

Even for ex-prisoners who stay out of trouble and get off parole,
their punishment does not end. Today a felony record functions like
an invisible scarlet letter, ensuring that former inmates are treated as
outcasts whose debt to society can never be fully repaid. By law, former prisoners in some states may be denied public housing, student
loans, a driver's license, parental rights, welfare benefits, certain types
of jobs, as well as the right to vote.

These myriad restrictions have transformed America into a two-tier
society, in which millions of ostensibly free people are prohibited
from sharing rights and privileges enjoyed by everybody else. The division between these two worlds falls along lines of race and ethnicity.
Nearly two-thirds of people leaving prison are African American or
Hispanic.

Nowadays, almost every criminal-justice dollar is spent on locking
people in prisons and keeping them there—and very little is spent on
transforming them back into civilians. Recently, the U.S. Department
of Justice did allot $100 million to state prison agencies to prepare in-

mates for their release. This is a marked change from the past, but it is still a minuscule amount compared to the $55 billion spent annually on the entire prison system.

In the last few years, the phenomenon of people leaving prison has become a popular topic in academic and criminal-justice circles, where it is referred to as "reentry." Experts debate the subject at national conferences; trade journals publish papers on it. These public discussions usually leave out the voices of former prisoners, relying instead on statistics. But the true story of America's exodus of ex-cons cannot be told only with numbers.

Coming home from prison is about learning to control your temper without using your fists. It's about finding a place to sleep. It's about remembering how to feed yourself. It's about accumulating a wardrobe. It's about rediscovering the opposite sex. It's about finding a way, legal or illegal, to make money. It's about trying to earn respect from the children you abandoned.

This book illuminates the hidden journey home from prison by documenting one woman's experience. In some ways, Elaine Bartlett is not representative of people leaving prison. Eighty-eight percent are male. Very few have earned a college degree. And virtually nobody wins clemency. The average prison term is twenty-five months—much shorter than the sixteen years Elaine spent behind bars.

In other ways, though, she is typical. Like about one-third of prisoners coming home, she served time for a drug crime. Like nearly half of all inmates, she is African American. And like the vast majority of people who go to prison, she grew up in poverty.

This book chronicles Elaine Bartlett's odyssey, from the streets to prison and back again. Parts One and Two recount how she got into prison and how she got out, covering the period from 1983 to 2000. Parts Three and Four follow her after she returns home, from 2000 to 2003, detailing her efforts to begin her life once again.

While no one prisoner's homecoming story is truly representative, there are many common threads. Often this story is actually two tales. There is the solitary journey of the ex-prisoner returning to a changed world. And if she is fortunate enough to have relatives waiting for her, there is the family's story, too.

Just as Elaine's imprisonment permanently altered the lives of her four children, her homecoming also changed their lives. This book is about all that they, too, endured. In the end, it is the story of the Bartlett family—a story about not only prison and poverty, but also departures and reunions, dreams and disappointments, loneliness and love.

PART ONE

An Easy $2,500
1983–1984

Twenty-six-year-old Elaine Bartlett cracked open the bedroom closet and surveyed her options. She picked out a T-shirt, a pair of Jordache jeans, a leather belt, and a brown knit sweater with suede patches on the elbows. She fastened a thin chain around her neck and slid a pair of gold hoops in her ears. Then she checked herself in the mirror. The day before, she had gotten a wet and set; the plastic rollers were still in her hair. She picked a beige silk scarf out of a drawer and tied it around her head.

Barefoot, she headed down the hall. She loved how the plush carpet felt between her toes. People had told her she was crazy to put carpet everywhere in her apartment, even in the kitchen, but she had been dreaming of wall-to-wall carpet for years. She had not been able to afford an interior decorator, of course. Instead, she had studied photos she had ripped out of glossy magazines. After seeing wall-to-wall carpet in the pictures of every celebrity's home, she had been determined to settle for nothing less.

There had not been enough money to buy furniture for every room, but she was especially proud of the living room, which she had done all in white: three white leather sofas, a white leather bar (even though she didn't drink), and, of course, white carpeting. Around the perimeter were statues: a tiger, an elephant, a giraffe. There was also plenty of glass. The record player had glass doors, and there were two glass tables. Not long ago, there had been three glass tables, including one with a zebra statue atop it. Then one day, her younger son, Jamel, had decided to play cowboy, jumped on top of the zebra, and crashed through the glass.

Friends had warned her about decorating her apartment with so much glass when she had four young children, but she hadn't listened. She thought her home looked glamorous. Anyone who saw a photograph of it certainly would not think she was broke, and that was precisely the point. Reality, of course, was a different story. Her apartment was located in the Wagner Houses, a large city housing project in East Harlem. Her rent was only $127, but she scrambled every month to make the payment.

To support her family, she collected welfare and worked off the books at a beauty parlor. Some nights she also poured drinks at a local bar. Still, the cost of caring for her four children—of buying food, clothes, and diapers—regularly exceeded her income. She got a little help from her boyfriend, Nathan Brooks, the father of her two daughters, but he was often in jail. As for the carpet and furniture, she hadn't actually paid for them all by herself. She'd had them on layaway for almost two years, then convinced her best friend, a drug dealer named Littleboy, to pay the rest of the bill.

Every year, her scramble for money intensified in the weeks before Thanksgiving. Today was November 8, 1983; Thanksgiving was only sixteen days away. Organizing a huge feast was a Bartlett family tradition, and this year she wanted to invite everyone over to her place. Now that she had all this new furniture, she was eager to show it off. The party promised to be expensive, but in recent weeks she had stumbled upon a plan to earn some extra cash.

All weekend long, Nathan had told her that her plan was a mistake. "It doesn't sound right," he'd said over and over. But now she did not have time to discuss the matter anymore. She dressed her daughters, three-year-old Satara and one-year-old Danae. Then she took them over to Nathan's mother, who lived next door. Her sons, ten-year-old

Apache and six-year-old Jamel, were already at her own mother's apartment downtown. It was nearly 8:00 a.m.; she had to hurry. As Nathan watched, she grabbed her pocketbook and marched out.

Most mornings, she headed to work, walking north three blocks, then west on 125th Street until she reached the 125 Barber Shop and Beauty Shop. Often she had at least two children with her. She could never make it down those four long blocks on 125th Street without sparking a small commotion. "Hey, Big Red!" the country boys would shout when she strolled by. "See her calves? She got good strong calves. She's a breeder. She can have some more kids. She ain't finished yet."

The men on the street always called her "Big Red"—the same nickname they gave every big-boned, light-skinned woman. The name stuck. Everyone at the beauty parlor called her Big Red, too. All day long, customers appeared in the doorway and asked, "Is Big Red in?" Four barber chairs filled the front of the shop, and a row of shoe-shine stands lined one wall. Elaine's customers knew that to get to the beauty parlor, they had to walk through the barbershop and into a back room.

She had been working here for nearly nine years, though she did not have a hairdresser's license. She rented a booth for fifty-five dollars a day, then kept everything else she earned. On a good day, she left with two or three hundred dollars.

While she worked, her children played at the arcade next door, with the older children minding the younger ones. Whenever they needed more quarters, they sprinted through the barbershop to find her. And whenever she got a break, she went next door, joining them in a game of Pac-Man or Frogger.

The barbershop was always buzzing with the news of the day. Nicky Barnes, the notorious drug kingpin, had been testifying recently in court, squealing on his former business partners. One year earlier, the movie 48 Hours had opened, and some people were calling Eddie Murphy the new Richard Pryor. And now Jesse Jackson had just announced that he was going to run for president. To most people here, he was far more appealing than the current crop of politicians: Mayor Koch, Governor Cuomo, and President Reagan.

Like many businesses along 125th Street, this barbershop was a magnet for anyone trying to make a dollar. Numbers runners stopped in all day long, taking bets from employees and customers alike. Boosters parked a van out front and walked in with armloads of stolen goods: sneakers, boots, underwear, cosmetics, socks, radios, even slabs of meat. Elaine rarely had to go shopping anymore; everything she needed, she could buy here for discount rates.

Almost everyone who came into the beauty parlor was black. One of the few exceptions was Charlie. He was the friend of a coworker, and he stopped in all the time. Elaine figured he had some sort of hustle, just like everybody else. Maybe he was a numbers runner; maybe a small-time drug dealer. She had seen him at parties, and he was always getting high. Although she'd known him for only a few months, she considered him a friend.

Charlie knew Elaine was always looking for a way to make some extra money. Four days earlier, at 10:30 on a Friday evening, he had visited her apartment to talk about a deal he wanted her to do for him. While her boyfriend Nathan was in the back room, Charlie had spelled out his plan. He knew a couple of people in Albany who wanted to buy a package of cocaine, but they didn't want to come to New York City. If she carried the package to Albany, a two-and-a-half-hour train ride away, he would pay her $2,500. The way he described it, the plan sounded perfectly simple.

Elaine flagged a taxicab and told the driver to take her to Grand Central Terminal. Once she got there, she looked for Tracy, Charlie's friend. She had spoken to Tracy on the phone that morning, and now she saw her standing near the ticket booth. Tracy handed her a shopping bag containing a package of cocaine, covered with a brown paper wrapper. Elaine went into the bathroom, loosened her belt, unzipped her fly, and shoved the sack down the front of her jeans.

The package contained four ounces of cocaine. It was enough coke for a one-hundred-person party, or to keep a daily user satisfied for a few months. Elaine patted the powder to flatten it out. Then she tugged up the zipper and tightened her belt once again, a little looser this time.

When she walked back toward the ticket booth, she saw Nathan. She was not too surprised to discover that he had followed her here. She knew he was worried about her going to Albany by herself. She'd never been there before, and neither had he. By now he'd given up trying to stop her from going. He figured that at least if he went, too, he'd be able to make sure nothing happened to her.

Nathan was twenty-four, two years younger than her, but he knew more about the drug business than she did. To him, every aspect of Charlie's plan sounded suspicious. Nathan was used to selling ten- or twenty-five-dollar bags of heroin—not four-ounce packages with a street value of a few thousand dollars. He had sold drugs on Harlem street corners, not carried packages to unfamiliar cities. Charlie's skin color made him nervous, too. He had played basketball with white men, but he had never done business with them.

He had told Elaine all his concerns, but she was convinced that she knew what she was doing. After all, she had been living on the periphery of Harlem's drug world since she was a child. She had never been arrested, but she had been going to jails for nearly ten years, visiting her brothers and her boyfriends. Like most people she knew, she had tried cocaine many times, snorting a line or two at parties. But she preferred marijuana, which she smoked like some people smoke cigarettes. Since age thirteen, she had been getting high three or four times a day.

Standing in front of the ticket window, she tried to figure out which ticket she was supposed to buy. She spoke to the clerk, then purchased two one-way tickets on the 8:45 a.m. train, known as the Maple Leaf. She did not have enough money for round-trip tickets, but she figured she and Nathan would be able to get home with the money Charlie was going to pay her.

That morning, she and Nathan were both tired. They did not talk much on the train, and he soon dozed off. She was too nervous to sleep. Twice, she went to the bathroom to check on the package in her pants. She wanted to make sure it wasn't leaking.

At 11:12 a.m., the Maple Leaf pulled into the station near Albany. Compared to Grand Central, the Albany-Rensselaer station was tiny. Elaine walked in and found a row of pay phones to her right. She called Charlie, then headed into the bathroom to check on the package once again. When she emerged, Charlie was in the station.

"C'mon," he said. "I've got a cab right here. Your train isn't going to go back for another two hours. I'm going to show you around."

Nathan and Elaine followed Charlie outside and into a yellow cab. Immediately, Elaine unbuckled her belt, pulled the sack from her pants, and handed it to Charlie. Now she figured her job was done. All she had to do was wait for her train back to New York City and collect her money from Charlie.

With Charlie giving instructions, the cabdriver crossed the Hudson River from Troy into Albany. The car navigated a maze of freeways and then headed north along Route 9. In the backseat, Elaine marveled at the scenery. "This is Albany?" she asked. "Oh my God, it's clean here." She had only been to upstate New York a few times. On each visit, her destination had been the same: the visiting room of a state prison.

As the cab continued along Route 9, they crossed over the border from the city of Albany into the town of Colonie. There were no high-rise apartment buildings here. No people hanging out on the sidewalks. No angry horns. Instead, two-story houses lined the road, with spacious yards and manicured hedges, paved driveways and painted mailboxes.

The ten-minute drive ended in the parking lot of what Elaine thought was an apartment complex. In fact, it was the Monte Mario Motel, a low-budget place that rented rooms by the day and the month. Charlie led Nathan and Elaine inside, up the stairs to the second floor, and into his room. Then he handed her a key. "I got you a separate room so you can chill out and wait," he said.

Elaine and Nathan headed down the corridor to their room. Like

Charlie's room, it had pink walls, a sink in one corner, two queen-size beds, and a television. It did not look like anyone lived here and so Elaine searched for clues to exactly where she was. When she looked out the window, she did not see a sign for a motel. All she saw was a parking lot.

Not long afterward, Charlie knocked on the door and invited them back into his room to watch television. By now, his friend Rich had shown up. Elaine had met Rich once before, at her apartment four days earlier. She and Nathan sat down next to each other on a bed, then leaned back atop the flower-patterned cover. Soon they were both asleep.

Less than an hour later, shortly before 1:00 p.m., Elaine woke to the sound of strange voices. Sitting up and rubbing the sleep out of her eyes, she surveyed the room. Now there were two more people here—a man and a woman. She saw the package of cocaine, minus its brown wrapper, lying on a table in one corner. Next to it was a scale. She did not know where the scale had come from. And she did not remember seeing the coke there before she dozed off.

The man wore jeans and a T-shirt. He looked about thirty and had a droopy mustache and wavy brown hair that hung past his shoulders. The woman, who appeared younger, was also clad in jeans. They were both white. The fact that Elaine and Nathan were the only black people in the room made Elaine very uncomfortable.

She heard Charlie talking with the man and woman. Then he turned to face her. "Elaine, these are my friends Ken and Sue," he said. "And Ken and Sue, this is Elaine and Nathan." Elaine watched Ken lift the plastic sack onto the scale, then lean close to examine it.

Ken pulled out a small plastic vial and scooped a tiny amount of powder into it. Then he turned toward her and Nathan and shook the vial. The powder inside turned pink, then blue. "What's that?" Nathan asked. Ken explained that it measured the quality of the cocaine.

After a brief discussion about the price of the cocaine, Ken sent Sue out to the parking lot. When she returned, she placed a stack of money, wrapped in paper, on the table next to the scale. For a moment, the whole group—Elaine, Nathan, Charlie, Rich, Sue, and Ken—beheld the powder and cash together. Then they heard a knock.

Rich walked over to the door and opened it. Suddenly a pack of men burst in. With their pistols and shotguns drawn, they shouted, "Down on the floor!"

CHAPTER 2

As Elaine would later learn, Charlie's name was not actually Charlie at all. His real name was George Deets. Just by looking at him, it was not easy to figure out where he was from. His olive skin led some people to assume he was Caucasian or Hispanic. In fact, he was Lebanese. Though his speech was peppered with the jargon of Harlem, he had actually grown up in Mechanicville, a small town north of Albany.

He had bushy black hair, a thick beard, and a tattoo on his right bicep of a skull with wings and red eyes. He was only five-nine and not very muscular, but he cultivated the persona of a gangster. He often quoted his favorite movie, *Scarface*. And when he was in New York City, he liked to eat at Umbertos Clam House in Little Italy, since it had been the site of a famous mob slaying.

Anyone who knew George Deets knew that he loved getting high. The more often, the better. His appetite for drugs seemed insatiable. Some addicts might go through a quarter-ounce of cocaine in a week or two; George could ingest that much in a single night. One of his favorite pastimes was speedballing, the sometimes-deadly practice of injecting heroin and coke. "George is here for a good time, not for a long time," his friend Richard Zagorski often said.

Everyone who worked in the narcotics unit at Troop G knew George and Rich. Troop G was the Albany-area office of the New York State Police. Since the 1970s the two men had worked off and on as informants for the narcotics unit, setting up undercover drug buys. Rich had been an informant since the early 1970s, while George had started several years later.

They made an unlikely pair. Rich was thirty-seven, while George was twenty-eight. Rich lived with his wife and two young sons; George still lived with his parents. They had met a decade earlier, when George was in high school and hung out at a motorcycle-repair shop that Rich owned. Ever since, they'd been good friends.

Among the several dozen informants who worked for Troop G, George Deets stood out. Not only did he know all the players in the local drug underworld, but he had many contacts in New York City. His ability to lure dealers from Harlem to Albany enabled him to set up larger deals than other local informants. Not too many men from upstate New York could befriend people on the streets of Harlem without everyone assuming they worked for the police.

George Deets's work for the state police almost always began the same way: He got arrested, then picked up the phone to call Troop G. He would offer to set up a drug deal, in the hope of getting his own sentence reduced. "Georgie set up a lot of good deals for us," says Senior Investigator Donald R. Weise, former co-leader of the narcotics unit. "If he told you something, basically, it was going to go down. He was an honest informant."

George was one of Weise's favorite informants. "I liked Georgie," he says. "I would say he was pretty intelligent. I'm sure if Georgie'd had a job and went to work, he would've done very well. He wasn't a real bad guy. He wouldn't kill anybody. He wouldn't stick any place up. He wouldn't do a burglary. He was a drug dealer, a likable drug dealer."

Not everyone in Troop G agreed with this assessment. "He was as bad as anybody that we dealt with," recalls Kenneth T. Cook, a former undercover officer who worked with Deets in the early 1980s. "Some informants work because they are trying to work a nut off;

they've been arrested, and in order to get a break on their sentencing, they cooperate. Other people do it for money. George did it for money at times. George did it because he had to work a nut off. And there were other times the only reason he would be doing it was because he was either trying to knock off some competition or to enhance his position in the drug scene."

Every time George set up a deal for the state police, Cook thought he tried to bend the rules. "If George had the opportunity to steal the dope on you, he would," Cook says. Cook did not often carry a gun when he worked undercover, but he always did when he worked with George. It was not hard for him to imagine George blowing his cover in a room full of armed drug dealers, pointing him out and announcing, "He's a cop." Cook often warned George about the consequences of such a betrayal. "If you ever set me up," the officer would say, gesturing toward his holster, "the first chamber is yours."

George Deets started selling drugs when he was still in high school. At that time, in the mid-1970s, Rich was running an elaborate operation importing marijuana from Mexico to upstate New York. Mexican families carried marijuana over the border to Arizona, where workers hid it in the back of an El Camino or packed it in boxes to be shipped via UPS. At first, George worked as one of Rich's distributors in New York. After George graduated from high school, he began flying to Arizona to set up deals and prepare loads.

Marijuana prices rose through the decade, and by the late 1970s, Rich and George were buying marijuana for $50 or $60 a pound, then selling it in upstate New York for about $250 a pound. Rich did not keep records of all his transactions, but he estimates he was importing about five hundred pounds a month. The operation grossed about a million dollars a year.

Despite their sizable profit margin, George was not satisfied. He urged Rich to expand their operation to cocaine, which promised greater profits and livelier adventures. George traveled to Colombia aboard a banana boat, leaving from the port of Albany. When he returned a couple of months later, he brought back a pound of high-quality cocaine.

George returned to Colombia several times by airplane. He made contacts, set up drop points, and laid the groundwork for a new trafficking operation. He and Rich arranged for the cocaine to travel from Colombia to Florida aboard a private plane. Then they had workers drive it up to New York.

They stored the cocaine in locked steel boxes, which they buried near George's parents' home in Mechanicville. This quiet part of Saratoga County offered plenty of good hiding places along abandoned logging trails and in the parking lot of a shuttered paper mill. Rich's challenge was to get the cocaine to their distributors before much of it disappeared up George's nose. George had a habit of digging up their steel boxes, then snorting the cocaine himself.

In the spring of 1981, George was arrested at the Albany County Airport with a packet of heroin in his wallet and a plastic bag of cocaine in the front of his pants. He was charged with a felony. If convicted, he could have received a prison sentence of 8⅓ to 25 years. The police offered him a deal: Switch sides and work as an informant. George agreed. The prosecutor allowed him to plead guilty to a lesser charge, and his sentence was reduced to five years probation.

Meanwhile, he and Rich continued to bring cocaine into New York; some of it came directly from Colombia, though not all of it did. They preferred to do their sales in upstate New York, where the profits were better and they knew most of the players. But there was not enough demand in these small towns for all of their product. They sold about 70 percent of their coke to distributors upstate, and George sold the rest in New York City. During their busiest years, the early to mid-1980s, Rich estimates they brought a kilo of cocaine into New York every two weeks, and that their profit was about $1 million a year.

Racking up drug arrests was the job of the state troopers assigned to the narcotics unit. Nobody walked over to their desks and handed them a memo spelling out specific quotas, but everyone knew they were expected to get arrests and convictions. The higher the conviction rate, the better. The agency's annual report published these numbers, which politicians and agency officials could then use both to illustrate the state police's successes and to argue for its expansion.

Like police officers everywhere, Troop G's officers needed informants in order to make drug arrests. This was a relationship that George understood well and regularly exploited for his own ends.

For any cocaine trafficker, telling the police about your trips to Colombia hardly sounds like a smart move, but George's modus operandi included many partial revelations. He often regaled Senior Investigator Weise with tales of his adventures in Colombia, bragging about the high-level dealers he knew and how he had even managed to find a "peep" down there. "What's a peep?" Weise asked. It was a police officer who could be paid off to facilitate a drug deal, George said.

Sometimes Weise pressed him for details. "What are you and Richie up to?" he would ask.

"Nothing," George would say.

The interrogation usually went no further. Weise considered George a valuable informant; he certainly did not want to scare him away. "You don't want to push Georgie too hard, because you'd lose him," Weise explains. "So it was kind of like a cat-and-mouse game."

In the back of Weise's mind, however, there was little mystery about why George had traveled to Colombia in the first place. "He wasn't going to Colombia to buy coffee, you know," Weise says. "You only go to Colombia for one thing."

George was always careful not to reveal any specific details about his own trafficking operation. He said just enough to whet Weise's appetite. "I'm working on a big deal for you," he would say.

He made it clear that he was not talking about setting up another four-ounce sale, or even a pound sale. He was talking about many kilos—the sort of drug bust that comes along only once in a career for a trooper in upstate New York. If George delivered on his promise, if he managed to lure a kingpin from Colombia to Albany County, the possible payoffs for Weise would be many: front-page headlines, promotions, award ceremonies.

"He had been to Colombia many times, or so he said," Weise recalls. "And I believe him, because he made numerous calls. We were trying to set up a major cocaine deal with people direct from Colombia, but it never materialized." From Weise's office, George made taped phone calls to Colombia, bantering in Spanish with various associates. "He had contacts in Colombia," Weise says. "He had phone numbers. As I recall, he didn't look in his book."

At the time, Weise was so convinced of George's ability to set up this deal that he got authorization to transfer $750,000 into an account in his name at an Albany bank. "Supposedly, from what Georgie said, the people in Colombia, through their contacts in a bank in Colombia, could check up here," Weise says. "They could supposedly call the bank and say, 'Hey, does Don Weise, at such and such address, have money in the bank?' And they'd say, 'Yes he does.' This was to show the people in Colombia—whoever they sent up—that I didn't have twelve dollars. That I had the money to pay for the keys we were buying."

Not everyone in the narcotics unit knew about George's plan. Cook says he heard that George might have gone to Colombia once or twice, but he does not remember a promise to bring Colombian dealers to Albany County. "George was always trying to make it look like he was the man in the know," Cook says. "Honestly, I think that's why Don liked him. Because he always envisioned that one day George was going to walk in and have this tremendous case—big kilos and kilos, a truckload of cocaine being delivered to Albany, New York."

George's cozy relationship with Weise and the state police provided the perfect cover for his own crimes. Twenty years later, after being told about George's cocaine trafficking, Cook does not sound surprised. "He was using Don Weise and the state police to protect himself in case he got caught," Cook says. "Then Weise would have to vouch for him, saying, 'Yeah, he's my informant. We knew he was going to Colombia, doing business for us in Colombia.' It's like hedging your bet."

. . .

In the fall of 1983, Rich Zagorski received a phone call from a friend who had just been caught with a few pounds of marijuana. The friend was panicked. He did not want to go to state prison, and the only way out was to become a snitch, which he also did not want to do. He knew about Rich's relationship with the state police, and he begged him to intervene.

The friend was a distributor for Rich and George, though on this occasion he had been arrested with marijuana he'd bought from someone else. Rich agreed to help, but because the friend had been busted with a competitor's marijuana, the favor would not be free. After his friend agreed to pay $10,000, Rich dialed Troop G.

He told the cops about his friend's arrest, and then he proposed a deal: He and George would lure a drug dealer to Albany from New York City if their friend could get his sentence reduced. This way, the troopers would get another arrest, and Rich's friend would avoid state prison.

"I told them, 'I know we can get someone,' " Rich recalls, "and they said, 'Bring 'em up and we'll talk to the district attorney.' "

This arrangement was unusual, but it was not the only time Rich had offered his services to Troop G on behalf of somebody else. George was willing to help, too, since Rich had promised him half the money.

By now, Rich and George had mastered the rules of the snitch game. They knew they could not simply go to New York City, purchase cocaine, and bring it back to Troop G's office. They had to set up a deal in upstate New York. An undercover officer would be the buyer, and the deal had to involve enough cocaine or heroin to constitute the highest-level felony, known as an A-1. Possession of at least four ounces or sale of at least two ounces qualifies as an A-1.

Troop G's undercover officers preferred to do buys on their home turf, in Albany County. Often they did their deals at local hotels, like the Howard Johnson on Route 7. This was not merely a matter of convenience. At the time, Albany County had two of the state's toughest judges. The troopers knew that anyone arrested for a drug crime in

Albany County was much more likely to be convicted. Albany County had the highest incarceration rate in the state among counties with any volume of cases.

To the officers in Troop G, it did not matter much who they caught. All that mattered was that whomever they arrested had a sizable amount of narcotics with them. It didn't matter if they were a first-time courier or a small-time dealer. From the police's point of view, every arrest and conviction was considered a success. And, of course, the easier the arrest, the better. "They didn't care who it was or what the circumstances were of why they got busted," Rich says. "They just cared about the numbers."

On Friday, November 4, 1983, Rich picked up George in his champagne-colored 1983 Chrysler Cordoba, got on the New York State Thruway, and headed south toward Harlem. It was a trip they had made many times before, and as usual they were shopping for anyone willing to carry drugs up to Albany. While some people invariably turned them down, a surprising number did not. "It was too easy to do, almost," Rich explains. "You go down there, sweet-talk them, flash them money, and they're on their way up."

On this night, George knocked on the door of Elaine Bartlett's apartment around 8:30 p.m. Her boyfriend, Nathan Brooks, answered. George had never stopped by before; usually he saw Elaine only when he visited the beauty parlor where she worked. Nate eyeballed the strangers, told them Elaine was not home, and shut the door. George and Rich rode down in the elevator. Soon after they left the building, George spotted Elaine, and she brought them upstairs with her.

Four days later, both Nathan and Elaine were laying facedown on a bed at the Monte Mario Motel, their wrists cuffed behind their backs. From the time the undercover officers walked into the room, the bust took less than ten minutes.

The setup could not have gone more smoothly. The troopers did not have to spend weeks or months hanging out on street corners, trying to win the trust of suspicious dealers. Instead, all they had to do was show up. In this case, the dealer was not only unarmed, she was so docile that she was asleep when the troopers arrived. Rich had promised only one arrest, and now the officers had two.

George and Rich also made out well. When George had rented two motel rooms, it was not to give Elaine and Nathan a place to rest, as he had claimed; he had done it in order to steal some of the cocaine for himself. While Elaine and Nathan napped in one room, a friend of George's had sneaked into the other room, taken some of the cocaine, and replaced it with inositol, a baby laxative and popular cutting agent.

By the time the officers arrived, the friend was gone and the cocaine still weighed four ounces, enough to constitute an A-1 felony. For the police's purposes, the purity of the cocaine did not matter.

The next day, Elaine Bartlett and Nathan Brooks appeared in the *Times Union* of Albany, on page B-4.

Couple held in cocaine sale

LATHAM—State Police arrested a Manhattan couple Tuesday night in connection with the sale of a quarter-pound of cocaine to undercover troopers, State Police said.

Nathan Augustis Brooks, 34, and Elaine Bartlett, 36, were charged with first-degree criminal sale of controlled substances.

Troopers said the pair was arrested in a "Latham area motel."

They were arraigned in Colonie Town Court before Judge Philip Caponera and sent to Albany County Jail without bail.

The arrest was made in conjunction with Colonie Police and federal Drug Enforcement Agency officers, troopers said.

While this article got Elaine and Nathan's ages wrong, all the other details were accurate. But, of course, there was no mention of the confidential informants who had set them up. It was the sort of news item readers would have seen many times before and quickly forgotten.

CHAPTER 3

Elaine stood and faced the camera, holding a white card in front of her chest. On the card, somebody had written her name; her police ID number, 478-G-13; and the date, 11-8-83. A row of horizontal lines marked the wall behind her. The chart indicated that she was five-foot-nine, though she was actually five-seven. The cops had made her remove her rollers before they took her photo, and so now her hair was full and wavy, adding two inches to her height.

She still wore the same outfit she had put on that morning: T-shirt, jeans, gold hoop earrings. But now she looked scared and confused, her eyes darting off to the side, away from the camera. There was no hint of the confidence or stubbornness that had propelled her out of her apartment and onto a train to Albany, a package of cocaine stuffed in her jeans. Now she held the card with her name on it so tentatively, it looked as if it were about to slip out of her fingers.

She had thought that by now she would be home, or at least riding on a train back to New York City. Instead, she was at the state police barracks in Albany County, posing for a mug shot for the first time in her life. She had seen Nate, but there was no sign of Charlie. The cops had put cuffs on him when they barged into the motel room, but that was the last time she had seen him.

After she and Nathan were photographed and fingerprinted, the cops whisked them into the back of a trooper car and drove them through town. They parked in front of a two-story house on a quiet suburban street. The officers opened the back doors for Elaine and Nathan, then escorted them across the grass, through the front door, and into a spacious kitchen. Apparently, the town courthouse was closed. On days like this one, the house of the town judge doubled as the local court.

The judge's kitchen looked like any other suburban kitchen: light green linoleum, yellow wallpaper, a refrigerator covered with magnets. The judge invited Elaine and Nathan to sit down at his kitchen table. Then he read the charges against them: sale of a controlled substance. The arraignment lasted only a few minutes. Afterward, the cops led Elaine and Nathan back to the car and then drove them to the Albany County Jail.

By now, it was late afternoon, and Elaine had been away from home for nearly ten hours. All she could think about were her children. They would all be wondering where she was. She assumed that her daughters were still at Nathan's mother's apartment, but she was supposed to have fetched them by now.

Elaine was told she could make one phone call. The last person she wanted to call was her mother, but she had no choice. She needed her mother to pick up her daughters. And, of course, she needed a much larger favor, too. She needed her mother to take care of all four children until she could get back to New York City. She did not know when that might be, but she hoped she would get home in time for Thanksgiving.

The phone rang in Yvonne Bartlett's kitchen, and everyone who was home heard what happened next. "What did you do?" she shouted into the receiver. "Where have you been? Where the hell are my granddaughters? I know you're not with that motherfucker Nathan! I knew he was going to get you in trouble!" Elaine was Yvonne's second child, her oldest daughter, the dependable one, the one who never got into any serious trouble. But now, here she was on the other end of the line, calling from the Albany County Jail.

Within the last eighteen months, Yvonne had received this same "I just got arrested" phone call from two of her sons. She knew what it felt like to sit for hours on a wooden bench in a courthouse, watch a prosecutor present evidence against one of her children, hear a judge pronounce him guilty, then watch a court officer whisk him out the back door. And she knew what comes after the conviction: the grueling bus rides to faraway prisons, the teary hours together in a crowded visiting room, the angry children left behind.

This was certainly not the future Yvonne Powell had envisioned for herself in 1950 when she left Birmingham, Alabama, and moved to New York City. Yvonne was the fifth of eight children. In the early 1940s, the oldest sibling, Arletha, had moved to New York City. Yvonne joined her at age nineteen, moving into Arletha's apartment on West 105th Street and Central Park West in Manhattan. Arletha worked as a domestic for a white family, and she found Yvonne a job as a domestic, too. Yvonne did not last long, however. She had little desire to spend her days scrubbing somebody else's house or cooking for somebody else's children. Yvonne's refusal to work angered Arletha; she thought Yvonne was lazy.

In 1953, Yvonne moved in with her boyfriend, Frank Bartlett. Three years later, she gave birth to her first child, Frank Jr. She had a daughter the following year, in 1957. Her name was Frances Elaine, but everyone just called her Elaine. At the beginning of 1958, when Elaine was five months old, Yvonne left Frank. A few months later, he tracked her down and attacked her with a pocketknife, stabbing her three times in the stomach and once in the left arm. The police report listed the cause of the assault: "jealousy."

Yvonne had a new boyfriend named Ronald Windsor, who was a year younger than she. In that pre–Civil Rights era, they made an un-

usual couple: She was black, he was white. He had recently been released from federal prison after serving two years for selling opium.
He had been caught with gum opium, a raw form that had not yet
been turned into heroin.

Between 1959 and 1963, Yvonne and Ronald had four children:
Ronald Jr., Kenneth, Sabrina, and Donjuan. Frankie and Elaine
thought of Ronald as their father, too; after all, they were too young to
remember Frank Sr.

Yvonne and Ronald fought often. Once he kicked her so hard she
went flying headfirst into a closet. By the time she emerged, one
of her eyes was bleeding. Whenever Yvonne and Ronald fought,
the children argued, too. Frankie would grab the telephone to dial
the precinct, and Elaine would try to snatch it away from him. "Don't
call the cops on my father!" she would cry.

To help support the family, Yvonne signed up for welfare. By 1963,
they were living in a decrepit hotel on West Eighty-first and Colum-
bus Avenue. One day, a welfare investigator showed up and discovered Yvonne's children in a room with five intoxicated adults. There
was no sign of Yvonne. Other tenants in the hotel said they had been
feeding her children for days.

The Department of Welfare cut off Yvonne's payments, accused
her of neglect, and reported her to Family Court. By now, the administrator of the local welfare office had known Yvonne for several years.
She explained that she was not going to help Yvonne anymore because doing so would condone a "veritable beehive of delinquent activity." However, the court requested that Yvonne's welfare checks be
reinstated while a probation officer sought to determine if her children should be taken away.

The probation officer visited the home and interviewed Elaine,
who was then five years old. "Elaine informed P.O. that she loved her
mother and siblings," the officer wrote. "The child views her home as
a 'tour of duty' to assist her mother to care for the younger children.
She verbalized these words with strong feeling and concern. Child
seems overidentified with her mother's responsibilities.

"Elaine enjoys playing with her sisters and brothers as their substitute mother. She related that she had only one toy and held it closely in her arms. The child related that she liked school . . . because it gave her the opportunity of traveling to and from home alone."

The officer described Elaine as "a very reticent child who refuses to speak at times. Her expression is usually sad almost mournful, distrustful and hostile. . . . She appears neglected; the child's hair is often unwashed and greasy but otherwise she is neat and clean although shabby."

On New Year's Day, 1964, the children stood around a bed and watched their mother cradle her boyfriend, Ronald, in her arms. They saw his blood oozing onto the sheets and heard her wailing echo through the room. The memory of this day would linger in Elaine's mind for decades as she tried to figure out exactly what had happened. All she knew was that Ronald had died. At the time, he was thirty years old.

In the years that followed, Yvonne told several different stories about Ronald's death. Sometimes she said he had been murdered. Other times she said he'd had a heart attack. She told at least one person he died of jaundice. And she told some of her children that she herself had shot him. An investigation by the city's medical examiner found that he had actually died of a heroin overdose.

Yvonne helped pay for Ronald's funeral with $265 from her welfare checks. When her caseworker found out, she closed Yvonne's case once again. Apparently, spending welfare money on funeral expenses was not allowed. For Yvonne, this loss of income was devastating. Not only did she have six small children to care for, but by now she was pregnant once again.

The probation officer assigned by the court spoke to her after Ronald's death. "Mrs. Bartlett stated she is without funds and means for caring for her family," the officer wrote. "She stated verbally that if her children were taken from her, she would jump off the George Washington Bridge."

The court sent Yvonne to Bellevue Hospital for psychiatric observation. Seven-year-old Frankie and six-year-old Elaine were taken to an orphanage in the Bronx. The younger children were placed with foster families. A few weeks later, Yvonne was released from the hospital, but she was not allowed to have her children back. In the summer of 1964, she gave birth to Michelle, her seventh child.

Later that year, Yvonne was arrested for selling heroin to two undercover cops. She sold a total of five glassine envelopes at three dollars apiece. "In the opinion of the officers, the defendant is a small-scale seller, who is not a drug user, but is selling for pocket money," the police report stated. Yvonne spent a few weeks in jail, pleaded guilty, and was sentenced to five years probation.

The following spring, she regained custody of four of her children, but not of Elaine and Frankie. They were sent to Mount Loretto, an orphanage run by nuns on Staten Island. A 1964 newsletter produced by Mount Loretto boasted that it was the "largest child-caring institution in the United States," larger even than Boys' Town in Nebraska. At the time, there were more than 900 children living at Mount Loretto.

Nobody explained to Frankie and Elaine why they could not live with their mother. They thought that if they could make her feel sorry enough for them, she would come to the orphanage and take them back home. One day, Elaine rolled around in poison ivy. Another day, Frankie leaned into a campfire and got first- and second-degree burns all over his back. Neither ploy worked.

In October of 1965, the welfare department restored Yvonne to its rolls and began sending her a check for $87.50 every two weeks. A year later, the court permitted Elaine and Frankie to move back home. At the time, Elaine was eight years old. She had been living away from her mother for two and a half years.

By now, Yvonne had a six-room apartment in Harlem, on West 139th Street, between Lenox and Seventh Avenues. Everybody in the neighborhood knew her. They called her "Big Yvonne" or "Big Mama." Yvonne was indeed a big woman; she stood six-one and weighed 415 pounds. She never went outside unless she thought she looked good. She always wore a wig, and she always wore handmade clothes—a skirt or maybe culottes, but never pants. Despite her considerable size, she had a small chest. To get the size of her breasts to match her girth, she would stuff her bra with a slip or a cotton diaper.

It was not always easy to figure out when Yvonne was telling the truth. She often told people she was Native American. No one knew whether this was true, but she did have a penchant for all things Native American. She liked to wear moccasins, and she gave her son Kenneth an Indian moniker, albeit one with a phonetic spelling: Shyan. Other times, she liked to say she was French. She would tell people her last name was Bartlette, which she pronounced *Bartlet-tay*.

She was a devoted Catholic who served fish every Friday, went to mass at least once a week, and read the Bible every night. She also had her share of vices. She cursed all the time, and she loved to play the numbers. If she put down a ten-dollar bet and her number hit, she would immediately pick another number and play again. She won so often that her friends were always calling, begging her to pick a number for them.

She supplemented her welfare income by playing the numbers and doing just about anything she could think of. She set up a stand on Lenox Avenue and sold watermelon, clams, and crabs. She poured drinks at the bar on the corner. She pushed a hot-dog cart around to local schools at lunchtime. She also continued to earn money illegally. One day, her son Shyan walked into the living room and saw her seated next to a large mirror that was covered with white powder.

Heroin was rampant in Harlem in the 1960s. New York City had more heroin addicts than any other city in the country, and within New York City, Harlem was the heroin capital. The spread of heroin had brought a wave of crime to the neighborhood. Muggings and purse-snatchings were so common that everyone knew someone who had been a victim. And every other day or so, it seemed that another person was killed.

The Bartlett children often walked by junkies shooting up in their building or in the park across the street. Some days they discovered a half-alive addict slumped in their building's stairwell. Whenever Yvonne saw one, she always tried to help, pulling the needle out of his arm, removing the rubber tourniquet, slapping him awake, leading him into her apartment, and pouring him a glass of milk. Then she would walk him around until he was alert enough to venture off on his own.

Growing up in this neighborhood required learning how to fight. School bullies often followed Elaine home, taunting her and calling her "white girl." Whenever Yvonne saw other children picking on Elaine, she would stick her head out the window and yell. "If they hit you, you hit 'em back," Yvonne would say. "No one is going to chase you home. You're going to walk these streets like anyone else!"

At first, Elaine was too frightened to fight, but eventually she started to like it. Sometimes she tried to provoke other girls into hitting her, just so she could punch them. When several girls tried to shove her head in a toilet, she brought a rug cutter to school and chased them down the hall. A security guard caught her and cuffed her to a pole. After that incident, Yvonne made sure to push her hot-dog cart to Elaine's school at lunchtime every day so that she could keep an eye on her.

While Yvonne approved of Elaine's defending herself from her peers, she had no tolerance for any child of hers disrespecting an adult. One day, Yvonne found out that Elaine had put tacks on her teacher's chair. She marched over to the school, removed her belt, placed Elaine facedown on her lap, and beat her in front of her classmates. "I don't think you'll have any more problems with her," she said to the teacher. "But if you do, just let me know."

At home, Elaine continued to play the role of second mother. She filled bottles, changed diapers, cooked meals. She took her brothers and sisters to school in the morning, then picked them up in the afternoon. When they all got home, she would set up a blackboard in the living room and run impromptu classes, helping everybody with their homework.

She intervened whenever one of her brothers or sisters got into trouble. Her brother Ronald needed the most protection, since everybody knew he was gay. Whenever neighborhood bullies picked on him, Elaine would beat them up. Whenever their brother Shyan called Ronald a "faggot," Elaine would shout at Shyan. And whenever Ronald wanted to put on a dress and practice his dance steps in front of the television, Elaine made sure Yvonne did not come in and beat him.

When Yvonne went out at night to work at the bar on the corner, she left Elaine in charge. One evening, while Yvonne was standing in front of the bar, an ex-boyfriend approached. Drunk and irate, he pulled out a pistol, shot her in the stomach, then fled north. According to the family story, Yvonne chased him up Lenox Avenue, across West 139th Street, and into a park before a group of men yelled at her to lie down.

Yvonne spent the next several weeks at Harlem Hospital, three blocks south of the family's apartment. The children trekked over to see her, but a guard told them they could not visit without an adult chaperone. While Frankie distracted the guard, Elaine sneaked into Yvonne's room with the other children. Nobody was going to stop them from seeing their mother. In the minds of her children, the scar that now stretched across her stomach was a mark of her courage.

Not long after Yvonne was shot, a fire tore through the family's building, likely started by the heroin addicts who lived on the roof. Nobody was injured, but their home had become uninhabitable. The Bartletts lived briefly in an apartment a few blocks north, and then Yvonne moved the family to the Bronx. Their new home was a tenement building on East 166th Street, in the Morrisania section of the South Bronx.

Heroin dealers did not hang out in this neighborhood, but in many ways the area was even more dangerous than Harlem. At the time, the South Bronx was rife with gangs: the Black Pearls, the Black Spades, the Savage Nomads, the Skulls. The gang members acted as if they were living in the Wild West, arming themselves with guns, chains, and machetes. Stories circulated about their assorted crimes: shootings, robberies, rapes. The Bartlett children learned to duck whenever they heard gunshots.

The Black Pearls had a clubhouse next door to the Bartletts' building, and Elaine met her first boyfriend there. His name was Robert Paschall, but everyone called him Bobby. Although he lived in East Harlem, he often played hooky and spent his days in the Bronx. Yvonne seemed to like him well enough, until the day she learned that her fifteen-year-old daughter was pregnant. From then on, Yvonne had nothing positive to say about Bobby.

In the summer of 1973, Elaine gave birth to Robert Paschall, Jr. The baby was Yvonne's first grandchild. She adored him, of course, but she despised his name. "Nobody in my house calls him Robert," she said. "His name is Apache as of today."

Two years after the Bartletts moved to the Bronx, a fire in an adjacent building spread to their apartment, and they had to move once again. This time, Yvonne found a two-story house on 100th Street in Corona, Queens. The beige frame house had aluminum siding, a brick chimney, a small dirt yard, and a driveway. The neighborhood was run-down, but living in a house certainly qualified as a step up. Now they would not have to worry about heroin addicts or anyone else setting their home on fire. And here, away from the violence of Harlem and the Bronx, Yvonne figured her children would be safe.

At first, Elaine hated living in Corona. She rode the subway to Manhattan every chance she got. On the weekends, she told her mother she was staying with relatives, but most of the time she was with Bobby. As Elaine headed out the door, Yvonne would shout, "I know that you're going to see that black motherfucker!"

Yvonne made no secret of the fact that she did not want her light-skinned daughters dating black men. Yvonne thought her daughters should do what she had done: find a white boyfriend, preferably one with a lot of money. Her children called her "color-stroked," and all three daughters ignored this advice.

Life in Corona got much better for Elaine after she met Althea Pough-Nimmons. Althea was a few years older, and she lived across the street with her mother, her three-year-old daughter, Tasha, and

Dude, her one-year-old son. Unlike Elaine, who was a tomboy, Althea liked to dress up. She took Elaine shopping for dresses and high heels, and she took her to get her first pedicure. Soon Elaine was stuffing tissue in her bra and sneaking out at night with Althea to go to a local bar with a dance floor in the back.

As Elaine grew older, tensions with Yvonne grew. The crux of their disagreements was always the same: Elaine, now seventeen, thought she should be able to come and go whenever she pleased. Though she had finally found a friend in Corona, she still dreamed of moving out of her mother's house and getting her own place with Bobby. One day, during yet another argument, Elaine shouted, "I'm leaving!"

Yvonne tossed Elaine's clothes out a second-story window. Some landed in the dirt yard. Others got stuck on the roof. "You can go," Yvonne said, "but this baby ain't going nowhere."

Elaine grabbed a bag, went outside, snatched up her clothes, and headed for the subway, leaving one-year-old Apache behind.

Bobby Paschall lived with his mother and three brothers in a city housing project on Fifth Avenue in East Harlem. Elaine moved in with them. She had stopped going to school in the tenth grade, and now she enrolled in a school for dropouts, run by the Urban League, which paid students about $115 a week. Several months after she left Queens, she paid her sister Sabrina fifty dollars to leave Apache on a bed next to an open window in their mother's house. While Yvonne was preoccupied, Elaine climbed in, grabbed Apache, and left.

Not long after Elaine moved in with Bobby's family, she started clashing with his mother, who was known as "Miss Tiny." Elaine thought Miss Tiny treated her like a maid, as if she were supposed to do all the housework just because she was female. One evening, Elaine overheard Miss Tiny criticizing her housekeeping abilities. Elaine put Apache in his stroller, grabbed her belongings, and walked out.

It was snowing that evening, but Elaine did not turn around. Instead, she pushed the stroller around the streets of East Harlem for an hour or two, until she spied an APARTMENTS FOR RENT sign on a building next door to a funeral parlor on East 118th Street. Elaine knocked, and a woman told her that she could rent an apartment on the ground floor for $150 a month. Elaine moved in.

Soon Bobby joined her, helping to pay the rent with the income he earned working two jobs: assistant stock manager at a plumbing company and dishwasher at a nursing home. Elaine's brothers and sisters often came to visit. Nearly a year after Elaine left Corona, Yvonne came to see her, too. She inspected the apartment, opening every drawer and cupboard. Apparently, she approved. "I knew you would make it, because you're my child," she said.

There was something suspicious about this building, however. Nobody lived here except for Elaine, Bobby, Apache, and the woman who collected their rent. After several months, a city official stopped by and informed Elaine that the building was about to be torn down. The woman who had rented her the apartment was running a scam; all along, she had known that the building had been condemned, and she had been putting Elaine's money into her own pocket.

Elaine's bad luck turned to good. Because she was living in a condemned building, the city granted her a lease for a subsidized apartment in the Wagner Houses, a municipal project four blocks north. Bobby and Elaine moved again.

The Wagner Houses cover twenty-six acres and are roughly the size of a small town, with enough apartments for 2,158 families. The project consists of twenty-two brick buildings, which stretch along the eastern edge of East Harlem, from East 120th Street to East 124th Street. Some of the apartment buildings are seven stories tall; others are sixteen stories. There are basketball courts and playgrounds, too. And back in the late 1970s, there were also plenty of drugs.

Elaine moved into a two-bedroom apartment, number 5F, on the fifth floor of a building at First Avenue and East 122nd Street. At the time, she was one of the youngest tenants to have a lease of her own. The apartment was twenty years old—older than she was—but it was in much better condition than the one she had just left.

By now, the Urban League's school had shut down. Through a friend, Elaine found work at a beauty parlor on 125th Street. She did not have a hairdresser's license, but she had plenty of experience doing hair. She had been practicing on her younger brothers and sisters for years.

Her friend took her to a wholesale supplier and helped her pick out supplies: rollers, shampoos, conditioners, gels, extensions, hairpieces, bows. When the boss was away, she let Elaine rent her chair. At the beauty parlor, Elaine expanded her skills, learning how to do perms, shape-ups, and cluster curls.

By now, Elaine's relationship with Bobby had become very tense. The two fought all the time. Often he came home late at night, reeking of gin. A few times, he locked her inside the apartment while he went to work. One day, they got into a fight and he knocked her off a ladder while she was painting. Elaine yanked open the refrigerator and hurled its contents at him—meat, eggs, whatever she could grab. Even after Bobby retreated into the hallway, she kept throwing food at him.

Elaine gave birth to their second son, Jamel, in 1977. The arrival of another child did little to improve relations between her and Bobby. One afternoon, Elaine took six-month-old Jamel and four-year-old Apache to nearby Mount Morris Park. Bobby showed up, too, and began shouting at her. Usually, nobody intervened in their fights, but on this day a twenty-four-year-old named Littleboy walked over and told Bobby to stop. Elaine did not know it at the time, but Littleboy would later become her best friend.

Bobby wanted their relationship to continue; Elaine wanted him to move out. To finally get rid of him, she figured she would have to start a relationship with somebody else. A young man she had seen around the Wagner Houses had attracted her attention. His name was Nathan Brooks. He was two years younger, and his mother lived next door. Elaine often saw him hanging out with Charlie Boo, the numbers man.

One night when Bobby was out, Elaine spied Charlie Boo and Nathan smoking marijuana in the hallway outside her apartment. "You don't have to stay out there," she said. "You can come in." While they sat around her kitchen table smoking together, she slipped off a shoe and rubbed her toes against Nathan's leg.

From the beginning, Elaine liked Nathan's shy, gentle manner and his basketball player's physique. He liked the way she looked, too. He did not want to get involved with somebody who already had two children; even so, he found it difficult not to think about this tall, older girl who he thought looked like a model.

Not long after his first visit, Nathan knocked on Elaine's door one night around 1:00 a.m. Elaine appeared in the doorway looking sleepy, her hair tousled and her eyes half-open. He could see her skin through her silky red nightgown.

"Is Charlie Boo here?" he asked.

"No," Elaine said. "But you can come in."

Nathan spent that night in Apartment 5F. After finally getting Bobby out of her apartment, Elaine was not eager to start a serious relationship with another man. Over the next few months, she saw Nathan often, but she considered him merely a "bed partner"—not her boyfriend.

Meanwhile, Elaine saw Littleboy whenever she went to Mount Morris Park, and sometimes he came into the beauty parlor where she worked. They had dated briefly soon after they met, but she'd decided he was not her type. He already had a wife and kids, plus a few more kids on the side. Nonetheless, they became close friends and spoke to each other almost every day.

Littleboy was a well-known drug dealer. He had moved to New York City from the South and had gone into business with friends from his hometown. They owned a gas station, a grocery store, a Laundromat, and a nightclub on 125th Street called the Pit Stop Lounge. At one point, he gave Elaine a part-time job in his grocery store. Littleboy had been arrested twice on minor drug-possession charges in the late 1970s, but he had spent only a few days behind bars.

Nobody would ever have guessed that he was a drug dealer, and that seemed to be part of the reason for his success. He did not wear a gold medallion on a chain around his neck. He did not cruise around the streets in a Cadillac or Mercedes. He did not stand on street corners, his pockets bulging with cash and drugs. He went to church every Sunday and never drank anything stronger than soda.

Littleboy was a valuable friend for a young woman who was nearly always broke. Anytime Elaine needed money, she could count on him. All she had to do was say, "Boy, I want to go shopping," and he would hand her $200. Sometimes they went to the movies together. Other times, he took her out for shrimp and lobster at City Island in the Bronx. She would order as much as she wanted, and he would always pick up the check.

Nathan Brooks had grown up on West 134th Street, not far from where the Bartlett family had once resided. As a child, he spent many nights fending for himself while his mother was out drinking. He would fix himself franks and beans, then sit in front of the television all night. As he grew older, he began spending his nights on the street, coming home whenever he felt like it. When he was in junior high school, he started selling heroin on his corner.

In the summer of 1979, Nathan was arrested with seventeen envelopes of heroin hidden inside his sweatshirt. Five weeks later, he was picked up with a loaded revolver tucked in the waistband of his pants. A few months later, he was arrested a third time—again for selling heroin. In exchange for pleading guilty in all three cases, he was given a sentence of one year in jail. At the time, he was twenty years old.

While Nathan was away, Elaine discovered that she was pregnant. She knew it was Nathan's baby, but she didn't tell him. She figured that if he found out she was pregnant with his child, she would never be able to get rid of him. It had taken her so long to get Bobby out of her life that she was leery of letting any boyfriend get too close.

Littleboy liked to pretend the baby was his. When they walked down the street together, he would rub her belly and tell people, "Big Red is having my baby." By now, the whole Bartlett family knew Littleboy. Most of them could not understand why Elaine was with Nathan, who was always broke, instead of Littleboy, who was flush. Elaine's family was not concerned about where Littleboy's money came from. They just knew that he had a lot of it, and that any time they asked, he would give them some, too.

Elaine gave birth to a daughter, Satara, in March of 1980. When Satara was a few months old and Nathan was out of jail, Elaine told him that he had a child. Satara had been diagnosed with sickle-cell anemia, a genetic blood disease, and Elaine needed Nathan to go to the doctor with her. Just as she had predicted, Nathan started spending more time at her apartment once he learned that he was Satara's father.

Elaine had another daughter two years later. She named her Danae, then gave the baby her own name, Elaine, for a middle name. This time, Nathan was at the hospital. Two months after Danae was born, Nathan received another one-year jail sentence for selling heroin. Elaine visited him every week, taking all four children with her.

By now, she had a few other reasons to visit the city's jails, too. Her eighteen-year-old brother, Donjuan, had recently been charged with murder and robbery after a shooting at a clothing store in Queens. In the summer of 1982, he went to trial. He was acquitted of murder, but convicted of first-degree robbery. A judge sentenced him to 8⅓ to 25 years in prison.

Elaine's brother Shyan, twenty-two, was also in jail on a robbery case, accused of having used a sawed-off shotgun to stick up four men on a Corona street, stealing their gold chains and their Nikes. Shyan pleaded guilty and was sentenced to 5-to-15 years in prison. In the fall of 1982, both Donjuan and Shyan entered the New York State prison system. Between visiting Nathan and visiting her brothers, Elaine spent nearly every weekend behind bars.

From all these trips to jail—plus her friendship with Littleboy— she learned a few lessons about the criminal-justice system: There was often little relationship between the crimes one committed and the amount of time one spent locked up. Repeatedly breaking the law usually meant you would get caught, though you might end up with more or less of a punishment than you actually deserved.

Nathan came home from jail in early 1983. This time, he was determined to go straight. Instead of resuming his old line of work—selling heroin on West 134th Street—he found a legal job. His father hired him to work as a late-night custodian, mopping and buffing office floors. Nathan had been out of jail for less than a year when George Deets, the police informant, walked into the apartment he shared with Elaine.

A few days later, word of Nathan's latest arrest trickled down to the streets of Harlem. None of his friends knew what he was doing in Albany, but they were not surprised to hear the news. Friends and acquaintances got picked up by the cops all the time. They figured Nathan would spend two or three years in prison, then return to the neighborhood once again.

CHAPTER 4

On the morning of January 3, 1973, Governor Nelson A. Rockefeller walked to the podium at the front of the Assembly Chamber in the New York State Capitol. State legislators filled the seats in front of him. As he did every January, Rockefeller was about to give his annual State of the State address. He was in the middle of his fourth term as governor, and he had already delivered fourteen such speeches. No one expected any big surprises this day.

At first, he covered all the usual topics: welfare, education, court reform. Then, halfway through, he turned to the subject of narcotics, and his tone changed. "The crime, the muggings, the robberies, the murders associated with addiction continue to spread a reign of terror," he said. "Whole neighborhoods have been as effectively destroyed by addicts as by an invading army. We face the risk of undermining our will as a people, and the ultimate destruction of society as a whole. This has to stop. This . . . is . . . going . . . to . . . stop."

To rid New York of the scourge of drugs, he proposed a seemingly simple solution: life sentences for drug pushers. If he could get his proposal through the legislature, the penalty for selling drugs in New

York State would be even harsher than for committing murder. Murderers, at least, would still be able to get released on parole.

Some state legislators burst into applause. Others remained silent, seemingly stunned by Rockefeller's words, their lips curling into a frown. The next day, the front page of the Daily News showed Rockefeller receiving a standing ovation. Above him, the headline declared, ROCKY ASKS LIFE FOR PUSHERS, CALLS FOR WAR ON DRUG MENACE.

Not surprisingly, Rockefeller's speech sparked a ferocious public debate. "Three cheers for Gov. Rockefeller's proposals for dealing with the drug problem!" a reader wrote to the Daily News. "The Legislature should approve them with no compromises. It's about time someone took hold of the reins in combating the nation's No. 1 domestic problem. Sock it to 'em, Rocky!" Another reader wrote: "Let's forget about life terms for drug pushers. Why should the taxpayers foot the bill for them? The only solution is to bring back capital punishment and execute pushers."

Much of the enthusiasm for Rockefeller's plan came from the residents of upstate towns; they feared what might happen if drug dealing in New York City was not stamped out. Throughout the 1960s, there had been a rise in media coverage about heroin abuse. Local papers reported that babies were being born addicted to heroin. News photos showed pictures of junkies sleeping on sidewalks. While heroin use was largely confined to New York City's ghettos, addicts had begun to appear in the state's smaller cities, too, fueling fears of a growing epidemic.

Meanwhile, on the streets of Harlem, Rockefeller's call for life sentences for drug pushers received a mixed response. "I'm afraid that only the poor people will get caught," a local pastor told The New York Times. A school principal said she envisioned the proposal leading to the "destruction of black and Puerto Rican people; I really feel it is a conspiracy, a way of destroying us." Another woman told the Times that people were worried the government was trying to "round up . . . young black boys and put them in concentration camps."

Rockefeller's proposal represented a radical departure from the mainstream approach to narcotics control—and from his own past record. At the time, most experts believed that addiction was an illness requiring treatment, not a crime that warranted prison. Rockefeller had long embraced this idea. In 1967, he had established the Narcotic Addiction Control Commission, known as NACC, which had converted jails into drug-treatment centers. He had also helped steer substantial state funds into New York City's methadone maintenance programs for heroin addicts.

But in recent years, his inability to curb the spread of heroin in New York City had become a source of increasing frustration. Many people had criticized NACC as a costly failure. In his State of the State speech, Rockefeller said, "We have allocated over one billion dollars to every form of education against drugs and treatment of the addicted. . . . But let's be frank—let's tell it like it is: We have achieved very little permanent rehabilitation—and have found no cure."

Rockefeller's failure to stamp out drug addiction was a blemish on his record, one that he hoped would not ruin his chances of becoming president. Already, he had tried three times to win the Republican party's presidential nomination. Every time he had lost, largely because he was perceived as too liberal. As the grandson of John D. Rockefeller, Sr.—the founder of Standard Oil, and once the richest man in the world—Governor Rockefeller was seen as out of touch with America's heartland. If he ever hoped to win the presidency, he needed a more conservative image. Launching a war on drugs seemed the perfect solution.

Virtually every expert in New York State opposed Rockefeller's proposal. There was no "army" of addicts overtaking New York City, they insisted. Arrests for drug crimes had actually decreased over the past two years. Mayor John Lindsay released a report predicting that by 1991 the state's prison population would swell to eighty thousand and the annual operating cost for the state's prisons would surpass $1 billion. Lindsay denounced Rockefeller's proposal as "merely a deceptive gesture offering nothing beyond momentary satisfaction and inevitable disillusionment."

Meanwhile, Rockefeller wielded a powerful weapon in his battle to win approval from the state legislature. He announced plans to create one hundred new court parts to handle all the new trials his proposal would spawn. Everybody knew that he had the power to appoint judges to fill all these new seats. Many state legislators aspire to become judges, and with the prospect of dozens of judicial jobs soon opening up, these legislators had an added incentive to support his plan.

In his speeches, Rockefeller did not reveal how he had devised his new antidrug plan. That job was left to Joseph E. Persico, the governor's longtime speechwriter, who gave a behind-the-scenes account in his book, *The Imperial Rockefeller*. At a party in March 1972, Rockefeller had chatted with William Fine, then the president of Bonwit Teller. The two men talked about narcotics—a topic Fine was especially interested in because his son was an addict. Rockefeller asked him to go to Japan and figure out why that nation had the world's lowest rate of addiction. Fine financed his own trip and returned with an answer: lifetime prison sentences for drug sellers.

Rockefeller's staff balked at the news of this proposal, but he refused to listen to any of their doubts. His drug proposal became an "are you with me or against me" test of loyalty, and staffers quickly realized that if they did not implement the governor's plan, they would have to start polishing their résumés. "I never fully understood the psychological milieu in which the chain of errors in Vietnam was forged until I became involved in the Rockefeller drug proposal," Persico writes.

One of the most unsettling moments he describes is a meeting between Rockefeller and the state's top drug-control official, Howard Jones, a former narcotics prosecutor from Manhattan, who was African-American. The governor never bothered to solicit Jones's input for his new proposal. In a meeting, Jones voiced his concerns, including his belief that drug dealers would recruit minors to work as couriers, and that the laws would create so many prisoners, there would be no place to put them. Rockefeller was not swayed. After Jones left the room, Rockefeller said, "He's just worried about his people."

. . .

On May 8, 1973, Rockefeller signed the package of bills that would come to be known as the "Rockefeller drug laws." The final version was less extreme than his original proposal. Instead of life sentences, the new laws established a system of "mandatory minimums." Anyone convicted of the highest-level felony, an A-1, would face a mandatory minimum sentence of fifteen years to life. The laws applied to heroin and cocaine, though cocaine use had not yet become widespread. Hashish and marijuana were not included. Rockefeller boasted to reporters that New York now had "the toughest antidrug program in the nation."

The new drug laws went into effect at the beginning of September. Three months later, Rockefeller resigned. Everyone assumed he was leaving Albany to prepare for a 1976 presidential campaign, but he got to the White House sooner than expected. After President Nixon resigned amid the Watergate scandal in 1974, his successor, Gerald Ford, asked Rockefeller to be his vice president. Five years later, Rockefeller died of a heart attack, never having won the presidency.

Arguably, his most enduring legacy is New York's mandatory minimum drug laws. During the decade after New York's laws went into effect, forty-eight other states passed their own Rockefeller-style drug laws. For politicians, the lesson from New York State was clear: Passing harsh antidrug laws was an effective way to curry favor with scared voters. Such laws enabled a politician to look tough on crime, without having to worry about the long-term consequences, such as figuring out what to do with all these prisoners once they were released.

At the time, New York State's prisons held 12,500 people. The state's rate of incarceration had remained steady over the decades, and the story was the same nationwide. In fact, the nation's prison population had actually decreased in the two years prior to Rockefeller's speech, shrinking from 198,061 to 196,092.

This picture of incarceration was about to change dramatically. Years later, it would become apparent that Rockefeller's speech had helped launch a new experiment in crime control, one that would have repercussions in every corner of the country for decades to come. Over the next three decades, mandatory minimum sentences for drug crimes would fuel an unprecedented prison boom. The nation's prison population would increase more than sixfold, from just under 200,000 to more than 1.3 million. Add in all the people locked up in county jails, and the total number of inmates would eventually exceed two million.

On the morning that Governor Rockefeller delivered his speech decrying the spread of drugs, Elaine Bartlett was fifteen years old, pregnant, and living in the Bronx, 150 miles south of Albany. Rockefeller had insisted that his tough penalties would act as a deterrent, scaring addicts and pushers out of the drug business. Ten years later, when George Deets asked Elaine to carry a package of cocaine to Albany, she did not think about the Rockefeller drug laws. In fact, she had never even heard of them.

CHAPTER 5

Elaine hardly looked her best when she arrived at the Albany County Courthouse on the morning of January 11, 1984. Sixty-four nights on a jail cot had left her completely exhausted. Her hair was straggly and flat. All the polish had peeled off her nails. Her jeans hung low on her hips. She was thinner now than she had been when she arrived in this city; since her arrest, she had been too stressed to eat.

Her bail had been set at $250,000, which was, of course, more than her family could afford. If she had come from a wealthy family, she might not have looked so haggard. If she had found somebody to bail her out, she could have spent the last nine weeks living in her own apartment. Her hair would have been bouncy and clean. She would have had on a fresh, well-pressed outfit to impress the jurors. Instead, she wore the same clothes she had been wearing for two months.

A sheriff's office employee, known as a "court matron," ushered Elaine inside the courthouse. She wore a waist chain, handcuffs, and leg irons. As she made her way across the rotunda, her leg irons scraped the floor. Another visitor might have marveled at the courthouse's three-story blue-glass ceiling, curved archways, and Ionic marble columns. Elaine's gaze remained fixed on the floor.

The court matron removed her shackles and took her upstairs to the courtroom of Judge John J. Clyne. This room was much larger and more impressive than the New York City courtrooms Elaine had visited whenever Nathan or one of her brothers was in trouble. The walls here were pale blue, with gold trim. A brass railing ran down the center aisle. Eight chandeliers hung from the ceiling.

The courtroom was the size of a small theater, with seats for at least one hundred people. This day, nearly every seat was empty. Elaine saw her mother and her sister Sabrina, and she spotted Nathan's mother, too. The families did not sit together. Elaine knew that her mother blamed Nathan for her arrest, even though she had tried to explain that the trip to Albany had been her idea, not his.

The court matron led Elaine up the center aisle to one of the oak chairs at the front of the room. Elaine's lawyer, Joseph Teresi, sat down beside her. A sheriff's deputy led Nathan to another table. Next to him was his attorney, Bernard Bryan. The chief drug prosecutor for Albany County, Thomas Neidl, sat nearby.

Judge Clyne soon appeared. He was tall and slim in his black judge's robe, and he wore his spectacles perched at the end of his nose. "Fill the box, please," he said. Elaine turned to the right and watched the jurors file in. Eight white men, four white women. There were also two alternates, both white.

The trial could now begin.

Everyone in Albany County knew Judge Clyne, who had been on the County Court bench since 1972. His penchant for giving out long prison terms had earned him the moniker "Maximum John." A local newspaper columnist described him as a "by-the-books conservative judge who coddled no one and cleaned the scum off the streets like a sponge." Among cops and prosecutors, he was very popular. "He doesn't give away the courthouse," they said admiringly.

The stories told about Judge Clyne took on a different tone in Arbor Hill and the South End, Albany's African-American neighborhoods. People there referred to him as the "hanging judge." Some doubted whether he liked black people at all. But nobody wanted to speak too loudly. You could never know for sure when you or one of your relatives might end up standing before him.

Some judges in New York City had denounced the Rockefeller drug laws as too severe. Judge Clyne did not share this belief. He usually gave people convicted of an A-1 drug crime the maximum 25-to-life—not the minimum 15-to-life. Albany's other County Court judge, Joseph Harris, often did the same, prompting courthouse talk that he was competing with Clyne for the distinction of toughest judge.

"They were giving out sentences like popcorn," recalls Bertrand F. Gould, a lawyer who worked in the Albany County public defender's office from 1968 to 2000. "It was, 'We'll teach those New York blacks to come up here and sell their damn drugs in Albany.' That's why the prosecutors and judges gave out such extreme penalties. I'm not sure whether it was provincial or racist. Maybe a combination of the two."

Most residents of Albany County appeared to have no qualms about Judge Clyne's stiff sentences. Rather, they took pride in their community's reputation as a place that did not tolerate crime. When Clyne ran for a second ten-year term in the fall of 1982, he won 78 percent of the vote. A year later, the case of Nathan Brooks and Elaine Bartlett was assigned to his court.

In the weeks following their arrest, Elaine and Nathan had to decide whether to plead guilty or go to trial. They didn't know it at the time, but their decision would ultimately determine the course of their adult lives. Some local defendants, hearing they would have to go before Judge Clyne, did everything they could to avoid a trial. But Elaine and Nathan had never heard of Maximum John. And at the time, they did not know that 95 percent of people indicted for a drug felony pleaded guilty rather than risk going to trial.

Nathan and Elaine had been charged with selling four ounces of cocaine—an A-1 felony, which carried the mandatory minimum sentence of fifteen years to life. The best way to avoid a lengthy prison term, they knew, was to become an informant. But Elaine and Nathan could not imagine returning to Harlem and trying to lure somebody else up to Albany with a sack of cocaine. Harlem was their home. If they set up their friends and acquaintances, where would they go?

The prosecutor offered them a deal: Admit your guilt and you'll get five years to life. To Elaine, the prospect of spending even five years behind bars was inconceivable. By the time she got home, her oldest son would be fifteen and her baby would be in kindergarten. She knew that she had made a mistake, but she did not think she deserved five years in state prison. She'd heard plenty of stories of people caught with drugs who did much less time.

Indeed, if she and Nathan had been arrested in Manhattan, a prosecutor would have likely offered them a better deal—probably three years. The disparity was partly a matter of perspective. Four ounces of cocaine wouldn't have seemed like that much to a prosecutor in New York City, but by Albany County standards, she was considered a big catch.

If Elaine and Nathan had actually been drug kingpins, they likely would have had the money to hire their own lawyers. But neither of them could afford a private attorney. So the court appointed lawyers for them. Separately, their attorneys warned them that if they lost at trial, they could receive up to twenty-five years to life in prison. Like many poor defendants whose counsel is paid for by the state, Elaine did not trust her attorney. She thought he worked for the system—not for her.

Elaine's mother advised her to plead guilty. "If you know you did it, take the five years," Yvonne said. Elaine ignored her advice.

She decided to go to trial, and she convinced Nathan to take the same gamble. "Everything is going to be all right," she told him. "They don't have anything on us." She figured the jurors would see that her crime had been manufactured, that her arrest was the result of Charlie's scheming. After all, he had picked her up at the train station, rented the motel room, brought the scale, and arranged the sale. Surely, they would see that she was not a major drug dealer.

. . .

The prosecutor stood and gave his opening statement, recounting the alleged crime. "These two defendants, for the amount of eight thousand eight hundred dollars, sold approximately four ounces of a narcotic drug cocaine to one Kenneth Cook," he explained. He then emphasized one of the most surprising details in this case. "These two defendants, like two peas in a pod, were, in fact, sleeping in a bed together when the police came."

When he stopped talking, Elaine thought her attorney would stand and say something. He didn't. Nathan's lawyer also declined to give an opening statement.

The prosecutor stood once again. "Your Honor, the People call George Deets."

Elaine turned around and saw a white man with a black beard that hung almost to his waist walking toward the front of the courtroom. At first, she did not recognize him. As he got closer, however, she saw that it was Charlie.

What was he doing here? Why did the judge call him George Deets? And why was he wearing a fake beard? Elaine had thought she might see him today, but she had assumed he would be seated at the front of the courtroom, near her, on trial just like she was.

She watched him settle into the chair on the witness stand, and then listened to him testify for the next half hour. He told the jurors about visiting her apartment, then returning to Albany and going to Troop G to tell the officers about her. He described picking her and Nathan up at the train station, then notifying the state police of their arrival.

Elaine quickly realized that he had set her up. She didn't know why he had picked her, but now it hardly mattered. She was the one seated at the defendant's table, and he was the one rewriting history. "She said she had . . . four ounces of cocaine for sale," he told the jurors. "I told her that I was living upstate and I had somebody that was definitely interested in buying this merchandise."

Elaine leaned toward her lawyer. "He's lying," she said.

When the prosecutor asked George why he had rented two rooms at the motel, he said, "She told me to get two rooms, so I did." When he asked George why he had brought a scale, George insisted that this, too, had been Elaine's idea.

Elaine tried to catch his eye, but he would not look straight at her. Listening to his words, she thought she might explode. Here he was, painting her as the instigator of this job, making her look like a big-time drug dealer, when he knew the truth. He had met her kids. He had been to the place where she worked. He had been to her apartment in the projects. They both knew big-time drug dealers, and they both knew she wasn't one.

The more she listened to George, the angrier she got. She found out that the state police had paid him $200 in "expense money" to lure her and Nathan up to Albany. She learned that he had worked as an informant more than twenty times. And she discovered that he had a rap sheet much longer than hers, including arrests for cocaine possession, heroin possession, reckless endangerment, and unlawfully dealing with a child.

George's friend Richard Zagorski was the next witness. Questioned by the prosecutor, Rich admitted that he too had been arrested for selling drugs in the past. In his case, it was hashish and diet pills back in 1971. By now, he said breezily, he had worked as an informant so often that he could not remember how many people he had set up, maybe fifty or sixty. "I just feel that, you know, cocaine is at a bad level and I think that, you know, it should be taken off the street," he said.

Elaine hoped the jurors were paying attention, and that they saw these two men for the liars they were. The hypocrisy might have been wholly apparent if they had revealed that they'd set up the deal as an off-the-books swap with the police for the freedom of a friend. But neither man revealed his true motive. And, of course, they did not say anything about the fact that they were running their own international drug-trafficking operation.

The next witness was Kenneth Cook, the undercover officer, who described his meeting with Elaine and Nathan. "I sat down at the table and I put the white powder on the scale and weighed it, and then I began negotiating in the first instance with Elaine Bartlett over price," he said. "I ascertained the price from Elaine and she indicated that they needed to get approximately . . . twenty-four hundred dollars for the four ounces of cocaine."

He said he had tried to bargain Elaine down to $2,000 an ounce by taking out a plastic vial—which he called his "field test"—to measure the purity of the cocaine. He admitted that his field test was merely a prop; it did not actually work. "It just helps in negotiations," he said. Nathan had asked about the test, and they had spoken briefly.

"I said that I'd be willing to pay twenty-two hundred dollars an ounce, and I asked what would the total be, and at that point Nathan said that would be eight thousand eight hundred dollars," he said.

Elaine's account of what happened in the motel room differs in one key respect: She insists she did not negotiate a sale. According to her, she only played the role of drug mule, carrying the cocaine to Albany. Why would I have fallen asleep, she says, if I was waiting for a couple of buyers to come? Wouldn't I have been anxiously pacing the room? And what black person would wake up in a room full of white strangers and immediately start negotiating a drug sale? These were the sorts of things she planned to say the next day, once she got her chance on the witness stand.

At 5:00 p.m., the judge announced that the trial would end for the day, then resume the next morning at 9:30. While everyone else headed home, Nathan and Elaine were escorted to the elevator, across the rotunda, and into the back of separate sheriff's vans.

At the start of the trial's second day, Ken Cook returned to the witness stand. Sue McDonough, the other undercover officer, testified after he did. The next witness was a senior investigator with the state police, who said he had been part of the "take-down team" that had stormed into the motel room. A forensic scientist was the last witness. He testified that the plastic bag of white powder seized by the police had indeed contained cocaine.

The judge announced a lunch break, and Nathan and Elaine were taken to separate holding cells in the subbasement of the courthouse. Replaying the morning's testimony in her mind, Elaine tried to figure out what she would say when she got her turn to take the stand. At 1:00 p.m., the trial resumed and the lawyers began delivering their closing statements. Slowly, Elaine realized that she was not going to get a chance to speak on her own behalf.

Both defense attorneys had sound reasons for not putting their clients on the stand. If Nathan had testified, the prosecutor would have brought up his prior felony convictions, which the jury would not otherwise find out about. If Elaine had testified, the prosecutor would have tried to find contradictions in her account. If she altered her story even a little bit, he could have indicted her for perjury.

In his closing statement, Nathan's lawyer tried to convince the jurors that Nathan was a "sad sack," who had merely come along for the ride. "What you have here, ladies and gentlemen, is overreaching," he said. "They lured, really, they lured defendant Bartlett into Albany County and they got an extra added bonus. She brought a companion along and . . . the authorities are seeking in this case to hang the companion as well."

Elaine's lawyer attacked the credibility of George and Rich, whom he described as "unsalaried employees of the State Police." He reminded the jurors of the many times the police had interceded on their behalf, ensuring they did not go to prison. "They owed a big debt to the state police, and whether or not somebody else had to pay for it unfairly and unjustly doesn't make any difference to George Deets or Zagorski," he said. "They had to score points with the state police and they would do it any way they could."

The prosecutor gave the final closing statement, defending his reliance on the two men. "The people in the State Police do not apologize for one second for the use of an informant in a drug case, because, simply as your common sense will tell you again, that is the way, ladies and gentlemen, it is done," he said.

He concluded by suggesting a motive for Elaine, which had not surfaced in earlier testimony: that her meeting with George in her apartment had been about much more than a single trip to Albany. "Mr. Deets was known . . . as a person who could possibly get people to buy drugs in the Albany area," he said. "For drug people in New

York City, [it was] a business opportunity to expand the business upstate into Albany." His words were convoluted, but his implication was clear: She had wanted to set up shop in Albany.

Elaine was irate. Surely, the prosecutor knew that she was not a kingpin planning to import cocaine to Albany; she had just wanted to earn an easy $2,500. But with only a sentence or two to the jury, he had suddenly made this trial about much more than a ten-minute transaction. He had tapped into the same fears that had helped Governor Rockefeller win support for his drug laws a decade earlier: that all the evils of New York City, the narcotics and violence and mayhem, would spread to the rest of the state.

Neither Elaine nor Nathan had uttered a single word to the jury. And both of their attorneys had declined to call any witnesses on their behalf. Now the jurors would go to the deliberating room knowing virtually nothing about them. All the jurors had was physical evidence: the bag of powder and the drug-test kit. And they had the words of six people—two informants, three troopers, and a scientist—all of whom worked, either officially or unofficially, for the state police.

To Elaine, it seemed that everyone who had worked on this case already knew one another. Nobody, though, knew her. On the witness stand, Cook had admitted that he had not even known her name while he was plotting her arrest; all he knew was that George was bringing up somebody from New York City with a bag of cocaine. In his testimony, Rich kept referring to her as "Eileen." Elaine could have been anybody—any person naïve or desperate enough to trust a smooth-talking man with a promise of easy cash.

At 3:05 p.m., the jurors filed out. Elaine waited near the back of the courtroom, sitting next to the court matron on a wooden bench. Yvonne and Sabrina sat near the front. Nathan was behind Elaine, locked inside a room with a sheriff's deputy. This room was empty except for two radiators and two benches. Metal grates covered the windows in order to deter disconsolate defendants from trying to jump to their deaths.

The jurors reappeared at 3:45 p.m. It had taken them only forty minutes to reach a decision. Elaine and Nathan were ushered to the front of the courtroom. Judge Clyne asked for the verdict for Nathan. "We find him guilty," the forewoman said. When he asked about Elaine, the forewoman said "guilty" again.

Elaine felt the room start to spin. Her knees went weak. She thought she might faint. She knew her mother and Sabrina had heard the verdict, and she could not bring herself to look at them. Even without turning around, she knew how her mother would react. She would be crying and cursing.

"Ladies and gentlemen of the jury, I want to thank you for the attention you have given the matter before you, the patience and cooperation that you have shown to the court throughout the trial," Judge Clyne said. "And again, as you are well aware, the criminal-justice system cannot operate without citizen participation as jurors. It's your system, ladies and gentlemen. In my judgment, it's the best in the world. . . . Thank you again for your service on this case."

After the jurors left, Judge Clyne turned to Elaine and Nathan. "Take the statement of defendant Brooks, please," he said. The judge's clerk asked Nathan several questions: "What is your name? What is your age? Where were you born? Where do you reside? What is your occupation? Are you married or single? What education have you received? What is your religion? Are your parents living or deceased?"

Only now, after the trial was over, did anyone seem interested in the defendants' stories. Nathan answered these questions, and then Elaine answered them, too. Their responses were recorded on a "Criminal Statistics" form—just another piece of paper to be added to their expanding court file. One question nobody asked was whether they had any children, or what would happen to the children now that they were going to prison.

Judge Clyne announced that he would sentence Nathan and Elaine in two weeks. On that day, they would find out exactly how long they would have to wait until they could return home. A deputy sheriff and the court matron led them downstairs to the subbasement and locked them in separate holding cells. From inside his cell, Nathan could hear Elaine wailing, her pain echoing down the concrete corridor.

CHAPTER 6

Yvonne Bartlett left the Lower East Side in the back of a livery cab, seated next to her daughter Michelle, early on the morning of January 26, 1984. Nearly three hours later, their cab arrived in downtown Albany, stopping in front of the courthouse. The day promised to be expensive and exhausting. And whatever happened, Yvonne knew the news would not be good. At least by the end of the day, there would be no more uncertainty. She would know when Elaine was coming home.

Over the last three months, Yvonne had spent many days traveling to Albany County—to its jail and its courthouse—and now here she was, back in Judge Clyne's courtroom, seated in a chair near the front. She was still angry that Elaine had not listened to her and had decided to go to trial, but now there was nothing she could do.

Before the judge arrived, the court matron permitted Elaine to speak to her. "Ma, I'm going to marry Nathan," Elaine said.

"Why the fuck do you want to marry this bum?" Yvonne asked.

Elaine had known that her mother would not approve, and so she had purposely not told her this news on the phone. Now there was no time for a discussion. Elaine and Nathan had already made their decision.

"Does anyone in the courtroom want to go to the wedding?" a court official asked. Across the room, Nathan's mother Juanita stood. Michelle rose, too. Yvonne did not budge.

A deputy sheriff led Michelle, Juanita, Nathan, and Elaine into the judge's chambers, which were located behind his courtroom. Hardcover legal books filled the shelves in this room, their spines visible behind sliding glass doors. In the center of the room was a long wooden table. Nathan and Elaine stood next to each other, holding hands, facing Judge Clyne. Juanita and Michelle stood behind them. The lawyer who had prosecuted them was there, too. And a few deputy sheriffs were stationed around the periphery of the library, presumably to stop the bride and groom in case they tried to bolt.

The ceremony lasted only a minute or two and concluded with the usual words. "I now pronounce you man and wife," Judge Clyne said. Nathan and Elaine were permitted one quick kiss. Then they were escorted back into the courtroom to be sentenced.

Elaine and Nathan had not had any wedding plans before they had come to Albany. After they had been arrested together, however, everything had changed. For the last three months, they had written long letters to each other almost every day, sending them through the jail mail. Stuck in Albany, away from their family and friends, they had felt as if they had only each other.

Before the trial, Nathan's lawyer had tried to get the two cases separated. Nathan would have had a much better chance of being acquitted if he had gone to trial alone. After all, Elaine was the one who had carried the cocaine to Albany—not him. But Judge Clyne had refused to sever their cases. And now that they had been prosecuted and convicted together, their fates were inextricably entwined.

By becoming husband and wife, they ensured that they would not have to do their time alone. Marriage gave them a few more privileges. They would be able to visit together in the Albany County Jail before they were transferred to the state prison system. And once they were at separate prisons, they would be permitted to speak on the telephone twice a year.

A few minutes after their wedding, they stood before Judge Clyne once again, this time peering up at him from the front of his court-room.

"I ask the Court to consider that this is the defendant's first involvement with the criminal-justice system, and she has a family," Joseph Teresi, Elaine's lawyer, said. "I will ask the Court to consider her family situation and to temper the sentence for this serious offense with a degree of mercy and understanding."

"Elaine Bartlett," the judge said, "do you wish to be heard in reference to sentencing?"

"Yes, I do," she said.

"Very well."

Finally, here was her chance to defend herself, to explain what had really happened, to make the judge understand her side of the story. All the words she had planned to say at her trial began to spill out. "I still say that I'm not guilty, and I did not make a first-degree sale, a felony," she said. "I feel that I am being railroaded and doing someone else's time for the man. George Deets should have been the one that should have sat in this Court and been tried for this matter, not me or Nathan Brooks."

Judge Clyne stared down at her from his perch. "The Court has read the presentence report in this case," he said, referring to the report prepared by a probation officer. "Further, the Court heard the trial testimony in this case. The trial testimony overwhelmingly established the guilt of this defendant beyond any shadow of a doubt. In addition to which, the presentence report indicates that this defendant conceded to the probation officer that she deals in cocaine."

"I told the probation I did that?" Elaine asked.

"That's what it says," the judge replied.

"Your Honor, I did not tell no probation lady that."

Judge Clyne glanced down at the report. " 'She states that she did deal in cocaine and her source is one George Deets,' " he read.

Elaine remembered a woman coming to the jail and interviewing her, but she had refused to answer her questions. Now she could not understand how something she had never said had ended up in her file as fact. It seemed that this piece of paper she had never seen was about to destroy any chance she had of winning over the judge.

"I did not state that to that probation woman," Elaine said.

"All right. And you were set up here by the police, right?" the judge asked. "Is that your posture?"

"I don't know what the police did or why he did it," she said, "but I did not make no statements to no police, and I did not wake up and sell no cocaine to no policeman."

"Everybody who took that stand in this case lied," the judge said. "Is that what you are telling me?"

"Everybody took the stand—you had two polices involved," she said. "Only one police claimed that I took a verbal statement in this sale. He did not say that I put that cocaine in his hand. He did not say that I took that money."

"Definition of sell includes an offer or agreement to do the same," the judge said.

"But he states he picks this cocaine off the table hisself," she said. "He did not state that I put this cocaine on the table."

Judge Clyne cut her off. "All right," he said. "You came up here from New York to see the South Mall. Is that it?"

Elaine had no idea what the South Mall was. She did not know that it had been Nelson Rockefeller's pet project, a complex of buildings and modest skyscrapers in the center of Albany. She did know, however, that the judge was mocking her ignorance, making her feel even more powerless.

"I came up from New York to see George Deets," she said. "I did not deny that."

"Okay," the judge said. "Do you wish to say anything further?"

"Excuse me?"

"Do you wish to say anything further?"

"Did you put my appeal in?"

"In answer to your question," Elaine's lawyer said, "we intend to file notice of appeal today or tomorrow, Your Honor."

No matter what Elaine said to the judge now, no matter how persuasive or articulate she managed to be, he was required by law to sentence her and Nathan to at least 15-to-life. It did not matter whether they had been caught with two ounces, two pounds, or two kilos of cocaine. Selling at least two ounces constituted an A-1 felony. And it did not matter whether they were kingpins or first-time dealers. The Rockefeller drug laws did not punish people according to their level of involvement; all that mattered was the weight of the drugs.

"Elaine Bartlett, having previously been convicted of the crime of criminal sale of a controlled substance in the first degree, a Class A-1 felony, it is the judgment of this Court that you be sentenced to an indeterminate sentence of imprisonment, which shall have a maximum term of life in prison. The Court hereby imposes a minimum period of imprisonment of twenty years."

Elaine stared at the judge in disbelief. Twenty years? For carrying a sack of cocaine to Albany? Of all the drug dealers she knew in New York City, she'd never heard of anybody getting that much time. She'd never even heard of anyone getting five years. Now this judge, with just a few words, had erased her entire future. By the time she got out of prison, she would be at least forty-six years old.

Judge Clyne offered no explanation for this 20-to-life sentence, no reason why this first-time felon merited five years more than the mandatory minimum. Maybe her plea for mercy had backfired. Maybe she was being punished for exercising her right to a trial. She had turned down the prosecutor's offer of 5-to-life, and now she would have to spend at least four times as long in prison. Yvonne and Michelle and the rest of the family would have to raise her children without her.

A few minutes later, Nathan fared even worse. Judge Clyne gave him 25-to-life.

Seven weeks after he sentenced Elaine and Nathan, Judge Clyne quit, explaining that he no longer found his job challenging. For many years afterward, his legacy would be evident in prisons across New York State. During his eleven years on the bench, he had sent nearly 2,500 people to prison. Some of these people were small-time drug dealers. Others were serious violent criminals, like former New Jersey

Teamster boss Anthony "Tony Pro" Provenzano, who was convicted of murder. "I do have a sense of accomplishment," Clyne told a reporter shortly before he retired. "I did what I set out to do—run a no-nonsense court."

On the morning after her sentencing, Elaine's name appeared on the front page of the *Times Union*. JUDGE WEDS 2, PUTS 20 YEARS BETWEEN THEM, the headline stated. The story prompted a junior high school teacher to send a letter to the newspaper.

> To the Editor:
>   I read the article about the life sentencing of Elaine Bartlett and Nathan Brooks who were convicted of selling four ounces of cocaine. The question I am asking myself is who has committed the real crime: two young people trying to make a quick buck who are snared by undercover agents or Judge Clyne who robs these youthful offenders of their entire future? This severe and inhumane sentence is something I expect to read about in the U.S.S.R. What ever happened to justice for all?
>
> Robin Geery
Voorheesville

Sitting alone on the cot in her cell, Elaine read and reread the letter several times, then ripped it out. She would take it with her when she went to state prison.

PART TWO

Thirty-five
Miles from
Harlem
1984–2000

The female prisoners scurried to the windows of their cell block so they could get a good view of the driveway. Usually, the vehicle coming through the front gate was a bus with a Department of Correction logo, carrying yet another batch of women from Rikers Island. Today, however, the vehicle rolling up the driveway was a gold paddy wagon with a red-and-gold star on the door. Everyone knew it was a sheriff's van, and that it had come from somewhere in upstate New York. If the inmates had been closer to it, they would've seen ALBANY COUNTY JAIL emblazoned on its side.

The prisoners watched five women emerge, each wearing steel cuffs around her wrists and ankles. They pushed open the windows and shouted their standard welcome:

"Look at the fresh meat!"

"You with the big butt! Move up here so I can take care of you!"

"Hey, bitch, I'm going to make you my wife!"

At the time, Elaine did not know that these threats were largely a joke, a way for bored prisoners to amuse themselves. In her mind, the words raining down on her confirmed her very worst fears. Over the last four months, locked in Albany County Jail, she had heard plenty of horror stories about Bedford Hills prison. These ugly rumors now swirled through her head: The women at Bedford will attack you, rape you, steal all your stuff.

Tears had been streaming down her face for two hours, the entire drive from Albany to Westchester County. It had not been easy to wipe them away with handcuffed hands, and so she had given up trying. Now her cheeks were wet, and her eyes were swollen.

An officer led her and the other women into a building designated RECEPTION. Elaine surveyed the dingy area. It was noisy and reeked of disinfectant. Along one wall was a row of grimy shower stalls with no curtains. The first thing she was supposed to do, she learned, was take a shower with lice-killing soap. In Albany County, she had posed for a mug shot and pressed her ink-wet fingertips onto a sheet of paper. But allow strangers to watch her strip down and shower naked? No way.

"This ain't going to be no fashion show," she said. "You're not going to be looking at my body. The judge sentenced me to twenty years. He didn't say I had to be subjected to all this."

She slumped in a chair and folded her arms across her chest.

A guard strolled toward her. "Get in the shower!" she shouted.

Elaine did not move.

"We've got a real live one over here," the officer announced.

From across the room, a voice boomed, "Who's that causing trouble?" Suddenly, a large woman in a blue guard's uniform appeared. She reminded Elaine of her own mother. She was shorter than Yvonne, but she was almost as heavy. This was Miss Dixon.

Elaine did not know her, of course, but almost everyone else did. After all, she'd been working here for nearly two decades. Over the years, Miss Dixon had seen hundreds of young women come through the front gates of Bedford Hills. Almost all of the first-timers were terrified. Most were angry, too.

"What are you here for?" she asked.

Elaine told her the short version: the trip to Albany, the trial, the 20-to-life sentence. "You're lying," Officer Dixon said. "This can't be your first offense. No wonder you're so damned angry."

Another guard handed over her new wardrobe: one green dress, two pairs of green pants, two matching green shirts, three white cotton panties, three white cotton bras, a pair of white canvas tennis sneakers. Elaine would later learn that certain colors were contraband: blue, black, orange, and gray. The guards wore these colors, and so the prisoners were not allowed to.

All of her clothes were marked with her new identity: 84-G-0068. By simply glancing at the tag glued to her shirt, everybody would know her prison history. The G revealed that she had started her incarceration at Bedford. Her number indicated that she was the sixty-eighth inmate to arrive here in 1984.

That afternoon, Miss Dixon gave her another name, too: "Rebel without a cause." It was a name that would stick for many years. Every time Miss Dixon saw her coming down the hall, she would say, "Oh, you're a rebel without a cause." For a time, the moniker was accurate. Eventually, though, Elaine did find her cause—one that perfectly matched her rebellious spirit.

Elaine did not know it at the time, but Bedford Hills has long been considered one of the most progressive women's prisons in the United States. When it opened in 1901, it was actually a "reformatory," not a prison. At the time, reformatories represented the latest innovation in the criminal-justice system. They sought to "reform" women without using chains or whips or any of the other punitive practices then common in penitentiaries. There was no stone wall around the grounds. No fence topped with coils of razor wire. No watchtowers or sliding metal gates. Only women found guilty of minor crimes, like prostitution and petty theft, were allowed to come here.

The Bedford Reformatory was built on a 107½-acre farm. Instead of cell blocks, the inmates lived in cottages, supervised by women, known as "matrons." Each cottage had the trappings of an upper-middle-class home: linen tablecloths and napkins, china, cut flowers in vases, framed paintings on the walls, a flower garden. Bedford's inmates attended classes on reading, writing, and math, as well as cooking, sewing, and crocheting. They also learned nontraditional skills, like how to repair shoes, cane chairs, milk cows, slaughter hogs, harvest potatoes, shovel coal, and pour cement.

John D. Rockefeller, Jr., Nelson's father, bought seventy-one acres of land next to the Bedford Reformatory in 1911. His interest in female inmates stemmed from his role as an antiprostitution crusader. On this property, he built the Laboratory of Social Hygiene, which he leased to the state. The purpose of his clinic was to identify inmates who were "mentally defective" and therefore incapable of reforming. These women were then sent to an asylum, where they were to be locked up indefinitely.

Despite their progressive ambitions, Bedford's officials soon began engaging in the worst sort of abuses found in prisons: flogging, sterilizations, shackling women to their beds for days, handcuffing them to the wall so that their feet barely touched the floor. If a woman screamed all night long, a matron took her to the reception building, also known as the "Screamery." There, she was left for days, and sometimes weeks, locked in a cell by herself.

Evidently, the reformatory experiment was failing. A report found that 60 percent of the incoming inmates were actually return visitors. In 1933, a women's prison was added, and the complex acquired a new name: Westfield State Farm. Although Bedford gradually abandoned its original mission, it held on to the designation Reformatory until 1970, when the two female populations were combined. The complex was renamed the Bedford Hills Correctional Facility.

Six decades after John D. Rockefeller set up a laboratory here to weed out incorrigible women, another Rockefeller played a crucial role in determining the makeup of Bedford's population. Governor Nelson Rockefeller's decision to punish drug felons with extra-long sentences led to a rapid increase in the state's prison population. Between 1975 and 1983, the number of women imprisoned in New York State nearly doubled, from 428 to 849.

By the time Elaine arrived here, the prison consisted of nearly fifty buildings, all enclosed by a fence topped with loops of razor-edged wire that sparkled in the sun. The cows and hogs were gone, and so were the linen napkins. Bedford Hills had acquired all the staples of a state prison: cell blocks, rec yards, law library, commissary, mess hall. Women who misbehaved were no longer flogged. Instead, they were sent to the brand-new building, which held the Special Housing Unit, or SHU, where they were locked alone in a cell for twenty-three hours a day.

Bedford Hills had long been the state's only prison for women, but after the Rockefeller drug laws went into effect, officials started looking elsewhere for beds. There were only 578 beds at Bedford—not nearly enough for all the women streaming into the state's prison system. Soon there were three more prisons with female inmates: Albion, a coed prison located west of Rochester; Bayview, a former YMCA for merchant sailors, in the Chelsea district of Manhattan; and Parkside, a work-release facility across the street from Mount Morris Park in Harlem.

Every woman entering the New York State prison system goes first to Bedford Hills to be tested, questioned, and classified. Women with short sentences, usually three years or less, are put on a bus to Albion. Those with longer sentences stay at Bedford Hills. If they have a choice, nearly all the women would opt to remain here. Most of the state's prisoners are from New York City, and the proximity of Bedford Hills to the city means they are more likely to get visits from friends and family. Albion is a seven-hour bus ride from New York City, while Bedford Hills is just thirty-five miles north of Harlem.

Bedford Hills is the only maximum-security prison for women in New York State. Violent crimes account for about half of its inmates; the other half are evenly split between those who've committed drug crimes and those convicted of property crimes. Elaine had an extraordinarily long sentence compared to most of the state's female prisoners. Seventy percent had a minimum sentence of less than four years. Of the women in New York's prison system at the end of 1984, only Elaine and thirty-four others had a minimum sentence of twenty years or more.

In many other ways, though, Elaine was typical of New York's female prisoners. Most were younger than thirty-five; had at least one child; had not finished high school; had been employed before they were arrested; and had never done time in a jail or prison before. In 1984, 23 percent of the women entering the New York State prison system were Hispanic, 26 percent were white, and 51 percent were African-American. At the time, blacks made up only 14 percent of New York State's population.

Prisoners with lengthy sentences were known as "long-termers," and Elaine definitely qualified. This group included Jean Harris, the former prep school headmistress, who had been sentenced to 15-to-life for killing her lover, Dr. Herman Tarnower, author of *The Complete Scarsdale Medical Diet*. Another prisoner destined to be a long-termer was Judith Clark, a political radical who had recently arrived. She had received 75-to-life for her involvement in the robbery of a Brinks armored car, during which two policemen and a Brinks guard were killed. Two months after Elaine's arrival, another radical who had also been involved in the Brinks robbery, Kathy Boudin, entered the prison with a sentence of 20-to-life.

Harris, Boudin, and Clark were the sort of women whose trials received front-page headlines and updates on the television news, bestowing them with notoriety long before they walked into Bedford Hills. In the fall of 1983, Clark's impending arrival had sent the prison into a minor frenzy. Officials came from Albany to inspect the fence around the perimeter. Guards donned bulletproof vests. Helicopters hovered overhead. When Elaine Bartlett trudged into the Reception building five months later, she attracted no outside attention. The arrival of yet another drug dealer, even one with a 20-to-life sentence, did not qualify as big news.

For Elaine, however, the day she arrived at Bedford Hills marked the end of one chapter in her life and the beginning of another. For years, a handful of dreams had sustained her. She had wanted to raise her children, furnish the rest of her apartment, maybe operate her own beauty salon. These were the ambitions around which she'd organized her life before she had been arrested and her world turned upside down. Now all she had was a long list of unanswerable questions. Would she really be here for twenty years? What would happen to her children? And what would happen to her? Would she even recognize herself by the time she finally got out of here?

CHAPTER 8

For Elaine, the nights were the hardest, when she was locked in her cell, lying on her prison cot in the dark. Sleeping alone felt strange. Growing up, she had always slept with her mother or a sister. After she had her own place, she usually slept beside one or more of her children, and maybe a boyfriend, too. In those early months at Bedford, she spent the last hours of every day crying into her pillow, trying to muffle her sobs so the other women wouldn't hear her. Eventually, after an hour or two, she would wear herself out. With her cheek pressed against her soggy pillow cover, she would fall asleep.

Every day began the same way, with a guard outside her cell shouting, "On the count!" at 5:30 a.m. This was the cue to get out of bed and press one palm against the cell window, so that she could be counted. On weekday mornings, she attended Adult Basic Education—the class for inmates whose skills are equivalent to those of a junior-high student. She thought the lessons were too easy, and she soon transferred to a GED class. In the afternoons, she worked as a porter in the kitchen. She usually went outside in the evenings and strolled around the yard. Like everyone else, she was locked in her cell from 10:00 p.m. to 6:00 a.m.

Her cell was about the size of the kitchen in her Wagner Houses apartment. It was number A29, on a second-floor tier known as Unit 113 A&B. Inside were a toilet, a sink, a bed, and a metal locker. There was, of course, no stove or laundry machine or refrigerator. The chores and responsibilities that had once defined her days were no longer part of her life. She did not have to feed herself or wash her own clothes. There was no changing diapers, no more picking up children from school, no more scrambling to pay the rent.

Now she had a new full-time occupation: waiting. She waited to leave her cell, to go to the mess hall, to call her family. She waited for the court to consider her appeal, for somebody to send her a letter, for a friend or relative to visit, for the chance to go home. Some women hung calendars in their cells. For Elaine, the prospect of ticking off one day at a time for twenty years—a total of 7,305 days—was too distressing to even consider.

Before arriving at Bedford Hills, she had never been a shoplifter or a pickpocket. But now that she was in prison, she, like just about everyone else, soon became a skilled thief. The first item she stole was a pack of sanitary napkins. Prisoners were allotted only two packs of napkins every month—a total of twenty-four pads. For most women, this was not enough, so everyone stole extra ones to stick in their underpants when their stash ran out.

In the evenings, when she went out to the prison yard, she often smoked weed with a few other inmates. Marijuana had always made her feel fantastic back in the days before she went to prison; after only a drag or two, she would be telling jokes and laughing uncontrollably. Now, whenever she got high in the yard, the fence drew her attention. Looking through the barbed wire and the many yards of trees, she could see cars whizzing down a highway. Some afternoons, she would stand right next to the fence and stare at the road for hours. Other days, she would climb onto one of the wooden picnic tables to get a better view.

The faint whoosh of cars reminded her that life went on in the outside world. People traveled places. They went on adventures. And all the time she was stuck here, living in a tiny concrete cage, waiting to go home. She smoked weed as often as she could, but every time she did, the same thing happened. The highway looked a little closer. The razor wire coiled atop the fence appeared a little less frightening. Escape seemed possible, and prison all the more unbearable. Getting high was supposed to make her feel better, but as her high wore off, she always felt more frustrated and more depressed.

Besides waiting and getting high, she had another part-time occupation: trying to make sense of her own situation, to figure how she had come to be doing 20-to-life in this maximum-security prison. What did I do to deserve this? She asked herself this constantly. Whenever she told anyone her story, they stared at her in disbelief. "Girl, you're crazy!" they said. Some people assumed she was lying. Inside Bedford Hills, it was not always easy to figure out who was telling the truth. The least popular prisoners—the "babykillers"—always tried to hide the nature of their crimes. Usually, they said they were doing time for drugs.

Of all the people Elaine knew who had committed crimes, she thought her crime was one of the less serious. Often she thought about her brother Shyan, who had started committing robberies at age ten and was first arrested at twelve. For years he had been a one-man crime spree. She had heard about him snatching pocketbooks on the subway, sticking up drug dealers, grabbing money bags from store owners, shooting people in the street. Now Shyan was in another state prison, farther north, serving a much shorter sentence than hers.

There was one prisoner Elaine heard about who had been at Bedford Hills longer than anyone else: Ruth Brown. She was a tiny seventy-seven-year-old black woman who tiptoed around the prison nursery, taking care of other inmates' babies. In the nursery, she was in charge, not the guards. After all, she knew this place better than just about anyone. Ma Brown had been a prisoner at Bedford Hills since the days when it was a reformatory.

In 1931, when she was twenty-four, she had been convicted of murder and sentenced to die in the electric chair—the first death sentence for a New York woman since 1895. She had stood by with a knife while a male friend had stabbed another man inside a speakeasy in Harlem. A judge sent her and a codefendant to New York's death house, then located at Sing Sing. He was executed, but Governor Franklin D. Roosevelt commuted her sentence to life in prison. She was moved to Bedford Hills.

Two days before Christmas in 1951, Governor Thomas Dewey granted clemency to Ruth Brown, enabling her to be set free. He cited her exemplary prison record and the fact that she had no prior criminal history. She left Bedford Hills at age forty-five after being locked up for twenty-one years. She was supposed to be on parole for the rest of her life.

Two years later, she was imprisoned for not obeying the rules of her parole. After spending another year behind bars, she was released once again. This time, she remained free for nine years, until 1964, when she was returned to Bedford Hills for another parole violation.

By then she was fifty-seven years old. She had a daughter, but she'd lost touch with her long ago. Nobody recognized Ma Brown on the streets of New York City; at least in Bedford Hills everyone knew who she was. She had been a prisoner for so long that she felt more at home inside Bedford than outside it.

Over the next twenty years, whenever she was scheduled to appear before the parole board, she simply did not show up. She remained at Bedford Hills until the summer of 1984, six months after Elaine arrived. That August, Ma Brown died of a heart attack. By then, she had spent forty-one of her seventy-seven years behind bars. Prison officials held a memorial service for her in the gym at Bedford Hills.

For years to come, the story of Ma Brown was passed down from one generation of Bedford prisoners to the next. Her story was part history lesson, part cautionary tale. Nobody wanted to lose all contact with the outside world like Ma Brown had. This fear was particularly strong among prisoners like Elaine, the ones with especially long sentences. Nobody wanted to discover that by the time they were finally permitted to leave, they had lost their desire to be free.

· · ·

Elaine's days were divided into two categories: the days when her family came to visit and the days when they did not. Nearly every weekend, her mother made the journey from New York City with all four of her children. To be able to see her, her family had to become prisoners, too. They had to step inside the fence, slip off their sneakers and sandals, walk through a metal detector, and pass through three electronically controlled doors. In those early months, the children did not mind. Everything about visiting Bedford Hills was a novelty.

A few dozen tables filled the visiting room, which was on the first floor of the prison's administration building. Every time Elaine's family came, they sat at their own table and tried to have a private conversation. This was not easy, though, since there were always guards nearby. When the children got bored, Elaine took them to the Children's Center at the back of the visiting room. Here, they could ride the rocking horse, paint at the easel, or play board games. The row of vending machines along one wall of the visiting room was also a source of entertainment. The children begged their grandmother for quarters, then skipped over to the machines to buy snacks.

Almost every weekend, the family gathered together and posed for a Polaroid, taken by the prisoner whose job was visiting-room photographer. In the summer of 1985, Elaine stood between her two sons, turning her head to one side and puckering her lips. Twelve-year-old Apache leaned over to give her a kiss, while eight-year-old Jamel pressed his skinny body against hers. Satara, age five, stood on a ledge behind them, one hand on her hip, the toes of her sandals pointing toward each other. Three-year-old Danae mimicked her older sister, lifting one arm and posing with a hand behind her head.

If not for the green pants Elaine wore, no one would guess this photograph was taken inside a prison. Jamel wears a big uninhibited grin, wide enough to reveal all his front teeth; Danae is smiling so hard, she's squinting. There is no hint of the trauma the children had endured over the past twenty months. No angry, sullen stares. No aloof poses. On this day, the family celebrated Apache's twelfth birthday. Other twelve-year-olds might have spent their birthday at Skate Key in the Bronx or at Coney Island, but Apache did not mind. The only place he wanted to be was with his mother, which meant he had to go to prison.

Elaine was more fortunate than some of her fellow inmates. There had never been any doubt about what would happen to her children after she got locked up—her mother would raise them. She often overheard other inmates on the prison pay phones, trying to navigate the bureaucracy of New York City's foster-care system. In a desperate voice, they would try to find out where their children were. Then they would plead with a social worker to bring their children to the prison. Over the years, some women lost track of their sons and daughters. Every now and then, children walked into the visiting room and looked around uncertainly, trying to figure out which woman was their mother.

Elaine listened to her children's stories—about their friends, their relatives' antics, the parties she had missed—but there was not much about her own life that she wanted to share. The Bedford Hills grapevine was always buzzing with news. Two ex-lovers had brawled in the yard. A crew of women had robbed another inmate on her way back from commissary. A prisoner had nearly died of a heroin overdose. Another inmate had performed oral sex on a guard just to get a few sticks of gum. These were the sorts of tales that could entertain a cell block of bored women for weeks, but they were certainly not subjects for the visiting room.

For Elaine, it was difficult to maneuver between these two worlds: the visiting room and the rest of the prison. In the cell blocks and corridors, she had to watch her back constantly, always ready to raise her fists if anyone tried to pick a fight. But then when she entered the visiting room, she had to play the role of mother. She had to be patient and affectionate, warm and loving. The visits with her mother and children were like oxygen. She needed them to hold on to her sanity and stop herself from becoming bitter. But at the same time, her family's visits always left her feeling unbearably sad.

Despite her children's grins, she could see the toll that her absence was taking on them. The sadness in their eyes was unmistakable, and frighteningly familiar. She was now twenty-seven, but she had not forgotten how she had felt when she was taken away from her mother at age six, then sent to an orphanage on Staten Island. The best times she had during those years were when she and her brother Frankie were permitted to go home for the weekend. But then, every Sunday night, when her mother took her on the ferry back to the orphanage, she would cry the entire ride.

Of all Elaine's children, the effect of her absence was most apparent in Jamel. He was the most needy and the most aggressive. In the visiting room, the only place he wanted to be was in her lap. If Apache, Satara, or Danae was already there, he would try to push them off. At the end of every visit, he cried and refused to leave, clinging tightly to Elaine's legs. When the guards tried to pull him off, he kicked and punched them. "Fuck that!" he shouted. "I ain't going nowhere!"

Elaine, too, cried at the conclusion of every visit, though she tried to hold herself together until after her family left. Then, once she joined the line of other prisoners waiting to be marched back to their cell blocks, the tears flowed.

"Why are you crying?" other prisoners would ask. "You should be happy. You just had a visit."

"Happy about what?" she would say. "I ain't going to see them for twenty years."

Not long after Elaine was arrested, her ex-boyfriend Bobby Paschall found out that she was in prison and that his sons were living with Yvonne. He took Yvonne to court and won custody of Apache and Jamel. When Elaine heard this, she was livid. Ever since her relationship with Bobby had ended, he had shown little interest in the boys. Why did he want them now? Was he just trying to get back at her for rejecting him in the past? Considering his penchant for alcohol and his ugly temper, Elaine imagined the worst sort of home for her sons.

Bobby had recently married and now lived with his wife in Brownsville, Brooklyn. According to him, he took Yvonne to court because he considered her a bad influence on his sons. "In the custody of that woman, they can turn out to be criminals and murderers and junkies and drug dealers and whatever," he explained years later. "The worst things of our culture they can turn out to be up under her. So that's why when I had the chance to seize custody of my kids, it was no problem. I wanted to offer them the best that I had. I didn't have much, but I did have moral standards."

The custody agreement required Bobby to take the boys to Bedford Hills every other weekend. In the visiting room, Elaine would refuse to talk to Bobby, leaving him seated alone at the table while she took her sons into the Children's Center. Soon she began hearing stories that confirmed her fears. Jamel told her that Bobby sometimes whipped him and Apache, using a leather strap, a metal dog chain, or even a rubber belt from beneath the hood of a car. When Elaine spoke to Bobby, she did not hide her rage. "I'm going to kill you when I get home," she said.

Yvonne had custody of the boys every other weekend. Apache and Jamel wanted to see her more often, so they frequently ran away from their father's house. On their own, they traveled from Brooklyn to their grandmother's apartment on the Lower East Side. Sometimes they took the subway. They got a free ride in a police car one time, when Apache convinced an officer that he and Jamel had lost their way. During one of their visits, Yvonne discovered bruises all over their backs. She snapped photos of their injuries, took Bobby to court, and won back custody of both boys.

Some weekends, Yvonne told Elaine that she could not afford to take the children up to Bedford Hills. So Elaine would be surprised when she heard that someone had come to see her. Walking into the visiting room, she would see Jamel seated at a table by himself, his skinny legs not quite touching the floor. He had sneaked out of his grandmother's apartment and come on his own. By now, he knew how to get to the prison. Ride the subway to Grand Central, transfer to Metro-North, get off at the Bedford Hills stop, flag a taxi. The guards were not supposed to let in children without a chaperone, but they had a hard time turning away a ten-year-old boy desperate to see his mother.

CHAPTER 9

Heroin and cocaine addicts flocked to the Lower East Side in the early 1980s. They came all the way from Connecticut and New Jersey to shop for drugs, double-parking their cars and then lining up in front of a dealer's storefront operation. To minimize police scrutiny, dealers recruited local children to carry drugs and act as lookouts. The *Los Angeles Times* published a front-page photograph of customers lining up to buy heroin on East Third Street. It declared the Lower East Side the "most open heroin market in the nation."

Three public housing projects make up the eastern border of the Lower East Side. They are comprised of fifty-one redbrick buildings, which cover fifteen city blocks, from Fourteenth Street to Delancey Street. The names of the projects reflect their original ambitions. The Riis Houses were named after Jacob A. Riis, the crusading reporter and photographer who produced the classic book *How the Other Half Lives* in 1890. The Wald Houses bear the name of Lillian D. Wald, the public health advocate and turn-of-the-century reformer.

When these projects opened in the early 1950s, the hope was that they would stamp out poverty in the neighborhood by providing better housing than the slum tenements in which most residents lived. But by the 1980s, the Riis Houses and Wald Houses had become synonymous with drugs and violence. Syringes littered their lobbies. Junkies nodded out on the benches inside the projects.

Avenue D, which runs along the west side of these two projects, was notorious. *The New York Times* dubbed it "one of the meanest streets in America, a narrow corridor of poverty and violence." It was, the reporter wrote, "a street where men gripping beer bottles in brown paper bags exchange prison memories." The *Daily News* ran a front-page picture of junkies sprawled on a sidewalk, with the headline, IS THIS ANY PLACE FOR CHILDREN?

Yvonne moved into the Wald Houses in 1980. She was assigned to Apartment 13B, on the thirteenth floor of a fourteen-story building near the rear of the project. This apartment was a step down from her house in Queens, but the cost of fixing busted pipes and making other repairs had forced her to find a cheaper alternative. Now her monthly rent was $153—down from the $350 she had been paying in Corona.

Apartment 13B had three small bedrooms, a living room, a tiny kitchen, and one bathroom. Yvonne shared the space with three of her children—Sabrina, Ronald, and Michelle—plus Sabrina's daughter, Michelle's husband, Michelle's two daughters, and Donjuan's daughter. While Donjuan was in prison, Yvonne was raising his daughter. After Elaine was arrested, her four children moved in, too. Their arrival pushed the apartment's population to thirteen. At night, every bed held at least two people.

Yvonne patched together an income from her monthly SSI checks, which amounted to $215. She got occasional handouts from her children, and sometimes Littleboy gave her money, too. But with an apartment full of people, the struggle for cash never stopped. And now that Elaine was in prison, Yvonne had four more children to feed.

Every time one of Yvonne's children got locked up, her expenditures increased. It was not just the cost of caring for the children left behind. It was all the prison expenses, too: the bus or train fare to get to prison, the Polaroids for each visit, the monthly collect-call bills, the packages of food, the occasional money orders needed to buy cigarettes or cosmetics in the prison commissary.

At the end of 1987, the state parole board released Shyan. By then, all the children in Apartment 13B had been hearing Uncle Shyan stories for years. They'd heard about his many crimes, as well as his propensity for getting women pregnant. Nobody knew exactly how many children he had, but they knew there were many. When he was sixteen and the family lived in Corona, two teenage girls in the neighborhood had been pregnant at the same time, both carrying his child.

After he got out of prison, Shyan moved in with a girlfriend in Corona, but he often stopped by Apartment 13B. Usually he had a gun with him, stuck in the waistband of his pants. Of all the children in the apartment, Shyan spent the most time with ten-year-old Jamel. He taught Jamel how to drive, introduced him to his friends, let him wear his gold jewelry, and took him to Florida for a vacation. He did not let Jamel use his gun, but he would sometimes let him hold it.

To satisfy his parole officer, Shyan worked briefly in the kitchen at the Marriott hotel near LaGuardia airport. Soon, though, he found a much more lucrative line of work. He teamed up with Darryl Whiting, the leader of a gang known as the New York Boys, that was exporting crack from Queens to a public-housing project in Roxbury, outside Boston. Whiting hired Shyan to be his hit man.

By the end of 1987, eight months after he came home, Shyan was back in jail for not reporting to his parole officer. He was released three months later.

Police officers and parole officers were regular visitors to Apartment 13B whenever Shyan was not locked up. They were always looking for him. Sometimes his family knew why; sometimes they didn't. Once a group of officers barged into the apartment and put a pair of handcuffs on Apache. With his curly hair, light brown skin, and lanky frame, the fourteen-year-old resembled his uncle.

"Grandma, what's going on?" Apache asked.

"That's not Shyan," Yvonne said. "That's my grandson."

Shyan cycled in and out of jail once more on another parole violation, and then in 1990, the police took him away for good. This time,
he was accused of opening fire with an AK-47 inside a bodega in
Queens. Three people were injured, including the bodega owner,
who had to have his leg amputated. A judge sentenced Shyan to five
to fifteen years in prison.

Meanwhile, law enforcement officials in Massachusetts were in-
vestigating his involvement in the New York Boys. After he was indicted, Shyan admitted to five murders in connection with his role as
Whiting's hit man. For these crimes, he received two life terms in a
Massachusetts state prison. (In Massachusetts, prisoners serving life
sentences are eligible for parole after fifteen years.) Shyan was also
indicted in a federal narcotics trafficking case. A federal judge sentenced him to twenty-two years in prison. These two sentences are
now running concurrently. His earliest possible release date is 2019,
when he will be fifty-nine years old.

When Elaine had first gone to prison, her sister Sabrina had played
the role of mother to Elaine's children, taking them to school and to
their doctors' appointments. Sabrina was an ideal surrogate mom; she
looked enough like Elaine to fool people. With Sabrina by their side,
Elaine's children did not have to reveal to anyone where their mother
had gone. There were no awkward pauses, no embarrassing explana-
tions.

Everything changed shortly after Sabrina gave birth to her second
child, Baby Regina. The infant was born prematurely and spent the
first two months of her life in a hospital. One morning, not long after
Regina came home, Sabrina woke up, checked on the baby, and discovered that she was blue. Sometime in the middle of the night, Baby
Regina had died in her crib.

In the weeks and months afterward, Sabrina sought solace in crack
cocaine. She began disappearing for days at a time. In order to support her drug habit, she started selling marijuana. By 1990, she was
getting arrested every few months, usually on Avenue D. Unlike her
siblings, she did not stay in jail for long. All her arrests were for minor

crimes—mostly possession or sale of marijuana. She seemed to have learned a lesson from Elaine's long prison term; marijuana is not covered by the Rockefeller drug laws.

By 1991, four of Yvonne's children were behind bars: Shyan, Donjuan, Elaine, and Sabrina. Of her three children who were free, Ronald and Michelle lived in Apartment 13B. Ronald was the artist in the family. He sketched portraits of his nieces and nephews, and he often danced around the apartment. Soon, though, Ronald started heading down the same path as Sabrina, getting high in order to deal with his despair. His family did not know it at the time, but he had learned he had HIV. Back then, a diagnosis of HIV was considered a death sentence.

Apache tried to cope with all the chaos in Apartment 13B by spending as little time there as possible. Every day after school, he headed straight to the basketball court behind his building. The neighborhood's drug dealers regularly recruited boys to join their business, but they did not target Apache because they could see he had athletic potential. "Stay on that court," they would say, handing him a few dollars so he could buy a soda or a snack. "I always want to see you with a ball in your hand."

Basketball became Apache's escape. He met older boys who encouraged him to keep practicing and told him that one day maybe he could win a scholarship to college. He joined New Life, an AAU basketball club, and he got the chance to leave New York. With his basketball team, he traveled around the country, playing in tournaments in Ohio, Nevada, Pennsylvania, and Georgia.

Now Apache had a sense of purpose—to be the best-possible basketball player—and a group of friends who shared his dream. His teammates became his new family. He called his best friends "brothers," and he took them to Bedford Hills to meet his mother.

Yvonne encouraged Apache's passion. She collected his basketball trophies and displayed them prominently in the living room. When

Apache's photo appeared in the *City Sun* after he scored twenty-seven points for the High School for the Humanities, Yvonne cut it out of the paper. When Apache wanted to transfer to La Salle Academy, a Catholic school with a nationally known basketball program, Yvonne helped scrounge together tuition money.

The more time Apache spent playing basketball, the less time he had to visit his mother, but he still thought about her all the time. As long as she was locked up, he felt as if he were locked up, too. All day, every day, he tried to imagine what she was doing at the same moment. Sleeping? Eating? Going to classes? At night, his mother appeared in his dreams. Other children might dream about a new bicycle or a trip to Disneyland. In Apache's dreams, his mother handed out lunch money to him and his friends.

When other children asked Apache where his mother was, he always told the truth. Nothing about her, not even her status as prisoner, could make him feel ashamed. Jamel was the opposite. Nothing got him more angry than when somebody asked him, "Where's your mother?" Jamel would refuse to answer. "Don't talk to me about my mother," he'd say. If that person asked the same question again, Jamel would attack him.

After Elaine went to prison, Jamel's energetic personality became laced with rage. In school, he threw erasers at teachers, tossed gum in girls' hair, sliced open other children's coats so the feathers spilled out. As Apache grew older and spent less time with him, Jamel felt abandoned once again. He missed having his older brother around. When Apache went out with his friends and did not invite him along, Jamel followed behind them as they left the project, throwing bottles and rocks.

When he was ten years old, Jamel joined the neighborhood's most lucrative industry. He became a runner, transporting packages of heroin and cocaine for the older dealers. Each trip to another block or another borough could earn him $100. Quickly, he learned that hanging out on Avenue D was an easy way to get whatever he wanted. After an hour or two of work, he could buy a meal, a new pair of sneakers, a gift for a girl. It may have been the only job in the city that a ten-year-old could get. No working papers needed. For a boy with no parents, no money, and a hunger for adventure, it seemed ideal.

Jamel bought his first gun at age twelve. He traded four bags of crack to a neighborhood junkie in exchange for a .25-caliber handgun. Purchasing a gun at such an early age might have seemed bizarre in another family, but Jamel had been around guns all his life. Not only did Shyan carry a gun, but Yvonne did, too. She did not take it out often, but everyone knew she kept a .38-caliber revolver in her purse.

Jamel began carrying his gun around in his bag or his pocket, and he practiced shooting it on the roof of his building. He did not bring the gun home, however. Instead, he buried it in the dirt in front of his building before he went into the apartment, so Yvonne would not see it.

Besides transporting drugs, he also had a few other ways he earned money. He sold marijuana. He played dice with other boys in the project. And sometimes he called a local Chinese restaurant, ordered food, and then robbed the deliveryman when he arrived.

By 1991, Jamel was fourteen years old and spending every night outside, looking for customers on Avenue D. Before dawn, he would return home. And a few hours later, somebody would wake him for school. Some days he went; some days he didn't. Other times he would work two or three days in a row before returning home and collapsing on a bed.

He spent a few months at Spofford, the juvenile jail in the Bronx, and there he acquired his nickname. When a fight between two boys broke out, Jamel jumped in the middle and beat up one of the boys. Another inmate dubbed him "Murder Mel." Jamel liked the name because he thought it made him sound tough. When he returned to the Lower East Side, his friends started calling him "Murder Mel."

Whenever Elaine called Apartment 13B and heard that Jamel was standing on Avenue D, she would order Apache to go downstairs and drag him home. But the younger brother no longer listened to the older one. By then, the boys in the street had become Jamel's new brothers.

Yvonne was determined not to watch another Bartlett child go to prison. Some nights, she stayed up until 3:00 a.m., waiting in the dark at the kitchen table for Jamel to come home. When he finally crept into the apartment, she would order him to strip. Then she would empty his pockets, take his money, throw his drugs in the toilet, and beat him.

Eventually, though, Yvonne gave up. After all, with Shyan back in prison, Jamel was now the family's main breadwinner; he often came back to the apartment with armloads of groceries. He bought alarm clocks, shirts, sneakers, and boots for his sisters. For himself, he bought puffy goose-down coats, leather jackets, a thick gold chain, and many pairs of Nikes. Family members began calling him "Little Shyan."

Nobody had ever told Jamel exactly why his mother was in prison. At first, when she'd left, he did not even know where she'd gone. Yvonne had told him that his mother was away at college. After noticing similarities between the uniforms of cops he saw on television and those of the guards at Bedford Hills, he had started asking questions. Eventually, he learned that his mother was in prison, but he did not know why.

Now Elaine decided to be frank with him about the details of her crime. In the prison visiting room, she told him the story of her arrest and trial. But even this first-person tale about the perils of drug dealing did not dissuade him. Soon, Elaine heard that Jamel was back on Avenue D. The next time he visited her, she became so frustrated that she punched him in the mouth. He started to cry, and soon she was crying, too. "Don't make me have to come over the fence, so the TV news says, 'Woman escapes from Bedford Hills,'" she said. "I don't want to have to come home and visit you in prison."

CHAPTER 10

Arlene O'Connor passed by Bedford Hills prison every time she drove south on Route 684. Peering through the trees on the right, just past exit five, she could make out a parking lot, a tangle of metal fences, a smokestack, and several redbrick buildings. If you didn't know the prison was there, it was possible to drive by and not see it at all. It was easiest to see the prison at night, when it lit the sky like a city in the distance.

Arlene lived just a few miles away. Like most of her fellow towns-people, she had never been inside Bedford Hills prison. For the most part, the lives of the area's residents and its inmates never intersected. Arlene did not know any prisoners, and she did not know anyone who worked inside. She had never heard about any riots or escapes, and so the prison's proximity to her home did not worry her. She would just glance over as her car barreled down the highway, and then she would go on with her day.

The first time she heard anything about life inside the prison was on the Sunday morning when Sister Elaine Roulet spoke at her church. Sister Elaine worked at Bedford Hills, and she had just started a new summer program. Many of the inmates rarely got to see their children, she explained, and so she was recruiting families who would be willing to let a prisoner's child stay with them for a week. The children would visit their mothers during the day and then spend evenings with their hosts.

The program appealed to Arlene. Her daughter was out of high school and no longer needed her as much. Maybe it was time to help somebody else's child.

Arlene and her husband, Patrick, lived in Katonah, a hamlet next to Bedford Hills. He ran a print shop. She worked as his bookkeeper and sold Mary Kay products on the side. They were certainly not rich, but they were not poor, either. Yet in recent years, they had begun to feel their financial pressures increase. The town of Bedford—which included the hamlets of Katonah and Bedford Hills—was rapidly transforming the northeast corner of Westchester County into one of the wealthiest regions in the country. The area's closeness to New York City, its easy access to the commuter railroad, and its rustic feel all contributed to its popularity. News that a house had sold for $2 million was no longer surprising.

Over the years, so many people in the entertainment business had bought homes here that it became known as the "Beverly Hills of the East Coast." Richard Gere, Christopher Reeve, Glenn Close, Tommy Mottola, Clive Davis, George C. Scott, and Chevy Chase all lived in the area at various times. As housing prices climbed, prison guards could not afford to reside here. Some lived in Davis Hall, a brick building on the grounds of Bedford Hills prison; others shacked up with coworkers in apartments in distant towns.

That Sunday morning, Arlene and Pat added their names to the list of volunteers, and soon they were told to expect a four-year-old girl. To their surprise, they ended up with a fifteen-year-old boy who was nearly six feet tall. His name was Apache Paschall. After Arlene and Pat recovered from their initial shock, they took him out to a Chinese restaurant. "He was the most beautiful kid," Arlene recalls. "So endearing. The best smile. We bonded right away."

Another fifteen-year-old might have been obsessed with sneakers and video games. Not Apache. His obsession was his family. He told the O'Connors that he was especially worried his younger brother would end up in prison. "From our very first conversation in the restaurant, he said, 'I have to break the cycle. I'm the oldest, and if I don't, my sisters and brother won't have the example to follow,'" Arlene says. "He was definitely taking on the role of father and nurturer. He didn't make it sound like a burden, but inside, he was in a lot of pain."

The O'Connors lived in a modest dark brown house with red trim on a hill above a small lake. Apache was pleased to discover they had a basketball backboard, albeit one with a crooked hoop. He and Pat shot baskets together in the driveway. In the evening, Pat invited Apache to walk their miniature poodle with him. The neighborhood was nothing like the Lower East Side. No sirens. No streetlights. The sky was pitch-black. Only the hooting of owls interrupted the silence. The possibility of a deer jumping out of the woods terrified Apache, and so he declined to walk the dog. Inside the house, Apache, Arlene, and Pat watched television together and roasted marshmallows in the fireplace.

Every day for a week, Arlene dropped Apache off in front of the prison at 8:00 a.m. In this mob of children, Apache was one of the oldest, and certainly one of the tallest. Standing outside the metal gate, he looked at ease; the prospect of passing inside this fence no longer fazed him. But sometimes Arlene would see a small boy or girl who appeared scared and confused. The horde of children, the guards in their uniforms, the strange host parents, the formidable fence, the countless rules—all of it overwhelmed and intimidated them, pushing them to the verge of tears.

When Arlene picked up Apache at 3:00 p.m., he was usually quiet for an hour or two. Eventually, he would reveal a bit about his visit with his mother, brother, and sisters. They had eaten lunch, played cards, swapped stories about their host families. The younger children had made arts and crafts and built sand castles on the patio outside. To keep Apache entertained, Elaine had convinced a guard to erect a basketball hoop on the patio. It was sort of like a summer camp, except that a fence topped with concertina wire loomed in the distance.

Before they met Apache, the O'Connors had been planning to remove the basketball backboard from their driveway because they thought it unsightly. When they saw how much he loved to play, they changed their minds. "That hoop will never come down," they told him. By the end of the week, the O'Connors had grown so fond of Apache that they told him he could come back whenever he wanted. They encouraged him to bring his sisters and brother, too. Listening to the stories of other townspeople who had participated in the summer program, they considered themselves lucky. Another child had stolen items from his host family's house.

Apache returned to the O'Connor home many times over the next several years. He came for a week in the summers, and during the year he occasionally stayed overnight. On one of his summer visits, Apache took Arlene with him into the prison. Arlene was nervous at first, until she sat down and talked to Apache's mother. "Elaine was just a mom trying to be a mom," Arlene says. "She was very warm and appreciative, and I think it was a relief to her to know who we were." Some mothers ignored their kids; Elaine was the opposite. "She was very aware of everything. Even if she was talking to someone, she was always very aware of what her children were doing. She thought they were incredible. She was very proud."

Every time Apache came to visit, the O'Connors felt their perspective on life shift slightly. He gave them updates on his family and told them about his plans to become a rapper and a professional basketball player. The O'Connors had never met a teenager with such grand ambitions, and they were impressed. For a middle-aged white couple who had never lived in a city, Apache's tales provided a window onto another world. Listening to him describe the turmoil in his grandmother's apartment, their own day-to-day worries began to recede. Sick parents, financial crises, and myriad health problems—Arlene had more problems than many of her friends. But she thought that if Apache could succeed with such odds against him, then she would manage, too.

The O'Connors missed Apache when he was not around. Sometimes they called him on the phone and tried to convince him to visit both his mother and them. "We wanted him to come out for her," Arlene says. "But we really wanted him to come out because we loved him and we wanted him around." Months would go by and the O'Connors would not hear from him. Then, out of the blue, he would call, saying that he wanted to visit. One weekend, he brought Satara and Danae. It was hard to know what the girls thought or how they felt, because they did not say much. At night, Arlene showed them a bedroom with several bunk beds and told them they could sleep wherever they wanted. In the morning, she discovered them in the same bed, curled next to each other.

Over the years, when Apache talked about his life in New York City, he often told Pat and Arlene that he wanted to show them where he lived. It seemed only right to reciprocate after they had opened up their home to him. Usually, at the end of each visit, the O'Connors would drive him to the Metro-North train station in Katonah. A few times, though, they drove him all the way to the Lower East Side. When their car neared the Wald Houses, Apache did not say anything about bringing them up to his family's apartment. Instead, he just told them to drop him on the corner.

CHAPTER 11

By the fall of 1992, Elaine had been at Bedford Hills for nearly nine years. She had worked as a "cook helper" and a "counter attendant," and after she got savvier about navigating the prison's politics, she had landed more desirable positions. In her sixth year, she worked in the Children's Center, next to the visiting room, planning games and projects for other women's children. The job paid 77.5 cents a day—a minuscule amount, but nearly twice as much as working in the kitchen did.

She continued to go to school, too. She took the high school equivalency exam so many times that she lost count—maybe five or six times—and then finally, in her seventh year, she passed it. It was an impressive accomplishment by the standards of the Bartlett family; of her six siblings, only Sabrina and Ronald had graduated from high school. After she got her GED, she enrolled in the prison's college program, which was then run by Mercy College.

Her obsession, though, was finding a way to get herself out of prison. She ordered the transcript of her trial and she read it so often she practically had it memorized. A public defender had submitted an appeal on her behalf, but it had been denied in 1985. Ever since, she had been on her own. So, like many prisoners, she puzzled over legal books and tried to figure out how to write her own court appeal.

She took a paralegal class, and then got a job as a paralegal assistant in the law library, helping other inmates obtain their rap sheets and trial transcripts. She had wanted the job in part so that she could investigate George Deets. Every time she met a woman from Albany County, she quizzed her about George, hoping for a few bits of information. Nobody had ever heard of him.

Working in the law library, Elaine met a few of the prison's best-educated inmates. In 1992, she and four other women brought a lawsuit charging that the prison was rife with asbestos. The suit was unsuccessful, but it did help launch a clean-up effort.

Elaine considered some of her fellow inmates good friends. Most of these women were long-termers, like her. They included Donna Charles, who was serving a seventeen-year sentence for an A-1 drug offense and whom everyone called "Jamaica" because that was where she was from; and Betty Tyson, a former prostitute who was serving 25-to-life for strangling a businessman with his necktie—a crime she said she did not commit.

By now, Elaine was thirty-five years old, older than most of the other inmates. Angry young women reminded her of herself in her first years here. Often, she pulled them aside and dispensed advice, urging them to get a job and go to school. She counseled prisoners when they were depressed, and she gave them birthday gifts when she knew they had no family. Most of the time, though, she just listened to them talk about whatever was bothering them. Soon these younger prisoners bestowed upon her their ultimate term of affection: "Ma." Elaine, in turn, referred to them as "my children."

Bedford Hills was full of such makeshift families, where one strong woman played the role of matriarch and cared for a few younger prisoners. At any given time, there were at least ten prisoners whom Elaine considered her "kids." When one of these inmates misbehaved—when a woman refused to come out of her cell in the morning—the guards would fetch Elaine. Soon the rebellious inmate would see her "mother" marching toward her, a belt in one hand.

"Get your butt up!" Elaine would shout. "Get in the shower! Let's go!"

Her children were scared of her, and they almost always did what she said. Some of them were still teenagers, and for many of them, prison marked the first time they had been away from home. Others had never even had a home. Their parents were dead or strung out on drugs. And so they had bounced around foster homes for years, eventually winding up in jail. For young women with no parents, a strong maternal figure was exactly what they wanted. "We knew she loved us," Tarsha Thompson, one of her children, recalls. "It was nice to be loved. That's something we were all lacking."

Every time a holiday arrived, Elaine took charge, playing the role of mother for her entire cell block. She convinced everyone to pool their food together—items their families had sent or that they had purchased in the commissary—and then she prepared a feast in the cell block's tiny kitchen. No matter the occasion, she always fixed the Bartlett family's favorites, including collard greens and rice and peas. She scooped the food onto paper plates and made sure every prisoner got one. It did not matter if they hadn't been able to contribute anything. Just like her own mother, who had always prepared enough food for their whole building, Elaine made sure nobody was left out.

Most of the letters Elaine received had the same return address: Green Haven Correctional Facility. In a prison cell in Dutchess County, thirty-five miles north of Bedford Hills, Nathan wrote to her a few times a week. His letters usually consisted of ten or more pages of lined paper, words covering both sides. "Nate doesn't write letters," Elaine would say. "He writes books." Sometimes his sentences oozed affection. Other times, he ranted for pages, lashing out about everything—the setup, their arrest, his prison term. At times, the purpose of his letters seemed less about relaying news than about exorcising his own demons.

After a few years at Bedford Hills, Elaine had stopped writing back. When she had news for him, she stored it in her memory until the next time they spoke. Prison officials permitted them two calls a year, usually for only fifteen or twenty minutes. Hearing his voice on the line, hearing him tell her he still loved her, she always felt less alone. At least there was one other person in the world who could understand both sides of her life: her day-to-day cell block existence and the family worries that never left her mind.

Nathan was always hungry for news, especially about Satara and Danae, and he asked a lot of questions. How tall were they now? How were they doing in school? Were they painting their nails yet? Despite his efforts to play the role of father, he had no contact with either of them. He had not even seen them since the arrest. Sometimes he called Yvonne's apartment, but she always said, "They're not here." He did not believe her; sometimes he thought he heard them in the background.

Every time Nathan spoke to Elaine, she could hear his frustration. "You get to see the kids. I don't," he would say. "Nobody loves me. Nobody cares."

"Stop your whining," Elaine would say.

Despite her tough words, she felt horrible about his loneliness. The only person who visited him regularly was his mother, and she came just a few times a year. "You ain't got nothing, so get one of your friends to hook you up with a girl to come see you," Elaine told him during one of their calls. "Everybody needs somebody. You need to try to find some type of happiness now wherever you can get it, because I'm in no position to give it to you. I'm in the same boat as you."

Not long afterward, he sent her a letter and enclosed a few Polaroids of himself with another woman.

"Why did you send me those pictures?" Elaine hollered at him during their next conversation. "Why the hell do I want to look at them?"

From then on, Nathan never mentioned visits from female friends. He continued to write often, but he stayed away from the subject of other women. Elaine did not talk about other men, either.

Over the years, Elaine had managed to find a few prison boyfriends. Some were men she had known before she got arrested; others were friends or relatives of women at Bedford Hills. They flirted with her in the visiting room and made her feel sexy, at least for a few hours. They sent her cartons of cigarettes and packages of food. And sometimes she convinced them to buy presents for her children. She picked toys and clothes out of catalogs, then asked the men to pay for them.

Eventually, though, they all got fed up with her. They would ask to meet her children, but she wouldn't let them. They would say they wanted a conjugal visit, which required that they marry first. "I'm already married," she'd say. And sometimes, when they leaned in for a kiss, she would give them her cheek. After a few months, they would realize she was not interested in having a boyfriend after all. What she really wanted was somebody who could help her get free. "I don't need another pack of Newports," she would say. "I need to get out."

Pictures of the children Elaine had left behind filled the photo album she kept in her cell: Apache spreading jelly on a slice of toast in the O'Connors' kitchen; Jamel posing next to a cake on his twelfth birthday; Danae grinning beneath a witch's hat, ready to go trick-or-treating; Satara in an outdoor pool, yellow water wings encircling her tiny arms. These photographs reminded Elaine of exactly who she thought she was—not 84-G-0068, but Elaine Bartlett, mother of four. She felt sorry for other prisoners who had no family and never got a visit or a piece of mail. Her children gave her a sense of purpose. By going to college, she hoped to set an example, one that they, too, might follow.

Yvonne still brought the children to see her, but these visits were less frequent than they had been in the beginning. Everybody was busy with their own lives. To find out what was going on, Elaine had to rely on the phone and the mail. Yvonne sent her photos of family parties, with everyone smiling and laughing, but Elaine knew this was only half the story. Nobody wanted to tell her any of the bad news. Whenever she called home, she always heard the same words: "Everything's all right."

Nobody told Elaine when her sister Sabrina started smoking crack.

Elaine found out through the Bedford Hills grapevine. Women arriving from Rikers Island told her they had met her sister in jail. Crack had not been a huge problem before Elaine got arrested, but now it seemed like every other woman coming into Bedford Hills was addicted to it. The fact that her younger sister had also become an addict infuriated Elaine. There were already too many Bartletts behind bars. "If she gets sentenced upstate, tell her to go straight to Albion," Elaine told her mother. "She better not come here, or I'm going to hurt her."

In 1992, Elaine heard that her brother Donjuan had been paroled from state prison and had moved into Apartment 13B. He was twenty-nine years old and had been locked up his entire adult life, since age eighteen. Sometimes, when Elaine called home, she heard reports that Donjuan had been acting strangely: Blasting Public Enemy at 4:00 a.m. Waking everyone at 5:00 a.m. Smacking the kids. Everyone said prison had changed him, and not for the better.

When Donjuan got on the phone, he told her how hard life on the outside was. "I left one prison to come home to another," he said. At the time, Elaine did not understand what he meant. All she wanted was to be free. She could not imagine how life on the outside could possibly be as bad as being in prison.

By now, her brother Ronald was extremely sick. The last time Elaine had seen him was several years earlier, when he had strutted into the visiting room wearing a knee-length black fur coat. She didn't know at the time that he was HIV-positive. Later, she wondered if he had purposely made such a grand entrance because this was the way he wanted to be remembered.

Listening on the telephone to details about his decline, she felt completely powerless. Maybe she never could have prevented Ronald from contracting HIV, but if she had been home, she at least could have helped take care of him. Now all she could do was wait. Bedford Hills had already provided her with a grim education about AIDS. Not a month seemed to pass without another inmate dying. In October of 1992, Ronald died, too. He was thirty-three years old.

Now she had only five siblings left. Of all her brothers and sisters, the oldest one, Frankie, had the most stable life. He had married Becky, his teenage girlfriend, whom he had met when the family lived in the Bronx. Together, they were raising four sons. For eighteen years, he had kept the same job, working at a piano-moving company. In a family with a dearth of role models, he was one of the few people everyone looked up to. Among his nieces and nephews, he commanded respect. Whenever he saw Jamel selling drugs and ordered him to get off Avenue D, Jamel obeyed him.

Frankie had never gone to Bedford Hills to see Elaine, but she did not hold this against him. She knew he had not forgotten her, because he sometimes sent her money. She also knew that he hated prison. Everyone still joked about the time Frankie had been picked up by the cops when he was a teenager. He had been in jail for only one night, but then spent the next few days in the bathtub. From that day on, he told everyone he was never going back to jail, not even to visit.

Long before Ronald's death, before anyone had ever heard of AIDS, the Bartlett family had been preparing itself for tragedy. From the time they were young, Yvonne's children had lived with the fear that one of them would someday be killed. Too many people had been shot on the streets of Harlem, Morrisania, and Corona for them not to worry that one of their family members would be gunned down.

If one of them did end up getting killed, everyone assumed it would be Shyan. Considering how many crimes he had committed while he was growing up, some relatives had doubted he would even make it to sixteen. Now he was twice that age, albeit locked up in yet another state prison.

In February of 1993, everyone's worst fears became reality. It was not Shyan or even Donjuan who was attacked, however. It was Frankie. At 8:00 p.m. on a Friday, he walked down East 138th Street in the Bronx, en route to a video store. On his way back home, a videotape in his hand, a group of men attacked him, stealing his weekly pay and stabbing him in the side. Frankie, who was seven feet tall and weighed 350 pounds, staggered back to his apartment.

He headed for his bedroom in the back and collapsed on his bed. While he waited for an ambulance, his wife pressed a towel against his wound, trying to stop the blood from pouring out. At the time, no one knew that the knife had punctured his spleen, and he was bleeding internally. Two weeks later, he died.

His murder devastated every member of the Bartlett family. Ronald's death had been expected, but nobody ever thought Frankie was going to die young, especially not at age thirty-six. After all, he had never been a criminal or a junkie. All he did was work, go home, and take care of his family. No matter how much one thought about his death, it made no sense. His family did not even know who had killed him. Nobody was ever arrested for the crime.

Prison officials permitted Elaine to attend Frankie's funeral, which was held in Harlem. When she arrived, she saw an ambulance in front of the funeral parlor. One of Frankie's sons was having an asthma attack, and Yvonne had become so hysterical with grief that she, too, could barely breathe. The paramedics wanted to take them both to the hospital. Yvonne refused. Elaine led her into a quiet office, fed her bits of ice, and tried to calm her. It was the first time mother and daughter had been alone with each other in nearly ten years.

That winter taught Elaine that prison is a terrible place to grieve. Surviving inside Bedford Hills required a show of invincibility at all times. She had learned this long ago. But after going to two funerals in four months, she became so depressed that she was having trouble getting through each day. The deaths of her brothers compounded her ever-growing sense of guilt. She was the big sister. She was the one who was supposed to be home, making sure everybody else was okay.

After her brothers died, Elaine started cleaning even more than usual. Ever since being sent to prison, she had tried to minimize her stress by cleaning. Scrubbing, sweeping, and mopping her cell always made her feel a little better. Sometimes she even got down on her knees and waxed the cell floor with a sanitary napkin. She might have had control over little else in her life, but at least she could control the cleanliness of her cell. After Frankie died, however, this old coping strategy did not work anymore.

All around Elaine were other women who had lost all that she'd lost, and more. At least she still had her sanity. Many of her fellow inmates were seriously mentally ill—schizophrenic, bipolar, or severely depressed. Some looked like zombies, stumbling around the prison in a Thorazine stupor. She heard about women swallowing safety pins, eating glass, dragging razor blades across their wrists, carving their initials in their arms, setting their mattresses on fire, hacking off their hair.

Some inmates were so depressed that they lied about hearing voices in order to get antipsychotic drugs, which they used to numb the pain of imprisonment. Elaine didn't want to do her time in a drug-fueled haze, but she didn't know how much longer she could stay in prison without losing her mind. Every morning, she stared at the mirror in her cell and asked herself, Is it me that's going crazy, or is it everyone else around me?

Now that she was older, she no longer mouthed off to the guards as often as she used to. When she felt angry about something or someone, she went to the gym and hit a punching bag. Exercise made her feel better, but she carried so much rage inside of her that she doubted she would ever be able to get rid of it all. After Frankie was murdered, she felt even more angry than usual.

It had always been difficult to straddle two worlds: the day-to-day prison life and the family dramas unfolding without her. Now they threatened to collide. Three months after Frankie's death, Elaine walked down her cell-block corridor shortly before 10:00 p.m. one evening. Next to the officer's station stood Michelle Plaza, a prisoner who was doing time for robbery, grand larceny, and an escape attempt. Soon she would be released on parole.

The two women were not friends, and on this evening they got into an argument. In response to angry words from Elaine, Michelle said, "I don't care. I'm going home. And all your family is dying while you're in here."

Elaine grabbed her from behind and knocked her to the ground. In full view of a guard, she punched Michelle in the head several times. An officer and a few of Michelle's friends rushed over. The officer grabbed Elaine, but she broke away from him. She slapped one of Michelle's friends across the face, then punched another.

By the time the officers broke up the brawl, the other women had managed to hit Elaine in the face several times. She would later learn that she had a blowout fracture beneath her left eye.

At a disciplinary hearing held the following week, Elaine was sentenced to sixty-three days in solitary confinement. Now she would only be allowed out of her cell for one hour of recreation a day. No eating in the mess hall. No sauntering around the prison yard. No attending college classes. She would have to sit in her cell all day by herself, alone with her thoughts. It was the prison's ultimate punishment.

CHAPTER 12

Apache boarded a bus to South Dakota in
the fall of 1992. The basketball coach at a high school in Pine Ridge
had recruited him and two other boys from New York City. Over dinner in Manhattan, the coach had talked about getting him a used car,
an easy $300-a-week job, and a starting spot on his team if he moved
to South Dakota.

Apache had already played four years of high-school ball in Manhattan, but he'd purposely not taken one class he needed in order to
graduate, knowing that he would now be eligible to play for another
year. This was a common strategy among inner-city boys who
dreamed of getting a basketball scholarship to college. A fifth year of
high school would enable Apache to sharpen his basketball skills and
raise his SAT scores, improving his odds of winning a scholarship.

Moving to Pine Ridge was like moving to a foreign country. Apache's
new school was on the Pine Ridge Indian Reservation. Everyone on his
basketball team was from the Oglala Sioux tribe, except for him and
the other boys from New York. The coach was not Native American,
either; he was white. Nobody in this new town was black.

Apache soon learned that the coach had sold him a lot of false
hopes. There was no job, and there was no car. Instead, there was just

a lot of controversy. Local parents complained that the boys from New York City were taking starting positions away from Indian players. A few times, angry fans shouted racial epithets at Apache and the other teenager from New York, who was black. They called them the "New York Nigger-bockers."

In a letter Apache sent to his mother, he described the coach as "a bum." Indeed, even the coach's recruitment of him was suspect. (The local athletic authority later investigated the coach, but it eventually cleared him of any violations.)

He had promised Apache that he could move into his house, but soon the coach sent him next door to live with a neighbor. Apache had no money, and the coach didn't, either. "You know I've never ever complained about a situation, even when I lived with my father," Apache wrote to his mother. "But this is the worst I've ever been in." He explained that he needed money to buy food, as well as underwear, socks, and a winter coat.

He knew his mother had no money, so he asked her to talk to Jean Harris, the former prep school headmistress serving time for murder. He had known Jean since he was a child; she had watched him grow up in the prison visiting room. When he had told her about his plans to go to South Dakota, she had said that maybe she could convince a few of her friends to sponsor him. "Please talk to Mrs. Harris for me," Apache wrote.

In the same envelope, he enclosed another letter for his mother. Although he was hundreds of miles from New York, overwhelmed by culture shock and money worries, he was determined to boost her spirits.

> Dear Mom,
>
> How are you? I hope your keeping your head up there. You know I miss you very much and I also love you with all my heart. I know you sometimes get mad because it seems like we don't try to come see you as much as possible. I know it bothers you a lot because on many occasions I heard you say, "You treat me like I'm going to be here forever." I really hate it when you say that because that's not true at all. I want you to realize that we all

love to come see you and we all think about you and love you very much. There should never be any doubt in your mind.

Ma, the reason I sometimes don't like coming up there is because I hate to see you like that. It really hurts me to see you there because to me you deserve more than that. Your my mother, the most wonderful mother in the world. . . . We never forget about you Mom we just hate to see you up there, and in a way I think that's kind of selfish on our part because we know you love to see your children and I'm going to try harder to get up there more often. I just want you to know we care, we love you, and will never abandon you.

Ma, to me you are a big part of my life. You're the reason I've been able to get through most of the bad times. Which there has been many in my life. So many times I could have gotten into bad stuff to make it ahead. But because of you I never let myself be led astray. Ma, I live for you and through you I find the will to succeed and survive. It makes me so happy when you say your proud of me because that's worth more than any trophy or award I ever got. . . . Ma, I'm going to be somebody no matter how much or how little world status I have. Because I feel that no matter what I do if you remain proud of your first son that's all that matters, and I'm always going to do the best I can to keep you proud.

Ma, I'm not ashamed of you nor am I ashamed of where you at. Ma, in my eyes you have done and will always do the best you can for us and the rest of the family. To me everything is done for a reason and I feel that God took you away to keep something bad from happening to you and I thank him for that because where would I be or any of us for that matter be if something happened to you? I want you to remember that and always know we love you with all our hearts.

Your son,
Apache

Apache did not travel home for Ronald's funeral, but then, at the end of 1992, he heard that his grandmother had suffered a heart attack. He asked Littleboy to buy him a plane ticket, and he flew back to New York City. He knew his mother would not approve of his leaving school, but it was obvious that his grandmother needed all the help she could get.

Elaine had bragged to her friends in prison about Apache's trophies, his move to South Dakota, and his college dreams. He knew that every time he racked up another accomplishment, she felt as if she had accomplished something, too.

"I want you to go back to school," she told him every time he visited her.

So as not to disappoint her, he always said, "I'm going back. I'm going back next month."

After Frankie died in early 1993, Apache could feel his college dreams slipping away. He decided he would have to stay in New York and put aside his own personal ambitions. Yvonne needed him, and he wanted to keep an eye on Satara and Danae.

Apache sometimes stayed at Apartment 13B, and sometimes he stayed on Long Island with his friend Fatso. At the time, Fatso was a student at a community college, and he tried to convince Apache to go to his school. Apache thought he had taken all the classes he needed to graduate from high school, but when he called Pine Ridge, he could not convince anyone to mail him a diploma. His formal education ended at age twenty, and so did his prospects of playing college basketball.

In the spring of 1993, two months after Frankie died, Jamel was arrested. According to the police, he and two friends got into a cab, rode to Queens, ordered the driver to stop on the side of the Van Wyck Expressway, pointed a gun at him, and robbed him of his day's earnings—$163. Jamel tells a different story. He says he and his friends got into the cab to go to Corona, but that they didn't know how to direct the driver there. When the meter hit $30 the driver got angry and demanded they get out. Jamel insists he did not have a gun, and that the driver made up the robbery story. Whatever the truth may be, Jamel was sentenced to one year in jail.

By that time he was sixteen years old—an adult in the eyes of New York's criminal justice system—and so he was sent to Rikers Island, the notorious penal colony, located in the East River between Queens and the Bronx. There are ten jails on Rikers Island, including one for teenage boys. Jamel had been hearing about Rikers for years, and in fact he had already been there several times to visit his uncle Shyan. The first time Jamel had gone to Rikers Island, he had been just five years old.

Now that he was locked up, he had plenty of time to write to his mother.

11/22/93

Dear Mommy,

How are you doing? Fine I hope. As for me I'm O.K. Well not really. I'll really be okay when I get out of here and get myself together. Mom all I do in here is just think I think about everything that have to do with my life but most of the time I think about you and when I come home I'm going to be coming to see you on the regular. Mommy you no why I was crying when I was talking to you on the [phone] is because I miss you I love you and I just can't take the fact that your not home with me and it ain't just when I talk to you every time I see you or think about you I cry mommy even now while I'm wrighting this letter I'm crying. Mom I now you got yourself together so when you come home you'll never do anything stupid again well while I'm here I'm going to get everything straight so when I go home I could do something with my life and make you proud of me well mother I have to go to bed now but you will be getting more letters from me. Sorry I didn't wright sooner.
P.S. I love you more than love it's self.

Love always,
Your Baby
Jamel

The other prisoners called him Murder Mel, but locked inside his cell at night, he didn't feel so tough anymore. At age sixteen, he was caught between two worlds. He was no longer the little boy who had clung to his mother's leg at the end of their prison visits, but he was not a hardened prisoner, either.

                                                                    1/17/94

Hello Mommy,

How is everything going in there? because I'm worried about you, but I know you'll be okay. Even though I still worry because it's hard being away from your loved ones, but just stay strong everything will be okay. I received the letter [you] sent and the pictures and stamps. Mommy, I need to ask you something because I'm stuck. I want to know if you think I should go live with my father. He's been asking me to come live with him, but I don't know if I should 'cause I need to take care of grandma, Satara, Dana. I also wanted to ask you something else I never asked before but I'm not afraid any more. I want to know the date that your suppose to come home. I was scared to ask before because I was young and it would made me evilier than I am and we don't need that. I need to keep myself on track from now on. Mommy I'm doing okay in here. I haven't had a fight in a while and all the girls are waiting for me to come home, they drive me crazy calling 24 seven. Mom when I came here I had 18 months but I'm doing good . . . so I should be out of here in six months. . . . Well I'll be writing again soon Mommy. Peace.

                                                          love you,
                                                          Mel

Jamel returned to his grandmother's apartment in the summer of 1994. He also returned to Avenue D. In early October, a police officer arrested him for selling a bag of cocaine. He returned to Rikers Island with another one-year sentence.

When Apache stayed on Long Island and Jamel was in jail, fourteen-year-old Satara was left to fend for herself. Since she was the oldest granddaughter, she got stuck with most of the chores. She cooked, cleaned, ironed, ran errands, changed diapers, filled bottles. Yvonne never made Apache or Jamel sweep or mop; only the girls in the apartment had to do those sorts of tasks. For three years, Satara had been working outside the apartment, too, starting when she was eleven years old. She was employed at a day-care center, where she worked off the books and earned about $180 a week.

Like Elaine had done when she was a teenager, Satara played the role of second mom in the apartment. She helped raise her younger sister Danae and her many cousins. With her income, Satara bought clothes and sneakers for Danae. When Danae mouthed off to her teachers in school, Satara lectured her about her behavior. When Danae fell off her bicycle and hurt herself, Satara took care of her.

Satara wrote to Elaine more often than her brothers and sister did. In careful schoolgirl script, she handwrote her letters on lined paper. Often she placed stickers in the margins and used Magic Markers to draw hearts around the letters of the word *love*.

L   O

11-4-94

Dear: Mommy

How are you? I miss you. But I still love you no matter where you at or what happen's you know that I will always love you mom. I wrote you a letter before but I did not send it out yet. I am sorry that I am sending it late. Ma you have to talk to Elaine Bartlette cause she is not doing right in school her teacher call's almost every day but not for her work for her behavior and fight's. I will bring you some money or send it to you but you know I don't like to send it cause they look in it and they will probly take it. By the way tell your friend's What's up.

By

Satara Bartlette

V   E

Satara often worried that her sister might end up in jail someday, too, just like their mother. They had the same name, Elaine, and both could be stubborn and rebellious. Just as Apache had tried to keep Jamel out of trouble, Satara was determined to stop her twelve-year-old sister from straying down the wrong path.

CHAPTER 13

Everybody who lived at 950 East Fourth Walk in the Wald Houses knew about Miss Yvonne. Her generosity was legendary. Sometimes she allowed the homeless man who slept on the bench in front of the building to spend a night or two in her apartment. When a neighbor could not stop fighting with her parents, Yvonne invited her to move in, too. In Yvonne's home, there was always a pot or two cooking on the stove, and she would feed anyone who was hungry. Friends and acquaintances stopped by all the time. They came for a meal, for advice, for a loan. Sometimes, they would just say, "Miss Yvonne, I need someone to talk to."

"Come on in, baby," she would say.

The neighbors knew she could decipher any piece of mail: confusing letters from the city's welfare agency, mistake-riddled cable bills, notices of phone service being cut off. They would bring her whatever bewildering piece of paper had just arrived in their mailbox. "Grandma, can you read this letter to me?" they would ask. She not only read the letters, but also gave tips on how to navigate the bureaucracy of whatever company or agency had sent it.

To her grandchildren and their friends, Yvonne was an endless source of entertainment. Every week, she wore a different color wig.

She would always wear perfume. Not just any kind of perfume—it had to be Elizabeth Taylor's "White Diamonds." Even if she were only going to do Tenant Patrol, sitting in the lobby monitoring visitors, she would douse herself with it. As she headed out the apartment door, she would say, "Yvonne Bartlett is going to find herself a rich man," prompting the children to laugh.

Yvonne dressed as if she were trying to prove a point—always in a skirt or dress, and always impeccably groomed. She might live in a housing project overrun with drugs and crime, but she was not going to let her surroundings keep her down. And she certainly did not want anyone to think that the stereotypes about people living in the projects applied to her. She did not want anyone to assume that she was dumb or unkempt. She might be poor, but she had plenty of pride. Her insistence on always looking good announced to everyone: I may live in this grimy project building, but this place is certainly not me.

After two of her sons died within four months, she started to lose the stamina and sense of humor that had once helped her get through the days. She had been diagnosed with diabetes many years earlier, and now her kidneys were starting to fail. Three mornings a week, she had to go for dialysis treatments. She still wore a wig every day and always looked immaculate, but her health was rapidly deteriorating.

Yvonne now traveled to Bedford Hills less frequently. She relied on a cane and could no longer make her way up and down the stairs of Grand Central Terminal. When she could scrounge together enough money, she tracked down Mario, a livery cab driver who usually parked on Avenue D. Mario would take her and Elaine's children to Bedford Hills, wait several hours while they visited, then drive them home. Because he liked Yvonne, he charged her only seventy dollars.

When Yvonne could not travel to the prison, she wrote to Elaine.

7-31-95

Dear Daughter,

How are you doing? I'm out of the hospital for a little while. Jamel has been home since the 19. He came home talking big shit. He stays here sometimes and sometimes he doesn't. . . . I told him to [go] and see you. Maybe he will. Maybe he won't. All he keeps telling me is that i did more for apache than him. None of the girls have any kind of respect at all. I don't feel like helping none of these children anymore. All the running i did for these kids and nobody appreciate shit. I am broke now so everyone treats me like a wet shoe. The grown people curse me out in front of these kids. Shyan told me just to walk away and leave them all alone. I am so tired of being sick all of the time. I'm going to try and come and see you before I'm gone. The pressure I'm going under now I don't think I'm going to make it. You have to call and talk to your daughters cause I can't put up with it anymore. I want you to be good so you can get home soon.

   I love you very much.

Love Mom,
Yvonne Bartlett

Two months after Elaine received this letter, Yvonne told her that she was coming to visit. The occasion was Elaine's thirty-eighth birthday. That morning, Elaine put on a long-sleeved white shirt, black panty hose, and a prison-issued skirt, which she hiked above her knees. Once she got to the visiting room and saw her mother, she almost started to cry. No words could have prepared her for how different her mother looked.

Yvonne was a shrunken version of her former self. She looked as if she weighed about 200 pounds—half as much as she used to. Gangrene on her big toe had spread, and a doctor had amputated part of one foot. Now she was confined to a wheelchair. She wore white stockings, a knee-length dress, a silk scarf, and a black trench coat. She looked put together, just like always, but her clothes could not conceal the truth about how frail she had become.

For the last year, Elaine had been trying to take care of Yvonne from inside Bedford Hills. She researched medications in the prison library, berated her sisters for not taking better care of their mother, and tracked down her doctors on the telephone. None of it was enough. She worried her worst nightmare was about to come true: that her mother would die while she was still in prison. She did not even want to think about the possibility that her mother would not be outside the prison gate to greet her on the day when she was finally set free.

The only reason she was still sane, Elaine thought, was because of her mother. Yvonne was her biggest defender. As long as Yvonne was around, nobody in the family was allowed to say anything negative about Elaine. Whenever anyone asked why Elaine had gone to prison, Yvonne said, "It ain't her fault. It's that motherfuckin' Nathan." The way Yvonne told the story, Elaine had followed Nathan to Albany. Falling for Nathan was her only real mistake. As far as Yvonne was concerned, her oldest daughter was a smart, proud, capable woman, just like she was.

Whenever Elaine called home, Yvonne gave her a pep talk. "It's going to be all right," she would say. "Don't worry. Keep your head up." Yvonne was the strongest woman Elaine knew. Over the last thirty years, she had endured enough tragedies for ten mothers. She'd lost her children's father, been shot in the stomach, seen three children go to state prison, watched one daughter become a crack addict, lost one son to AIDS, and lost another to the streets. Still she had managed to persevere, raising not only her own seven children but nearly a dozen grandchildren, too.

Yvonne rolled up her sleeve and showed Elaine the scars her dialysis treatments had left. She complained that her skin was getting darker as her kidney problems worsened.

"You still look pretty," Elaine said.

"Stop lying," Yvonne said. "I look like shit. I wish somebody would take care of me. I wish you were home to take care of me."

Seeing her mother in a wheelchair, tears filling her eyes, Elaine vowed to do absolutely everything she could think of to get herself out of prison. She knew that every now and then the governor let an inmate out early, and so she decided she was going to write him a letter.

Near the end of their visit, she pushed her mother toward a corner of the room so they could pose for a Polaroid. Yvonne folded her hands in her lap and stared straight ahead. Even in her best church clothes, she appeared tired and sad. Elaine leaned close and glanced at the camera with worried eyes. Neither woman smiled. On this day, there was nothing to celebrate.

CHAPTER 14

The long-termers at Bedford Hills remembered the names: Sandra Keller, Luz Santana, Aida Rivera. All three women had been sentenced to 15-to-life and all of them had convinced Governor Cuomo to give them clemency, reducing their minimum sentences so they could go home. Any woman who managed to get out early became an instant celebrity inside Bedford Hills. Their story became a source of hope, passed down through the years by other inmates hungry for any reason not to give up.

Convincing the governor to give you clemency was the Bedford Hills equivalent of winning the lottery. The odds against you were almost as steep. During his twelve years as governor, Cuomo had awarded clemency only thirty-five times—an infinitesimal number, considering there were seventy thousand inmates in New York's prisons when he left office. By the fall of 1995, George Pataki was governor, and nobody yet knew how generous he would be about granting clemency.

There were no posters on the bulletin boards in Bedford Hills explaining how to win clemency. Figuring out the process required research and savvy. Elaine went to the law library, found out which prisoners were eligible, and learned she met all the basic qualifica-

tions: Her minimum sentence was longer than one year; she had finished half of it; and she had more than a year to go before she would
see the parole board. In fact, she was not eligible for parole for another eight years.

"To whom it may concern," she wrote in a letter to the clemency
bureau. "My name is Elaine Bartlett, and I am currently in my twelve
year of a 20 to life sentence for a drug sale. I have no prior arrests
record." She summarized her family history, then added, "Since my incarceration I have taken programs and completed high school attended five semesters of college and worked in jobs that can bring a
pay check home. . . . I want to be a productive member of society, and
a mother to my children. I would also like to take some of the burden
off my mother who is 65 years old, who is on dialisis and needs to
have some time for herself. I also would like to break the chain of
prison and poverty for my children. Very Truly Yours, Elaine Bartlett
84G0068."

To improve her odds, Elaine solicited pointers from an older inmate, who suggested she collect letters of recommendation. After
twelve years in prison, Elaine didn't know many people outside of
Bedford Hills, except for her family. She had lost contact with her
friends long ago. And so she solicited letters from the people she saw
every day. She asked every civilian and officer she knew to write the
clemency bureau on her behalf.

Helene D. Holohan:

I have been acquainted with Miss Elaine Bartlett (84G0068)
since May of 1984 when she first came as a student into my
GED class. During the ensuing years, I have watched her grow
from an angry, purposeless young woman to an adult who is determined to make something of her life.

Ms. Bartlett's academic career at Bedford Hills began in a
negative manner. There were many failures and few successes.
Nevertheless, she kept coming back to try again and finally managed to turn herself around.

Officer Knox:

> I can say only good things about Ms. Bartlett's attitude which always seems to be a positive one. I have went to Mrs Bartlett on several ocassions and asked her to help with inmates who had poor hygein habits or personal problems. Inmate Bartlett would often show them how to properly clean their cells, wash laundry on the unit, or whatever the problem might be. If ever the facility asked for her help on the paint crew to finish a job in a limited time frame Mrs Bartlett would work throughout the night for days at a time when it wasn't manditory.

Officer Jennings:

> Approximately two years ago, Inmate Elaine Bartlett prevented another inmate from seriously injuring me. At that time, I . . . was working on the seven to three pm shift . . . when I received a call requesting me to come up to 113AB Housing Unit, where Inmate Elaine Bartlett was housed . . . A verbal argument had come up between the inmates, and they were ready to exchange blows, and I came between the two inmates. One of the disgruntled inmates then decided to vent her anger out on me. . . . And she proceeded to verbally harass me and threaten me with serioius physical injury.
>
> At that point the inmate was in the kitchen area with *boiling, hot water*, supposedly making coffee. All of a sudden the inmate came rushing out of the kitchen stating "Motherf—er, I'm going to throw this (boiling) hot water in your face!" The inmate was approximately fifty feet away and headed in my direction, hot pot in hand, when Inmate Elaine Bartlett took action. Inmate Bartlett stepped between the assaultive inmate before she could throw the coffee in my face. She then demanded the pot from the assaultive inmate and quieted the inmate down. She then told her what the consequences would be if she did me harm in any way, and escorted the inmate back to her cell.

New York's governor typically grants clemencies just before Christmas, but Christmas came and went without any news, good or bad.

The first six months of 1996 also passed without any word from Albany.

Meanwhile, Elaine missed the birth of her second grandchild. She already had one granddaughter, born at the end of 1994. Apache was the father; the mother was his former girlfriend. She named the infant Nytaea, but Apache called her Baby Tara, after his sister. In the spring of 1996, Elaine heard that Jamel's girlfriend had given birth to a son. His name was Little Mel.

At the time, Jamel was on Rikers Island, charged with another felony: selling heroin to an undercover officer. A few months after his son was born, he pleaded guilty. A judge sentenced him to two to four years. This time, he was going upstate. In New York, everyone who receives a sentence longer than one year gets transferred from Rikers Island to the state prison system. "Oh, Elaine, don't feel responsible," her friends told her. "It's not your fault." But Elaine did feel responsible. She thought that if she had not gone to state prison, Jamel would not have gone, either.

Her only consolation was the news she'd received from her counselor: she'd been invited to meet with the parole board for a clemency interview. She began to think that she might actually get out early. She heard that a parole officer had visited Apartment 13B to interview her family and check out the residence. Everyone assumed this meant she was finally coming home.

Even all these years after her arrest, Elaine was still obsessed with George Deets. She continued to spend much of her time trying to figure out who he was, where he had come from, and why he had set her up. She did not know anything about his trips to Arizona or Colombia, but she suspected he was a serious drug dealer.

At her clemency interview in the fall of 1996, two commissioners interrogated her about her crime. She ranted about George Deets for a while, probably longer than she should have. But she could not stop herself. By the time the interview ended, most of her optimism had vanished. "I think my mind shut down," she explained later. "I wasn't really prepared for it. And I never experienced anything like that before."

Christmas did not bring any good news from Albany, and soon she received a letter.

December 31, 1996

Dear Ms. Bartlett:

   I regret to inform you that, after a careful review of your case, it has been determined that there is insufficient basis to warrant the exercise of the Governor's clemency powers.

   A grant of executive clemency involves intervention in the normal course of the criminal justice process. Such action constitutes extraordinary relief and is taken in only the most compelling of circumstances.

Sincerely,
JAMES V. MURRAY
Director
Executive Clemency Bureau

Elaine had been a prisoner for thirteen years. Her teenage daughters had no parents at home, her mother was dying, one son had just gone to state prison. Didn't this qualify as "the most compelling of circumstances"? What circumstances could be more compelling? When Elaine called home and relayed the bad news, her children were stunned. In prison, the only thing worse than having no hope, Elaine discovered, is to believe you are going home and then find out you are not.

Flashbacks to her clemency interview would haunt her for years, filling her mind with unanswerable questions. "You constantly ask yourself, What did you do wrong? What did you say wrong? Was it because you didn't talk the way they wanted you to talk? Was it because you didn't answer the questions the way they wanted you to answer them?" she explains. "You'll kill yourself worrying about what you did wrong."

For the last two years, Elaine had worked on the prison's construction crews. She had fought hard for these jobs; they were the best-paying ones in the prison. Once she even received a typed thank-you note from Elaine Lord, the prison's superintendent. "I would like to express my appreciation for the accomplishments you have created on renovating the Nursery at Bedford Hills," Superintendent Lord wrote. "I am very proud of the work done on the 3rd floor and the progress on the 2nd floor of Building 5. Keep up the good work!"

Now, every time Elaine walked around the prison, she became enraged. She saw evidence of her own labor all over the place. She had painted, plastered, laid down tiles, poured concrete, sanded floors. She had worked as an electrician, a plumber, and a landscaper, too. The institution looked better. But what had she gained, working so many hours at slave wages? Elaine thought the parole board's message was clear: "I'm good enough to fix up this raggedy joint, but I'm not good enough to go home."

The last few months of 1997 were especially rough for the Bartlett family. On a rainy fall day, Elaine's sister Sabrina slipped a heavy knapsack over her shoulders, filled her jacket pockets with cans of vegetables, and jumped in the East River. She likely would have drowned had she not been wearing a bright red-and-blue jacket. Somebody spotted her bobbing in the water, and a police officer fished her out, foiling her suicide attempt.

Not long after she was released from the hospital, she was back to her old ways, hanging out on Avenue D. In mid-December, she and her brother Donjuan were arrested for selling heroin to an undercover cop. They were both sent to Rikers Island.

Eight days later, Apache, Satara, and Danae trekked to Bedford Hills for their annual Christmas Eve visit. Today the visiting room was crowded with adults and children, just as it always was on the day before Christmas. At the moment, Jamel was 370 miles away, locked up in Attica prison. Yvonne had stayed on the Lower East Side; she was too sick to make this trip anymore.

Neither Elaine nor her children were in a festive mood. They had already spent too many holidays in this room with fluorescent lights, ever-present guards, and the lingering stench of microwave popcorn.

By that time, Danae was fifteen, Satara was seventeen, and Apache was twenty-four. Nobody wanted to climb in Elaine's lap anymore, or ride the rocking horse in the Children's Center.

Suddenly, another prisoner's table erupted in cheers. The news spread through the visiting room: Angela Thompson had just received clemency. Elaine's children knew Angela and her son from the summer program. She had been a prisoner at Bedford Hills for eight years, six years fewer than Elaine. But unlike Elaine, she had influential supporters. A retired State Supreme Court justice had written her clemency application, and a *New York Times* columnist had publicized her case.

The Bartlett family listened to the whooping across the room. They watched prisoners and guards congratulate Angela. Suddenly, Danae shoved back her chair and jumped up. "Why did she get clemency and you didn't?" she railed, loud enough for everyone to hear. "What makes her need to go home any more than you? What are you really here for? Don't lie to us! You can't be doing twenty years just for drugs. What did you really do? Who did you kill?"

CHAPTER 15

Lora Tucker struggled to keep calm as she walked down the prison corridor, carrying a satchel filled with pencils and paper. Would the women be hostile and aggressive? Would there be a guard in the room while she taught? How was she going to entertain fifteen prisoners for two hours? These questions had consumed her for days, but she did not dare pose them to the guard who was escorting her. Once she walked into her classroom, she realized she didn't have to worry about entertaining fifteen women. Only five had showed up.

Ten eyes followed her as she walked to the front of the room. That day Lora wore a blouse, a vest, and a felt hat with a piece of lace tied around it in a bow. "I'm Lora Tucker," she said. "This is my first time in a maximum-security prison." There was no point in trying to fool this audience. No point in pretending she had grown up in the ghetto, or that she knew anything about life on the inside.

Just the week before, Lora had been working at the Federal Reserve Bank in Manhattan as a $48,000-a-year interior designer. Tired of feeling stressed and unhappy, she had decided to quit, take a $15,000 pay cut, and get a job at WomenCare, Inc., a nonprofit organization that ran a mentoring program for prisoners. And so now here she was, standing before a classroom of felons.

Like many of the women at Bedford Hills, Lora is African-American. Unlike most of them, she is from an upper-middle-class family. Her father is a psychologist; her mother worked as a teacher and a school administrator. They raised her in Howard Beach, Queens. The neighborhood was Jewish and Italian; the Tuckers had been one of the very few black families. For Lora, it was not hard to imagine that if she had grown up in another family in a poorer neighborhood, she, too, might be wearing prison greens at the moment.

For the next ten weeks, throughout the fall of 1997, she was supposed to teach a class at Bedford Hills. The class did not have an official name, but she thought of it as an "empowerment workshop." "We're going to figure out what your needs are, and how I can help you," she told the prisoners. "I know what I want to do, but I want to know what you want to do, too. I'm willing to learn, and we're all going to learn together."

Lora was still thinking like an interior designer, as if the prisoners were her clients and it was her job to please them. She did not know it at the time, but this was not the way classes at Bedford Hills usually went. Teachers told the inmates what they were going to teach; they did not solicit prisoners' input about what they wanted to learn.

"Let's go around the room and have everybody introduce themselves," Lora said. "You don't have to say why you're here. Just say anything you feel I should know about you. And tell me one of your dreams or desires."

The women followed her instructions. They seemed willing to give her a chance, Lora thought. All of them, that is, except for one, who slumped in a chair in the second row. This particular inmate looked especially angry and sullen. "I'm Elaine Bartlett, 84-G-0068," she said. "I'm doing 20-to-life under the Rockefeller drug laws. My dream is to be out of here and home with my kids and my mother."

By now, Elaine explained, she had already attended almost every program the prison offered. For this class, she had just one wish.

"Please make these groups interesting," she said. "Because I am grouped out."

The Labor Day holiday threw off the class's schedule, and two weeks passed before Lora returned to Bedford Hills. She arrived at her classroom early. The only student already there was Elaine. One quick look at her teacher's face and Elaine could tell that something had changed. All of Lora's enthusiasm from the first class had disappeared.

"What's going on?" Elaine asked. "Are you okay?"

"Don't worry about it," Lora said.

The following week, Elaine showed up early again and asked the same questions. Lora knew she was not supposed to reveal too much information about her personal life, but this time she could not stop herself.

"Listen," she said. "I just found out I've been diagnosed with HIV. Just bear with me."

In fact, Lora had been diagnosed with AIDS, not HIV, which meant that her case was particularly advanced. She had been infected by a boyfriend, and now she felt like her life was over, as if she might die any day. Ever since she'd received the diagnosis, she had been thinking about her will.

The next week, Elaine showed up with a fistful of pamphlets about AIDS. So many women at Bedford Hills had the virus that the prison had a peer-counseling program for HIV-positive inmates. Free literature was not hard to obtain.

On this day, Elaine brought not only reading material, but also Diane, an inmate who had been living with the virus for nearly fifteen years. They showed up before class started, so that Diane could offer Lora a few encouraging words.

Over the next weeks, Lora's class tripled in size, partly because Elaine had been recruiting new students. Many of the women were long-termers serving time for drug crimes. Elaine and the other students told Lora what they wanted: tips on winning clemency. Lora tailored her lessons accordingly. The subject of one class was "How to Do Your Own PR and Marketing." She called another lesson "Make Yourself a Name, Not a Number." She even ran mock parole board hearings, casting herself in the role of inmate and the prisoners as parole commissioners.

Meanwhile, Elaine continued to show up early every week. "Are you taking your medications?" she would ask Lora. "Are you eating? Did you have lunch?" Lora would always insist she was fine, but Elaine knew better than to believe her. "Don't you be talking about dying," Elaine would say. "Don't be walking in here thinking you're going to die next week or next year. You're going to live, girl. We need you."

Lora and Elaine started to talk about the possibility of Elaine applying for clemency again. Elaine explained she did not want to put her family through the trauma of another rejection. Lora encouraged her to try once again, and she offered to help.

"I could see she felt hopeless," Lora said later. "She was resolved that she was going to be in there for twenty years, and that there was no one there to support her. She was pretty much alone. I could see that what she needed was someone on her side. She needed someone to say, 'I care. I believe in you.'"

Part of Lora's desire to help stemmed from her belief that her own days were numbered. At least I can free one person before I die, she told herself.

Elaine gave Lora her children's telephone number. On one of her days off, Lora drove to the Lower East Side and met Apache. They rode around the city together in her car and talked for an hour or two. Lora explained that she wanted to try to get his mother out of prison. To win clemency, she said, Elaine would need help from him and his sisters. Her application would be much stronger if it included letters from all of them. Apache promised to talk to Satara and Danae.

Lora's ten-week course concluded at the end of 1997, and when she started teaching another course in January, Elaine attended that one, too. Over the weeks, the two women grew closer, despite the prison's ban on volunteer-inmate friendships. In whispered conversations before class, they discussed Elaine's clemency application. And every week, Elaine smuggled in sandwiches from the prison kitchen so that Lora would have something to eat on the train ride home.

While Lora was trying to figure out how to free one Rockefeller drug law prisoner, two men in Manhattan were strategizing about getting rid of the laws altogether. One of these men was Anthony Papa, who had recently left Sing Sing prison, after serving twelve years of a 15-to-life sentence for cocaine sale and possession. He had managed to win clemency from Governor Pataki in large part by painting. His provocative works about prison life had won him a spot in a show at the Whitney Museum and myriad stories in the New York press.

Shortly after his release, he had appeared in a debate about the drug laws, which aired on C-SPAN. Randy Credico, a stand-up comedian, saw Tony on television and tracked him down. Many years earlier, Randy had befriended William Kunstler, the legendary radical lawyer, who died in 1995. Now, Randy wanted to set aside his comedy career and do something in the Kunstler tradition of battling injustice. Trying to repeal the Rockefeller drug laws seemed the perfect fight. Randy and Tony met and hashed out a strategy.

Randy talked about starting a movement patterned after the women who had started marching weekly in the mid-1970s in Argentina. Known as the mothers of the disappeared, they sought to draw attention to loved ones killed by the military. Randy suggested he and Tony recruit the relatives of drug prisoners and hold similar vigils in New York City. He already had a plan for the first one. It would be held on May 8, 1998, the twenty-fifth anniversary of the signing of the Rockefeller drug laws. He had an idea for the perfect location: outside Rockefeller Center.

Meanwhile, Lora had been researching the Rockefeller drug laws on Elaine's behalf. Her research led her to the Correctional Association, a prison watchdog group that had long been trying to repeal the laws. Lora joined the group on its annual lobbying trip to Albany, and on the bus she sat next to Tony Papa. Lora told him about Elaine's clemency bid, and Tony told her about the upcoming vigil. He also suggested she call Randy Credico.

By now, Randy was working with a brand-new organization, the William Moses Kunstler Fund for Racial Justice. When Lora called him and told him about Elaine, he was excited. He needed prisoners with sympathetic stories, and this one sounded particularly good. He added Elaine's name to the list he had been compiling. And he collected the basic facts of her story. He planned to make posters to represent all the drug prisoners who contacted him. At the upcoming rally, the posters would play a crucial role.

Fourteen years after she had arrived at Bedford Hills, Elaine was finally starting to get what she had always wanted: people on the outside who were concerned about her and her family. At the same time, however, she knew she was about to lose the one person who had kept her strong and sane all these years.

On the morning of March 12, 1998, she was led out of the prison and into the backseat of a van. The guards up front tried to chat, but she didn't respond. As they rode toward New York City, she leaned back and closed her eyes.

The van stopped on the Upper East Side of Manhattan, outside Beth Israel Medical Center. The guards climbed out, then opened the passenger door for her. She shuffled across the sidewalk and into the hospital lobby, wearing steel cuffs around her wrists and ankles.

The chain between her legs permitted only baby steps; walking through the hospital seemed to take forever. She could feel everyone's eyes on her. At the moment, though, she didn't care what anyone thought. She had too many other worries.

When she finally got to her mother's room, she discovered her amid a tangle of tubes and machines. Her mother's six-one frame extended the length of the extra-long bed. Elaine could see that she was even more frail than the last time she had seen her, two and a half years earlier.

Yvonne was now sixty-six years old. She had five remaining children, thirty grandchildren, and four great-grandchildren. For forty years, she had been the matriarch of the Bartlett family. But Elaine could see that the huge, proud, sassy woman who had reared her was already gone. She had rarely seen her mother without a wig on, but now, as Yvonne lay in her hospital bed, Elaine could see her real hair.

Elaine hovered over Yvonne, trying to figure out how to give her a hug. She bent down and rubbed her cheek against her mother's face. Then, with her bound hands, she caressed her shrunken body. Yvonne did not respond. Elaine shuffled close to the bed, then threw her body onto it. She lifted both legs and swung them onto the bed, too, the chain between her ankles rattling as she moved.

Elaine rolled over so she could press her body against her mother's, just like she had done when she was a child. Two guards stood across the room, watching. Elaine spent a half hour in this position, stroking her mother's skin and whispering in her ear. "Ma, I understand you can't take it no more," she said. "You can go now. It's all right."

Two days later, Elaine was watching *Soul Train* in the dayroom when she heard a guard shout her name. "Elaine, you've got to go see the chaplain right away," he said. She knew there was only one reason the chaplain would have called for her. Her mother was dead.

CHAPTER 16

The sky released a steady drizzle onto midtown Manhattan on the afternoon of May 8, 1998. Anyone riding in a taxicab down Fifth Avenue that day would have seen a sea of raincoats and colored umbrellas on the sidewalk between West Fiftieth Street and West Fifty-first Street. Fifty people had gathered in front of Rockefeller Center to mark the twenty-fifth anniversary of New York's drug laws. Many held handmade posters with a picture of an imprisoned relative. Two people held a red nylon banner with the slogan TOO MUCH TIME FOR NONVIOLENT CRIME!

The crowd included prisoners' relatives, former inmates, a state assemblyman, and eighty-eight-year-old Al Lewis, who played Grandpa on the 1960s sitcom *The Munsters*. To Randy Credico's delight, more than a dozen journalists showed up, too. Every time a reporter walked toward him with a microphone, he was ready with a sound bite. "You take a person like Joel Steinberg," he told WNBC-TV. "He's doing eight to twenty-five years, and he killed his kid. The whole thing here is, you're better off killing someone than you are selling drugs or possessing drugs. You'll do less time. That's the message."

Lora Tucker stood nearby, chatting with Apache, Satara, and Danae. Even Elaine's sister Michelle had shown up. They took turns holding Elaine's sign, which was made of white poster board. Her name appeared across the top, written with a red marker. Underneath was a photocopy of a Polaroid showing her and Apache crouching on the visiting room floor, their arms wrapped around Baby Tara and Little Mel. The details of Elaine's story—her age, crime, sentence, and years served—appeared next to her picture.

In the years since the Rockefeller drug laws went into effect, the population in New York's state prisons had soared from 12,500 to nearly 70,000. This rapid rise in the prison population had been fueled by the drug laws as well as by the Second Felony Offender Law, which was also passed in 1973 and mandates prison terms for two-time felons. Of New York's 70,000 inmates, 21,000 were serving time for a drug crime. Ninety-four percent of the state's drug prisoners were African-American or Latino.

The Rockefeller drug laws had altered the profile of the typical New York State prisoner. Between 1980 and 1999, the number of new prisoners serving time for drug crimes had risen from 11 percent to 45 percent. The laws had also sparked a prison-building boom. New York State now had sixty-nine prisons, up from eighteen in 1973. In the last fifteen years, the annual budget for state prisons had grown from $450 million to $1.7 billion. In New York state, the cost of imprisoning one person for a year is about $32,000. By this point, the price tag for Elaine's incarceration was nearly $500,000.

Nearly every poster at the vigil outside Rockefeller Center told the story of a first-time prisoner who had been convicted of an A-1 felony and was serving at least fifteen years to life. These were the most sympathetic cases in the state. There were not too many of them, however. At the end of 1997, only 631 of the state's 21,000 drug prisoners were serving time for an A-1 felony.

Many more of New York's drug prisoners had been convicted of a B-level felony. Posters do not convey the injustice of their sentences quite as easily, but in some ways these cases are just as troubling. Selling only one bag of heroin or one vial of crack constitutes a Class B felony. Under New York's penal law, this offense is equivalent to first-degree rape, first-degree manslaughter, and armed robbery.

It was a testament to Randy's perseverance that he had managed to find and recruit so many families of A-1 drug prisoners in just a few months. His posters revealed a shrewd strategy: Promote the most sympathetic prisoners while pushing for widespread change. Randy's mission was to rewrite the narrative that had led to the laws' creation. While Governor Rockefeller had characterized drug pushers as violent thugs who deserved to be in prison for the rest of their lives, Randy sought to portray these same people as victims of unjust laws whose lengthy prison stays were destroying their families.

From the moment Rockefeller first proposed his new drug laws, activists across New York State had been waging battle against them. Their weapons included detailed reports, damning statistics, and well-crafted op-ed pieces. The people most directly affected by the laws—the state's drug prisoners and their families—had not been included in the public debate. Now Randy sought to change this by publicizing their stories.

His timing could not have been better. Crime rates had fallen over the last few years, and fears about violence and drugs had started to subside. State legislators appeared willing for the first time in years to reassess the Rockefeller drug laws.

The afternoon vigil was fairly quiet. There were no chants. No whistles or bullhorns. No marching up and down Fifth Avenue. To the shoppers walking by, the gathering no doubt seemed a minor event. But for Elaine's family and all the other prisoners' families, the vigil was a much-needed morale boost. Shame, frustration, despair, embarrassment—these were the emotions that arose when a relative went to prison. But here there was no need to feel ashamed. The prisoners' relatives could see that their predicament was not so unusual, that their pain was shared by many other people across the city.

For the next few months, Randy held vigils every Friday at Rockefeller Center. When he tired of that location, he moved his demonstrations around the city—to Brooklyn State Supreme Court, the State Office

Building on 125th Street, and Governor Pataki's midtown office. Wherever he went, he carried his cell phone. He had a 1500-minute plan and had programmed thirteen reporters' numbers into the speed dial. Over the next year, he managed to convince virtually every local media outlet to cover his vigils. They even received attention in the international press, including the *Financial Times* and BBC Radio.

When reporters called, looking for a prisoner to interview, Randy sometimes steered them to Lora, who hooked them up with Elaine. A *New York Times* columnist wrote about Elaine. Her photograph appeared on the front page of the *Times Union* of Albany. Geraldo Rivera went to Bedford Hills to interview her. With Lora's coaching, Elaine figured out how to tell her story without dissolving into tears. Talking to strangers about her predicament was not easy, but her confidence increased each time she was interviewed.

Elaine knew her mother would never have approved of all these interviews, of speaking publicly about her arrest and conviction. Yvonne had always been a private person. When Elaine had first gone to prison, her mother had told her not to send letters directly to her brothers Donjuan and Shyan, who were also in the state prison system. Her mother said to mail the letters home instead and that she would forward them. "You don't let everyone know your whole family is in jail," Yvonne had said. "That's embarrassing."

But by now, Elaine had decided to tell her story to as many reporters as possible. She felt she had no choice. To win clemency, somebody would have to deem her extraordinary, and the best way to attract the governor's attention was by using the media. If she had to reveal personal details about her family's pain in order to improve her chances, then that's what she would do. Just as there had been a group of people who had put her into prison—the informant, the state police, the prosecutor, the judge—now there was another group of people who might be able to help her get out—activists, liberal legislators, reporters.

Of all the journalists who came to see her, there was one who turned her cause into his own personal crusade: Charles Grodin, the veteran actor, who was then hosting a late-night talk show on CNBC. In many ways, Grodin was the ideal person to champion Elaine's cause. Since he was not a mainstream journalist, he was under no obligation to remain "objective." And he had enough celebrity to risk the sort of ratings dip that inevitably occurs when a television show tackles serious political topics.

While other late-night hosts were obsessed with Monica Lewinsky, Grodin became fixated on the Rockefeller drug laws. He invited experts to appear on his show, and he aired interviews with prisoners. According to Grodin, New York's drug laws were the "most appalling injustice that's taking place in America." He went to Bedford Hills to see Elaine several times, sometimes with a TV camera, sometimes not. He often talked about her on his show, and when he aired an interview with her, he introduced her as a "political prisoner."

In the spring of 1998, Satara, now eighteen, wrote a letter that she hoped would get her mother out of prison. Her words filled one and a half pages of lined school paper. At the time, she did not know what would become of her letter. Following Lora's instructions, she slipped it in an envelope and mailed it to Randy. He had offered to help compile Elaine's clemency application and send it on to Albany.

4/22/98

I am writing this letter to let you know that it's time for my mother to come home. Because I really need her. Ever since my grandmother Mrs. Yvonne Bartlett died on March 14, 1998 I haven't been the same. I've been lonely, uncomfortable . . . and very sad. . . . I just don't feel like being here sometimes without my mother or grandmother. And I know what she did was wrong but she did the best because she was a single parent on welfare. I know she was wrong but its time for her to come home because I need to support her. She lossed her mother and it hearts her 'cause she wasn't out here to take care of her and I know it hearts her alot but she just don't show it but I am her daughter and I know she needs me. . . .

I am 18 years old and everytime I look back she was never their for me to hold. I have dreams about my mother and this is when I really need her with me. Because I feel that it's been long enough, and me, my sister and brothers are really struggling right now and we need her help. Also my family is falling apart and times are hard, but I am really tring. Look I have sickle cell diseases and I take medicine for it. Sometimes when I go to the hospital I have to stay. . . . I get scared that they might find something else wrong with me. So I just cry and pray to get better so I can live as long as I could. Sometimes I feel like killing myself because my mother lefted me and know my grandmother is gone. She should of took me with her.

I am a stressed out girl who needs my mother right know to be their for me. But I am just trying my hardest to get out of school. I am doing it because I love myself and I promised my grandmother because she was suposed to go to my 12th grade graduation and it is really going to heart me that she is not going to be their. Please allow our mother to come home and be with us for she has been gone to long. . . .

> Thank you!
> Yours truly,
> Satara Bartlett

A few months after Satara wrote this letter, Apache came home late one night after a basketball game. He turned on the television and collapsed on the couch in the living room. *Ever since my grandmother Mrs. Yvonne Bartlett died on March 14, 1998 I haven't been the same.* . . . Apache saw Satara's handwriting on the screen and he heard Charles Grodin reading her words. He had never seen his sister's letter to the clemency bureau; he did not even know she had written it.

Lately, he had been so busy with his basketball teams that he had spent little time in the apartment. Even when he did stop in, he and his sisters rarely talked to one another about how they were feeling. Instead, they all kept their sadness and grief to themselves, trying to be strong for one another. *Sometimes I feel like killing myself because my mother lefted me and know my grandmother is gone.* . . . Alone in the living room, listening to his sister's words, realizing how much pain she had been hiding, Apache began to cry.

CHAPTER 17

The sixteenth anniversary of Elaine's arrest found her still imprisoned in Bedford Hills, still trying to figure out how to get home. By now, she had missed nearly one hundred family events. Fifteen Easters. Sixty of her children's birthdays. Seven grandchildren's birthdays. Three grandchildren's births. Four elementary school graduations. Four middle school graduations. Countless basketball games, barbecues, baby showers, and welcome-home-from-jail parties. The only family events she had attended were the saddest ones: three funerals.

She had already done everything she could think of to win clemency. Over the last few years, she had moved from a regular cell block to the prison's "honor floor," and then to Fiske Cottage, the "super-honor" dorm, located atop a hill at the rear of the prison grounds. This three-story building was one of the last vestiges of Bedford Hills' reformatory past. Faced with a space crunch in the early 1980s, prison officials had renovated and reopened the cottage. Twenty-six women lived here, and each had her own room and a key to her door. There were no cells, no metal bars, no steel doors.

Most of Fiske's residents liked living here. Not Elaine. The only reason she had asked to move to Fiske was because she thought it

would make her look like a model prisoner—and a better candidate
for clemency. She would rather have lived on a regular cell block, surrounded by her inmate "children." The women chosen to live at Fiske
were the prison's elite: long-termers, often Hispanic or white, who
frequently had one or two academic degrees and a record of good behavior. In Elaine's view, many of them thought they were better than
the other prisoners, and there was nothing she despised in a fellow
inmate more than snobbery.

Elaine also disliked Fiske because she hated the idea of the guards
having yet another way to control her; the downside to living in this
super-honor dorm was knowing that at any moment the privilege
could be taken away. In addition, she had heard that the Rockefeller
family had once used this building as a hunting lodge. She did not
know if this was true, but she was unnerved by the possibility that she
was living in a room where a Rockefeller had once slept.

To boost her odds of winning clemency, Elaine had joined the
prison's newest program, Puppies Behind Bars, in which inmates
trained Labrador retrievers to be guide dogs for the blind. Though
Elaine loved dogs, she had qualms about the program. Training a
guide dog was a very time-consuming process; it required walking
around for at least a year with a dog leash in one hand. For their work,
though, the prisoners were paid nothing. This fact bothered Elaine,
but she did not complain. She did not want to do anything that might
hurt her bid for clemency.

By that time, she was convinced that clemency had little to do with
merit and everything to do with politics and publicity. When she had
gone before the parole board the first time, she already possessed a
thick stack of certificates, diplomas, and glowing letters of recommendation. Yet all of those pieces of paper hadn't gotten her released.
Now she had an associate's degree, too, but she did not think that was
going to get her out of prison, either. For all the talk of rehabilitation,
she believed it was really the media's attention she had needed the
most.

Nobody had given her more publicity than Charles Grodin. Not
only had he talked about her on the air many times, but he had gone

to Albany and lobbied on her behalf, organizing a luncheon for State Senate Majority Leader Joseph Bruno and ten other state legislators. At the luncheon, he had shown video clips of her and three other prisoners. Not long afterward, Bruno had announced that he endorsed clemency for all four women.

Bruno has no official role in the clemency process—the governor makes these decisions—but Bruno does have influence. Apart from the governor, he is the most powerful Republican in the state. And his willingness to support clemency for anybody was surprising. He is a conservative who favors harsher punishments for criminals, including eliminating early release on parole.

Inside Bedford Hills, tensions among clemency applicants increased every year as Christmas approached. For Elaine, the previous few months had been especially stressful. Every time her name appeared in the newspaper, every time her odds of going home seemed to improve, she could feel the resentment toward her grow. Everyone knew which long-termers had a shot at clemency, and the competition was intense. Women researched one another's crimes in the law library to see how they stacked up, and they snubbed those inmates who managed to snag an interview with a reporter.

Getting a lot of media coverage was not a guarantee of early release, however. One year earlier, Elaine's friend Donna Charles had received some media attention and had even managed to get a letter of support from the judge who had sentenced her. She, too, was an A-1 drug prisoner who had never been arrested before. In the days after her clemency interview, her odds of getting out seemed so good that prisoners had started congratulating her. "Girl, you've got it!" they said. "You're going home!"

But when Christmas arrived, Governor Pataki had declined to give anyone clemency. Donna was still at Bedford Hills, in year eleven of a 17-to-life sentence.

At noon on December 19, 1999, Elaine sat in the hall of the prison's main building, staring at the second hand on the clock above the officer's desk. She wore her best shirt; it was mint green and had gold buttons up the front. Instead of her usual state-issued green pants, she had put on a green skirt. Behind the closed door of the room next to her, two parole commissioners were grilling another inmate. Any minute, she knew, it would be her turn.

Jan Warren, who was in her twelfth year of a 15-to-life sentence, was inside the parole room. Elaine hoped Jan was not saying anything to anger the commissioners. She wanted them to be in a good mood when it was her turn. She pulled a Newport out of her pocket, asked the guard for a light, walked to the end of the hall, and pushed open the door. She stood for a few minutes in the doorway, her eyes fixed on the entrance to the conference room. Soon Jan emerged, a soggy tissue in one hand.

Elaine tossed her cigarette on the ground, said a silent prayer, and headed down the hall, toward the same room where two parole board members had interrogated her three years earlier. This time, two different commissioners sat side by side at an eight-foot-long table. A U.S. flag hung from a pole on the side of the room. Looking through a window, Elaine could see the prison's parking lot, filled with officers' cars.

The parole board members introduced themselves as Irene Platt and Joseph Gawloski. Elaine recognized Platt's name. According to the prison grapevine, she was very tough. Elaine noticed James Murray seated off to the side; he had introduced himself earlier. Of course she had recognized his name, too. He was the head of the Executive Clemency Bureau and the author of her rejection letter.

She sat down in the chair across from the commissioners. A stack of papers with her name on them was on the table. Gawloski flipped through her file, while Platt interrogated her.

"Do you really expect us to believe this was the first time you ever sold drugs?"

Sometimes they like to play devil's advocate, Elaine thought, to provoke prisoners into revealing how angry or unremorseful they are. Last time around, she had launched into a bitter diatribe about being entrapped by George Deets. Today, she wasn't going to take the bait.

No ranting about the injustices of the drug laws. The parole commissioners did not want to hear that.

"I don't really expect you to believe anything," she said. "But it's the truth."

"Why didn't you leave the drugs at the train station?"

Two years ago, she would have become hostile and defensive if asked this. But by now, she was convinced that these questions were designed to rile her, to test her resolve, to see whether she could keep her emotions in check. Don't get angry or annoyed, she told herself. Stay cool.

"I've asked myself that question every day for sixteen years," she said. "I don't have an answer for you."

"How have you changed since your last appearance before the parole board? What programs have you been involved in?"

Elaine thought she knew what the commissioners wanted to hear. She figured they wanted her to say that Bedford Hills—and its many programs for prisoners—had reformed her. But the truth was that she did not believe the prison had rehabilitated her. In her opinion, she had not needed much "rehabilitation" in the first place—just a decent education and a few more job skills.

Elaine did not explain any of this to the commissioners. Instead, she served up a few calm words in explaining what had changed her. "Education and the death of my mother," she said.

In Elaine's opinion, clemency was a cruel and unfair game. She saw it as part of the governor's political dance, a way for him to show concern about the injustices of the laws without actually changing them. She did not think the governor should give anyone clemency; instead, he should just repeal the laws. She kept these thoughts to herself, however. She figured these weren't the sorts of statements that would help her win over her audience.

At the end of her thirty-eight-minute interrogation, she thanked the commissioners, smiled sweetly, and leaned over the table to shake their hands.

.   .   .

By now, the people who had put Elaine in prison barely remembered her, if they remembered her at all. Officer Kenneth Cook had risen to the job of deputy superintendent in the New York State Police. Thomas Neidl, who had prosecuted Elaine and Nathan, was now a criminal defense attorney and, in fact, a critic of the Rockefeller drug laws. Bernard Bryan, Nathan's lawyer, worked for the state legislature. Joseph Teresi, Elaine's lawyer, had become a county court judge. The judge who had presided over their trial, "Maximum John" Clyne, was no longer alive; he had died of throat cancer in 1998.

After setting up Elaine, George Deets had continued to work for the state police. In the mid-1980s, his friend Richard Zagorski had severed ties with George after meeting a clean-cut young woman he wanted to marry. George was arrested for an A-1 felony, a cocaine sale, in 1988. He pleaded guilty to a lesser charge, got 6-to-life, and managed to get out of prison while his appeal was pending.

In early 1993, while partying at a friend's house, he ingested heroin, cocaine, marijuana, and Xanax. He went into seizures and was rushed to the hospital. There, he was pronounced dead, at the age of thirty-seven. His body was placed in a cemetery on the outskirts of his hometown, next to a patch of dandelions, not far from where his smuggled cocaine is likely still buried.

CHAPTER 18

By the time she walked out of the deputy superintendent's office, everybody in the prison had already heard the news: Elaine Bartlett was going home. "Congratulations!" women shouted at her as she strode down the corridor. "I knew you were going to get it!" When she went out into the rec yard, women sprinted toward her and threw their arms around her. For the next hour or two, tears streamed down Elaine's cheeks. She had sobbed hundreds of times since coming to prison, but this was the first time she had cried tears of joy.

The only thing standing between Elaine and freedom was one more hearing before the parole board. Unless she broke a lot of prison rules within the next month, she would be released. The governor had reduced her minimum sentence from twenty years to sixteen, enabling her to be released early. Clemency was not the same as a pardon, however. She still had a felony record, and she would have to be on parole once she left.

The news from Albany marked the beginning of four giddy weeks. When guards told Elaine to hurry in the hallways, she just laughed. "Have your fun now," she said. "I'm going home soon. Just try to tell me what to do on the other side of the fence." Women she had known for years congratulated her, and she could tell that most of them really meant it. She received hugs from dozens of women, and she got a letter from Kathy Boudin, who was serving time in connection with the 1981 Brinks robbery.

> Dear Elaine,
>
> I don't know, my friend, what a hard battle you have fought and I am writing to tell you how much I hope that you triumph and go home. You have never given up, you have fought hard for everyone and I send you my support and respect.
>
> It is hard to fight to get out—the ups and downs, the hopes, the disappointments, a roller coaster of emotions, and you're dealing with your whole family and their ups and downs. We have known each other, forever, it seems. It will feel strange here without you but it will feel better because I know that you are home. . . .
>
> Love ya,
> Kathy

The Bedford Hills grapevine was always buzzing with news about women who had left. The news was sometimes good, sometimes not. The prisoners heard which of their friends had become pregnant, moved into their own apartments, reunited with their husbands, landed jobs, moved in with their prison girlfriends, been arrested again, started smoking crack. There were few secrets between parole office waiting rooms and the cell blocks of Rikers, Albion, and Bedford Hills.

Elaine's friend Betty Tyson had left Bedford Hills in 1998, after a judge reversed her murder conviction. By then, she was the longest-serving female inmate in the state prison system; she'd been locked up for nearly twenty-five years. Before she left, she had given Elaine a parting gift: a piece of fabric from the green prison coat she had worn every day, which she signed, "Godspeed and good luck." Six months later, Betty's friends at Bedford Hills heard good news. She had brought a wrongful-imprisonment lawsuit against the city of Rochester, and the city had agreed to pay her $1.25 million.

Once Elaine was freed, she did not plan to spend much time thinking about Bedford Hills. Other women made elaborate promises—to send letters, packages, money—and then were never heard from again. This always enraged the women left behind, who imagined their friends were now too full of themselves to remember them. "She walked away and didn't look back," they would say. Elaine did not want anyone talking badly about her after she left, so she purposely made no promises.

In some instances, it seemed, the longer a woman stayed at Bedford Hills, the less she wanted to leave. Some inmates had discovered love for the first time inside this prison, and they were dreading the day they would have to leave their girlfriends behind. Some women had nowhere to go after they were released. The family they had in prison was more than they had on the streets. Compared to them, Elaine considered herself fortunate.

She knew that everyone would be watching her, analyzing her successes and failures, searching for clues about what they could expect when they got out of prison. She did not want to disappoint. The ultimate failure, of course, would be to come back here with a pair of cuffs around her wrists. Women were constantly returning to Bedford Hills because they had committed a new crime or disobeyed the terms of their parole.

Some came back with stories about parole officers who were more determined to lock them up than to help them. There was even a rumor that parole officers earned a bonus for every parolee they sent back to prison. This wasn't true, but the state's parole officers had become noticeably stricter, especially since Governor Pataki had been elected. The percentage of parolees arrested for breaking parole's rules had more than doubled over the last decade.

Elaine was a very different person from the angry twenty-six-year-old who had mouthed off to Officer Dixon on her first day in prison. She was now forty-two years old. The toll of her prison term was written all over her body. Gallstone surgery a few years earlier had left a scar running diagonally across her stomach. Her big toenail on her left foot was half-missing, crushed by a metal locker while she was re-arranging her cell. And the bottom of her left eye was slightly lower than her right, a lingering reminder of the fight that had left her with a fractured eye socket.

Like everyone else, Elaine carried many invisible scars, too. Prison damages everybody, no matter how educated they become or how much they believe they have not changed. Despite her best efforts not to become bitter, Elaine still carried with her sixteen years of frustration and rage. Her wounds were not yet visible, but in the days and months to come, the true toll of her lengthy imprisonment would become apparent.

In the days before her release, she created a "To Do" list of all she wanted to accomplish once she got home. Spend time with Apache, Satara, and Danae. Visit Jamel in jail. Visit Nate in prison. Quit smoking. Go out for a seafood dinner with Lora. Ride the Cyclone at Coney Island. Stop cursing. Find a job. Go to the movies. It was too late to repay her mother for raising her children, but at least she could go home and try to make up for some of the lost years. And now there was a new member of the family with whom she was eager to spend time. Satara had recently given birth to a daughter she'd named Tenéa.

Already, though, there were signs that rejoining her family would not be easy. Elaine knew that her sister Michelle resented her for being away all these years. At thirty-five, Michelle was raising nine children, five of her own and four of Sabrina's. "I'm going on vacation for two weeks and you're taking the kids, so you can see what it feels like," Michelle had said on the phone.

Elaine had no plans to take care of nine nieces and nephews. First, she wanted to help her four children. She'd heard that Danae had been losing weight because there was no food in the apartment; Jamel had been charged in yet another drug case; and Satara had been in and out of the hospital with crises related to her sickle-cell anemia.

Apache seemed to be doing all right—he had recently found a job coaching basketball at Saint Michael Academy, a Catholic school for girls. Still, she worried about him, too.

The parole board scheduled Elaine's release for January 26, 2000. The date was already etched in her memory; coincidentally, it was the same day that Judge Clyne had sentenced her. That morning, she woke in her Fiske Cottage room at 4:00 a.m. Next to her was Winston, the black Labrador puppy she had been training as a guide dog. Winston usually spent the night locked in a cage in the corner, but on her last night in prison, she had let him sleep on her bed.

She took Winston for a walk, then returned to her room and began singing along to her radio. This morning, she spared no effort to look good. She curled her hair and put on black eyeliner. She couldn't decide which shade of lipstick to wear, so she put on several. The combination made her lips look cranberry. In her prison greens, she went to the state shop building and signed her parole release papers. Then she slipped on a brand-new outfit.

Lora had bought her an electric-purple pantsuit and a black trench coat. Jamel's girlfriend had sent her a black Victoria's Secret bra, matching panties, and black suede boots. Elaine pinned a button she had made just for today on the lapel of her new coat. It was a small photo of her mother inside a plastic frame, decorated with a pink ribbon, a tiny silk rose, and a message: "Yvonne, I Carry You in My Soul."

After 118 days in Albany County Jail and 5,805 days in Bedford Hills, she could hardly believe she was going home. In her first years here, she had spent hundreds of hours choreographing the moment of her release, imagining what she would wear and who would greet her. But as the years dragged on, this image faded from her mind. She had started to think that she would need a cane by the time she was allowed to walk out.

In recent weeks, she had begun to picture this moment once again. The fantasy scene she liked to replay in her mind featured three white doves soaring toward the sky at the moment of her release. It also included the sound of Diana Ross singing, "I'm Coming Out."

The time has come for me
To break out of the shell
I have to shout
That I'm coming out . . .

At 9:54 a.m., Elaine stepped out the prison's front door and heard a different sort of music. "We love you, Elaine!" Dozens of women filled the windows of the school building, waving their hats, mittens, and scarves. "You go, girl!" they shouted.

Elaine stopped, spun around, and waved good-bye.

PART THREE

**Life on the
Outside**
2000–2001

It felt strange to ride in the backseat of a van without steel cuffs around her wrists. The guards had made sure to cuff and shackle her the four times they'd taken her from Bedford Hills to New York City—for Ronald's funeral, Frankie's funeral, Yvonne's hospital stay, and then Yvonne's funeral. Now, finally, she was free. She slipped one hand inside her bra and pulled out a slim stack of bills.

"They gave me forty dollars," she said, massaging the money with her fingertips. "Can you believe that?" Forty dollars is the standard parting gift of the New York State prison system. "Can you buy lunch for forty dollars now?" she asked.

"You can't even buy a hamburger for forty dollars," Lora Tucker shouted from the driver's seat.

Elaine giggled. On this day, everything seemed funny. It was not yet noon, and already she had been laughing for five hours, ever since she had woken up. And now, here she was, halfway home, heading south on the Saw Mill River Parkway toward New York City. If all went well, she would be at her welcome-home party in an hour or two.

Apache dialed home on a cell phone. "Where's Tara at?" he asked. "Go wake her up and tell her her mother wants to speak with her."

He handed the phone to Elaine. She had never held a cell phone before, but she had no trouble figuring out how to use it.

"You know who you're talking to?" she asked Tara. "Do you know where your mother is at? That's right. I'm in the car on my way to Manhattan. Listen. At three o'clock, I want you and Nay-nay to meet me at the restaurant. Do you have a pen? Take this address. We'll be outside waiting for you, so you'll definitely see your mother. You remember what your mother looks like, right?"

Elaine laughed once again. After all, she'd just seen Satara in the visiting room one month earlier.

Lora steered the van along the New York State Thruway, then exited in the South Bronx. Soon they were near the Mott Haven Houses, where Elaine's brother Frankie had lived with his family before he was murdered. Apache dialed Becky, Frankie's widow, and told her to come downstairs. By the time the van reached 139th Street, Becky and her twenty-year-old son, Frank, were standing outside.

Elaine burst out of the van and threw her arms around Becky, whom she had known since they were teenagers. The last time Elaine had seen her had been at Yvonne's funeral two years earlier. Since then, Frank appeared to have grown six inches; now he was nearly seven feet tall.

Elaine noticed him staring at her blankly. "What do you mean you don't know who I am?" she asked.

She turned to Becky. "You were supposed to tell them who their aunt is. Didn't you show them pictures of me? I'm not dead."

"You didn't send me no pictures," Becky said.

"We're family. You hear that?" Elaine said to Frank. "Look how tall he is. Boy, you better be a basketball player."

Elaine had a few plans for the afternoon, but she wanted to spend the night celebrating at her sister's apartment in Harlem. "I want you all to come to Michelle's tonight," she said.

"I ain't got no money," Becky said.

Of course, Elaine barely had any money, either. Nevertheless, she slid her hand in her bra, pulled out a ten-dollar bill, and handed it to Frank.

"Bring the kids," she said to Becky. "I don't want to hear about how you have no money."

Back in the van, Elaine directed Lora to stop at the nearest bodega. "I want every kind of gum you have," she told the man behind the counter. She emerged from the store with a bag of Doritos, another bag of chips, and a fistful of gum.

Inside prison, gum is contraband, since a well-placed wad can jam a door lock. Elaine had been craving gum for years. She unwrapped a stick of Big Red and chewed it slowly, savoring the hot cinnamon flavor flooding her mouth.

"Do you have the address for the parole office?" Lora asked.

"Apache, where's the green paper I gave you?" Elaine asked. "That's for the parole man. The green sheet with the rules and regulations about what I can and can't do."

Like all new parolees, Elaine had to report to her parole officer within twenty-four hours of leaving prison. Lora steered the van through the Upper East Side and midtown, then stopped in front of 119 West Thirty-first Street, one block from Madison Square Garden. There was no sign on this fifteen-story building, but inside was Elaine's parole office.

She swept into the lobby, her three-inch heels clicking against the floor as she strode toward the guard at the front desk. He directed her to the parolee waiting room on the second floor. There, a receptionist informed her that her parole officer was not in. She would have to report back tomorrow.

The next stop was Gus' Place, a restaurant in the West Village. Elaine, Lora, and Apache arrived at 3:30 p.m. Just as they neared the front door, Elaine saw a taxi stop in front and let out three passengers: her nineteen-year-old daughter Satara, Satara's boyfriend, and a female friend. Elaine hurried toward Satara and squeezed her arms around her.

At the same moment, a photographer and cameraman ran over to record the reunion. Apparently, there was no time for a private hug. Elaine grabbed Satara's hand and led her into the restaurant.

Randy Credico, the anti–drug law activist, had organized this welcome-home party for Elaine and the two other women who had just been released. Already, the restaurant was packed. Satara retreated to a corner with her friends, while Elaine bounced from reporter to reporter, reveling in the media spotlight.

"When you heard that [twenty-to-life] sentence, what were you thinking?" asked a WPIX-TV reporter.

"That I was railroaded out of my life," Elaine said. "It didn't take me sixteen years, two weeks, and three days to learn my lesson. You could have put me on probation. You could have had me do community service. There were different things you could've done with me other than throwing me in jail and throwing away the key like I was Charles Manson or somebody."

Everybody at the party wanted to talk to Elaine—activists, reporters, ex-cons, prisoners' relatives. Charles Grodin gave her a hug and a kiss. Margaret Ratner—widow of William Kunstler and founder of the Kunstler Fund—gave her a bouquet of flowers. Strangers slipped her their business cards. And when she lifted a forkful of linguini with shrimp into her mouth, a television camera zoomed in for a close-up.

The party, the press, the cocktails, the free food, the hugs and the handshakes—this was her victory lap, the beginning of her new life as a free woman. But even with all the attention and accolades, Elaine was distracted. Every time she got a break, she scanned the restaurant for the one person she had not yet seen: her younger daughter, Danae. There was no sign of her.

Finally, after two hours, Elaine decided to leave. With Apache and Satara, she rode over to the Lower East Side in a taxi. A crew from a local television station trailed behind. Her children took her to JHS 22, the school near the Wald Houses where Danae practiced basketball in the afternoons.

Walking up the stairwell, Elaine heard the sound of balls smacking against the wooden floor. She stepped inside the gym, and, surveying a group of teenagers, she picked out her daughter. Danae was the one with her shorts riding low, a husky seventeen-year-old with a ball in one hand.

"Oh shit!" Danae shouted. "There's my mother!"

Danae looked as if she did not believe what she was seeing, as if she'd never thought this reunion would be a reality. "My mother! My mother!" Elaine opened her arms, and Danae sprinted toward her.

Finally, Elaine had tracked down three of her four children. Jamel would have to wait until she could get to Rikers Island. The family walked across East Houston Street, then north on Avenue D toward the Wald Houses. To Elaine, this housing project looked like the one she had lived in when she was a young mother: a complex of towering redbrick buildings, asphalt pathways, basketball courts, wooden benches, fenced-in grass, and jungle gyms.

Her children led her toward the rear of the project, stopping in front of a fourteen-story building. The address above the front door— 950 East Fourth Walk—was familiar, too. Elaine had scribbled it on hundreds of envelopes over the years. Elaine, her children, and the camera crew waited in the lobby for an elevator, then rode it up to the thirteenth floor.

When the elevator door opened, everyone stopped talking. Even in her euphoric state, Elaine could sense that something was wrong.

Once she got to Apartment 13B and glanced inside, she understood. Pieces of a kitchen table leaned against one wall, held together by duct tape. Broken chairs spread across a grimy linoleum floor. The ceiling, once white, was now filthy gray, stained by smoke. To the left, a tattered sheet hung in the doorway to the living room, a sorry substitute for a door.

All those years she'd been away, she had never even considered the possibility that she might be living in better conditions in prison than her children were in the free world.

"Oh my God," Elaine said loudly enough for everyone to hear. She whirled around. "Turn that camera off! Do not show that on TV!"

CHAPTER 20

Elaine had planned to celebrate her release by going to City Island for a dinner of shrimp and lobster. But after inspecting Apartment 13B, she knew she couldn't relax yet. Everywhere she turned, she saw something that needed to be fixed: the toilet seat, the curtain rod in the living room, the kitchen table, the lock on the front door. There was no garbage pail in the kitchen. No cleaning supplies under the sink. No toilet paper in the bathroom. The cupboards were empty, and the refrigerator, too.

The morning after her release from prison, Elaine decided to go shopping so she could fix up the apartment. Cassandra Rivera offered to drive her. Cassandra was the mother of Jamel's son, Little Mel. Although she was no longer Jamel's girlfriend, she still spent time with his family. She was only twenty years old, but she was one of the very few people Elaine knew who had her own car—a hunter-green Range Rover.

Cassandra picked up Elaine, Satara, and Danae, then drove to a bank. She got out of the car, leaving them behind. When she returned, she was carrying a thick envelope. "Here," she said to Elaine, "this is for you." It was a welcome-home present.

Elaine stared at the number on the front of the envelope: $1,500.

She opened the envelope, pulled out a stack of crisp bills, and counted each one slowly, as if she did not actually believe the dollar amount she'd just read. "I haven't held this much money in almost seventeen years," Elaine said, staring at the cash. She threw the envelope out the car window and clutched the bills tightly in one hand.

"Put that money away," Cassandra said, glancing over at Elaine as she drove. "In your pocket." Elaine ignored her. She did not dare let the cash out of her sight, for fear it would disappear.

Cassandra was the wealthiest person Elaine knew—at least the wealthiest by legal means. She came from a working-class family but had received a large amount of money two years earlier, when she turned eighteen. The money had come from a lawsuit stemming from a car accident. Cassandra had broken her back and spent three months in a body cast when she was six years old; all her injuries eventually healed. Nobody in the Bartlett family knew exactly how much money she had received, but they knew she had paid half the bill for Yvonne's funeral, which had cost $10,000. And they knew she owned a Lexus and two Acura Legends, in addition to the Range Rover.

Cassandra turned into the parking lot of Costco in Long Island City, Queens. Everybody got out of the car and walked toward the store's entrance. At Bedford Hills, Elaine had shopped in the prison commissary, which was actually a hole in a wall, covered by a metal grating. To purchase a pack of Newports or a bar of soap, she'd had to wait for a guard to call her name. Then she had to show her ID, hand her order form through the window, and wait for someone to put her items in a wire basket.

Costco seemed like another planet in comparison. Elaine had thought she was going to a supermarket, but this place looked like a warehouse. The ceiling was thirty feet high, and the products were stacked at least twenty feet into the air, far above the shoppers' heads. This store seemed to sell everything: computers, leather jackets, jewelry, contact lenses, groceries. Elaine stopped just inside the entrance and tried to take it all in.

In prison, nobody ever hurried, but now everywhere she looked there were shoppers moving decisively through the store, pushing carts filled with products. Surveying the scene, Elaine felt like her senses were working overtime. Another person just out of prison might have become so overwhelmed that they would want to retreat to the parking lot. Not Elaine. The stack of bills in her hand seemed to energize her.

"What are you standing here for?" she asked Cassandra and her daughters. "Let's go shopping."

She grabbed a cart and headed for the food section. Every few minutes, she paused to marvel at the displays—the packages of meat, the boxes of cereal. "Look at that!"

"Ma, they've been had that," Satara said. "You act like you've been gone a hundred years."

Elaine wandered from aisle to aisle. She did not examine each product, checking its size and price. Instead, she just grabbed whatever looked like it might be good, then tossed it in her cart. And since this was Costco, every product was super-sized. The bags of Doritos were twenty-five ounces. Sixty waffles came in a box. The packages of Oreos weighed three pounds. One box of Snickers held thirty-six bars. Elaine dropped one item after another into her cart, filling it almost to the top.

Satara, Danae, and Cassandra watched in disbelief. "What you're doing has been done before," said Cassandra, who had bought plenty of groceries for the Bartletts over the years.

"They need food," Elaine said.

"Four gallons of orange juice, Elaine? That's ridiculous."

"You know we need that. Somebody always needs orange juice."

"That's it, Ma," Satara said. "Nothing else."

Elaine pushed the cart toward them, then walked off. "I'll be right back," she said. "I forgot something."

She headed to the entrance, took a second cart, and kept on shopping. "Ma, stop!" Danae and Satara shouted. Elaine ignored them. She walked up and down every aisle two or three times, picking up one item after another. After wandering through the store for nearly three hours, she finally wore herself out. By now she had filled three carts, each of which was slightly larger than a standard grocery cart.

There were chicken patties, beef patties, pork chops, sausages, hot dogs, bacon, popcorn shrimp, crab cakes, linguini, Ragú sauce, Rice-A-Roni, Pop-Tarts, Cap'n Crunch, Frosted Flakes, Bisquick, Wonder bread, Sunny Delight, Pepsi, Frito's, Doritos, Tostitos, Ruffles, Pringles, pretzel sticks, Oreos, Ritz Bits, Kit Kats, miniature Snickers bars, mayonnaise, catsup, vegetable oil, olives, pickles, coffee, tea bags, a broom, a mop, rubber gloves, sponges, Comet, Soft Scrub, Lysol, liquid bleach, trash bags, shampoo, soap, lotion, deodorant, mouthwash, toothpaste, and a toothbrush.

In the checkout line, Elaine watched closely as a cashier swiped each item. At the East Harlem supermarket where she'd shopped in the early 1980s, the cashiers had punched in the prices. Now everything moved much more quickly. On a screen above the cash register, the total appeared: $868.94. Elaine opened her fist, counted out $880, and handed over the crumpled, sweaty bills.

Before Elaine arrived, Apartment 13B had six full-time residents—four adults and two children. Satara and her eight-month-old daughter, Tenéa, stayed in the back room. Apache slept in the middle room. Sabrina's twenty-one-year-old daughter Star and her one-year-old son shared the room closest to the front door. And Sabrina, thirty-eight, slept in the living room, which she had converted into her bedroom; she had hung a sheet in the doorway and taped photos of her children to the back wall.

Elaine had not seen her sister Sabrina in nearly nine years. After Sabrina had started getting high, she had stopped going to Bedford Hills to visit. Elaine still thought of her as pretty, smart, and independent. Now, though, she was a completely different person. Sabrina plodded around the apartment in a housecoat, her hair askew. Dark spots covered her arms. Tiny scars dotted her face. Half her teeth were missing.

Everyone said she was much better now than she had been in years. At least she wasn't living on the streets anymore, and each morning, she commuted to a methadone clinic in Harlem. But to Elaine, it looked as if Sabrina were trapped in her own invisible prison, one from which there was no escape. Though she had survived her suicide attempt a few years earlier, she appeared to have given up on life. Everyone knew she was HIV-positive, but she refused to discuss the matter or to seek any treatment.

When Elaine went to prison, her older daughter Satara had been three years old. Back then, Satara had liked to slip on Elaine's high heels and prance around their apartment. During visits at Bedford Hills, she had always been the one primping in front of the bathroom mirror. With her long hair, almond-colored skin, and pretty smile, she never had trouble attracting boys.

But now, it seemed that Satara no longer cared how she looked. She had dropped out of high school after she got pregnant, and she spent nearly all her time inside the apartment, minding her baby and watching soap operas. Some days, she did not bother to change out of her pajamas or to brush her hair. She had always been quiet, but now she seemed even more withdrawn than usual.

Elaine thought Satara was very depressed, but she did not know exactly why. Maybe she was still in mourning over her grandmother. Maybe she was suffering from postpartum depression. In recent months, she had been in and out of the hospital many times because of crises related to her sickle-cell anemia. Now that Elaine was home, she was determined to do all she could to lift Satara's spirits and keep her healthy. She gave her pep talks, nagged her to fix her hair, and encouraged her to go out with her friends.

Danae, Elaine's younger daughter, had been just fifteen months old when Elaine was arrested. Now Danae was a senior in high school. Most days, she dressed like a tomboy, in baggy jeans, an oversized basketball jersey, and a baseball cap turned backward. She had an athletic build, a chipped front tooth, and the same large brown eyes as Elaine.

Everyone in the family thought Danae was gay. They had thought this for a while, but nobody had told Elaine. The news surprised her, but it did not upset her. After all, her brother Ronald had been gay, and they had always gotten along well. What bothered Elaine much more was the fact that Danae seemed very angry. Whenever Elaine told her to do something, like fix her chipped tooth, Danae shot her a look that said, "You've been gone my whole life. Who are you to be telling me what to do?"

Soon after Elaine moved into Apartment 13B, she discovered that Danae did not even live there. Two years earlier, Danae had moved out and joined another family in a nearby building. Nobody had told Elaine; they knew she would be furious. Indeed, Elaine refused to accept that she would not get to be Danae's live-in mother. Several times during her first week out of prison, she stormed over to Danae's other home and screamed at her to return. Once she even snatched an armful of Danae's clothes and took them back to 13B.

Danae refused to relocate, though she did stop by sometimes. "You're not going nowhere!" Elaine told her one day. "Stay here!" As soon as Elaine stepped into the shower, Danae headed for the door. Naked and dripping, Elaine grabbed a robe, streaked out of the bathroom, and chased her into the building's hallway. "You're staying right here!" she shouted. Danae followed her back into the apartment and sat down in the kitchen. When Elaine returned to the bathroom, Danae darted out the door.

At night, Elaine slept in Satara and Tenéa's bedroom at the back of the apartment. The room was 120 square feet, almost twice the size of a standard prison cell. The linoleum floor had once been ivory, but was now so scuffed that it was gray. Yellow paint peeled off the radiator in the back. The room did have a spectacular view, however. A window looked out over the East River toward Brooklyn. Barges floated by during the day, and at night it was possible to count the lights on the Williamsburg Bridge.

This was the biggest bedroom in the apartment, but there was little room in it for Elaine. Satara and Tenéa's possessions already filled every corner: a baby swing, diapers, teddy bears, sneakers, clothes, books, CDs, tapes, a television. The closet was so packed that its two doors would not close. Elaine stored her belongings—a few plastic bags of papers, letters, and photographs—in the hallway outside the bedroom door. At night, she slept next to Satara and Tenéa in their queen-size bed.

The evening after her Costco outing, Elaine decided to cook. First, though, the apartment had to be cleaned. She enlisted Satara, Star, and one of their friends to sweep and mop. Then she prepared the meal she had been craving for years—spare ribs, collard greens, yams, potato salad, corn bread. These were the dishes she had grown up with, the same ones Yvonne had always cooked.

Everybody devoured Elaine's dinner, but the family spirit she tried to promote did not last long, and soon her cleanup efforts were undone. Garbage overflowed the plastic can in the kitchen. Nobody replaced the toilet paper when it ran out. The sheet she had snatched down from the living room doorway reappeared. And, as Cassandra had predicted, all the groceries quickly vanished.

In those first days out of prison, Elaine thought about Yvonne all the time. Mostly, she thought about how angry her mother would be if she could see the state of this apartment. Elaine remembered growing up in a household where appearances mattered. No sheets hung in doorways. If someone slept on a sofa bed in the living room, they reassembled it during the day so everyone could use the room. Even if the family was broke, even if the cupboards were empty, their home had always been tidy. This was not just a matter of neatness; it was a matter of pride.

Every time Elaine looked around Apartment 13B, she got mad. She did not want to live in a dump. Even more disturbing, though, was the realization that this apartment reflected the state of her family: Everybody had given up.

Elaine had a lot of ideas about how her daughters should fix their lives. Nobody was interested in hearing them. When she told Satara to stop spending so much time in the apartment "laying up" with her boyfriend, Satara ignored her. When she badgered Danae to move back home, Danae ignored her, too.

In Elaine's opinion, the respect and authority a mother should be accorded were missing. But Satara and Danae had never really known their mother out of prison, and now here she was, bossing them around all the time. Some nights Satara refused to sleep in the same bed with her and instead stayed in the living room. Some days Danae snubbed her, refusing to acknowledge her when they passed on the street. Whenever Elaine felt especially hurt, she shouted at them, "You treated me better when I was in prison!"

All the ecstasy and optimism of her release day vanished during her first week home. The place Elaine had dreamed of returning to was comfortable and familiar, but nothing about this apartment was comfortable or familiar. And every bedroom door had a lock on it. Over the years, Elaine had heard stories about Sabrina stealing money and jewelry from everyone; she figured this was the reason for the locks. Still, the locks bothered her. After so many years of cell-block living, she wanted to be in an apartment where all the doors were open.

Whenever anyone asked her how she felt, she said, "I left one prison to come home to another."

CHAPTER 21

Parole Officer Alfonso Camacho first heard Elaine Bartlett's name in November of 1999, when he was assigned to check out Apartment 13B. At the time, she was a candidate for clemency. Before she could even be considered for release, however, he had to determine whether the place she wanted to move into was suitable. His decision carried enormous weight. If he deemed the apartment unsatisfactory, she had little chance of receiving clemency.

He drove to the Lower East Side, walked through the Wald Houses, found her family's building, and banged on the door of 13B. Once inside the apartment, he surveyed the living room and kitchen, then strode down the hall, and glanced in each of the bedrooms. It was certainly not the cleanest or most comfortable place, but in his eight years as a parole officer, he had seen much worse. Nobody appeared to be selling or using drugs. He did not see any pipes or hypodermic needles. He did not smell any crack smoke.

Camacho interviewed Elaine Bartlett's children and determined that the family's income was $1,240 a month, or $14,880 a year. All the money came from government checks, either welfare or SSI. If the apartment had been outfitted with wall-to-wall carpeting and brand-new furniture, it would have raised questions about illegal sources of income. But that was hardly the case here.

To Officer Camacho, it seemed that Elaine's children were doing the best they could, considering how young they were. What they needed more than anything else, he thought, was their mother. He returned to his office and typed up a two-page report, listing the apartment's address, residents, and sources of income. He also gave his verdict: "satisfactory." If the governor did grant clemency to Elaine, she would likely wind up on his caseload.

Like many of the parolees he supervised, Camacho had grown up poor. He came from a large Puerto Rican family and had been raised in Bedford-Stuyvesant, Brooklyn. Of his nine siblings, he was the only one who had made it to college, graduating from the State University of New York at New Paltz in 1987. A few years later, he had joined the state Division of Parole as an officer with a starting salary of $42,000.

New York's parole agency oversees 50,000 former prisoners, and at any given time, Officer Camacho supervised about forty or fifty of them. Like every parole officer, he was required to enforce numerous rules. No drugs. No leaving the city without a travel pass. No owning a knife or gun. No hanging out with other felons. No going to visit anyone in jail without permission. No owning a pit bull or rottweiler. No staying out past curfew (usually 9:00 or 10:00 p.m.). No skipping parole appointments.

Parole officers play two roles: cop and social worker. They protect the community and also help people coming out of prison. Every officer interprets his duties differently. Within a single parole bureau, one officer may lock up a parolee every week, while another will arrest one every few months. Inside the Thirty-first Street parole office, Camacho had a reputation for being tough. "I've locked up a small city in my eight years," he often said.

After the governor granted clemency to Elaine Bartlett at the end of 1999, her case was assigned to Camacho. Even if her name had not appeared in the newspaper, she would have stood out. Most of the parolees on his caseload were male. While roughly half of them had done time for drugs, virtually all had served much shorter sentences than she had. Her education also made her unusual. Parolees rarely possessed college degrees. Most did not have a high school degree, and many could not even read and write.

By giving Elaine clemency, Governor Pataki reduced her sentence from 20-to-life to 16-to-life. Since she still had *life* on the back of her sentence, she would have to spend at least three years on parole. As long as she obeyed the rules, she had a chance of being discharged from parole in 2003. But, of course, there were no guarantees. Technically, *life* could mean just that; she could be on parole until she died.

Every parole officer has strategies for getting new parolees to comply. Some try fear. They issue threats, shout, toy with a pair of handcuffs when they talk. Camacho took the opposite approach; he tried to coax parolees into obeying parole's rules by putting them at ease. He had found that this usually worked better than intimidation. His casual attire was part of his strategy. He usually wore a Mets cap, a gold hoop in his left ear, a gold cap on his front tooth, a goatee, baggy jeans, and Timberland boots.

On January 27, 2000, he met Elaine Bartlett for the first time. In his office, he gave her his standard "welcome to parole" speech. "I only expect three things from you," he said. "Report regularly. Let me know where you live. And don't do drugs." He actually expected a lot more, but he didn't want to overwhelm her. "Try not to get arrested. Try to stay away from people who have criminal records. If you're going to move, let me know where you're living. You've got some rules you've got to live with. Do anything else you want. You live your life with parole as part of it. Parole is not trying to tell you how to live your life."

Elaine had an aura of grandeur about her, he thought, as if she were a celebrity who did not expect to be treated like a run-of-the-mill parolee. He would have to humble her a little, or else she would never obey parole's rules.

At that first meeting, Elaine asked for permission to visit her son on Rikers Island. Camacho refused. He explained that he wanted her to get her own life in order before she went running off to jail. He advised her to apply for public assistance, and he told her to report the following Thursday for her weekly visit.

She followed his orders and returned the next week with a Medicaid card. This time, he could see that she was distraught. As he did every time he saw a parolee, he took notes about their meeting on a form known as "Chrono Notes." Using the standard abbreviation for parolee, he wrote, "Ⓟexpressed concerns at household with daughter Elaine who is being confrontational toward her due to her desire to reside at another location."

Camacho knows as well as anyone that the first weeks out of prison are the most precarious. On their first visit to the parole office, most people are excited and optimistic—thrilled to be out of prison and back on the street. But by the second or third week, it's not unusual for them to come dragging into the office, frustrated and depressed. The more years they spend in prison, the better life on the outside looks to them. But eventually, the euphoria disappears and they all learn the same brutal lesson: Life after prison is a constant struggle.

Five days later, Camacho paid a surprise visit to Apartment 13B. He knocked on the door at 10:35 p.m.—ninety-five minutes after Elaine's curfew. She was home. They spoke briefly, and he reminded her to check in with him on Thursday.

Elaine showed up at the parole office for her weekly visit two days later. This time, Camacho handed her a plastic cup and sent her into the bathroom with a female officer. Like every parolee, she had to submit to a drug test. The female officer was supposed to watch her pee in order to make sure she didn't scoop up toilet water or try another ploy to alter her urine.

This week, Elaine had a new request: She wanted permission to leave the city. She explained that she had been invited to speak to the state legislature's Black and Puerto Rican Caucus in Albany the following week. Camacho authorized the trip, but there was one condition: She would have to return to the parole office in a few days to pick up a travel pass.

The next Thursday, Elaine did not check in with Camacho. He did not know if she was in Albany, but he did know she had never picked up the travel pass he had prepared. In her file, he recorded this lapse: "FTR" for Failure to Report. Elaine had been on parole for only twenty-two days, and already she had broken one of parole's cardinal rules.

The next week, Elaine showed up at the parole office with an explanation: She had gone to Albany but had forgotten to pick up her travel pass.

Camacho gave her a stern lecture, but he did not reach for the pair of handcuffs attached to his belt. He might have arrested her if she had also violated a few more rules—if she had been getting high and staying out past curfew. But she had been home whenever he visited her after 9:00 p.m., and the lab test on her urine showed she was drug-free. "Ⓟ admonished for FTR's," he wrote in his notes. "Ⓟ reminded to obtain travel passes prior to trip to Albany."

It was, of course, too early to know how his relationship with Elaine Bartlett would end. Maybe with a handshake and a hug. Maybe with her in the backseat of a parole car as he drove over the bridge to Rikers Island. As Camacho had learned long ago, one can never really predict which parolees would stay out of jail and which would return. Even though she had the governor's stamp of approval, there were no guarantees that Elaine Bartlett would remain free.

CHAPTER 22

On a Friday in early March, the temperature on the Lower East Side hovered just above freezing. Elaine zipped her granddaughter Tenéa, now ten months old, into a bright pink snowsuit. Elaine did not yet own a parka herself, so she borrowed one from Apache. It was a few sizes too big, but she figured it would do. She pulled it on, then slung Tenéa's diaper bag over her shoulder. Shortly before 11:00 a.m., she picked up Tenéa and carried her out of the apartment.

In those first weeks out of prison, Elaine had trouble finding her way around the city. Sometimes she would stand still on a sidewalk for several minutes, staring at street signs. "Are you lost?" strangers would ask. "Can I help you?" She found the subway system particularly confusing. Before prison, she used to ride the trains every day; now she kept forgetting which line to take or where she was supposed to get off.

Rikers Island was one of the very few places that she knew how to get to. By now she had already been there twice. Today would be her third visit.

She carried Tenéa through the Wald Houses, across Avenue D, and down East Third Street. At Second Avenue, they boarded the F train, rode it to Forty-second Street, then switched to the number 7 train. For once, Elaine was not lost, but she still felt miserable. The long lavender nails she had sported the day she left prison had disappeared weeks ago; all that remained were half-bitten stubs. As the 7 train rumbled toward Queens, a tear started down her cheek.

At Queens Plaza, Elaine and Tenéa transferred to the Q101 bus and settled into a seat near the back. On other days, when Elaine pushed Tenéa around the East Village in her stroller, strangers stopped to admire her granddaughter's eyes and near-constant grin. But now, as Elaine looked down, she noticed that Tenéa was frowning. Worried eyes peered out beneath a ski hat adorned with Baby Minnie Mouse. "You look like you know where you're going," Elaine said.

This afternoon, the Q101 was crowded with women—likely the wives, girlfriends, sisters, mothers, and grandmothers of prisoners. All were African-American or Latino, and everybody looked about as happy as Tenéa. A young woman seated next to Elaine appeared especially distraught; she kept her arms crossed tightly in front of her chest.

Elaine had tried to convince Satara and Danae to go with her, but they had refused. After all these years, she figured, they were probably tired of going to jail.

Ever since leaving prison, Elaine had felt as if she were living in a strange new world. People used Metrocards instead of subway tokens. Welfare offices were now called "job centers." Food stamps came on a swipe card, instead of paper coupons. Newports, once a dollar a pack, now cost $4.50. But there was one aspect of her life that had not changed: She was still going to Rikers Island. In the late 1970s and early 1980s, she had gone to see her brothers and boyfriend. Now she was making the same trip to see her son.

At 12:30 p.m., the bus pulled up to the security checkpoint at the base of the bridge leading to Rikers. Elaine braced herself for all that awaited her on the other side: the metal detectors, pat frisks, dingy waiting rooms, gruff guards, slow lines. The Q101 passed through the checkpoint, crossed over the East River, cleared another checkpoint, and turned into a parking lot.

"All right," she said to herself, "I gotta put on a happy face."

As Elaine and the other women exited the bus, a guard shouted, "No beepers or cell phones allowed inside!" Elaine already knew these rules; she had left her beeper at home.

She carried Tenéa into the visitors' center. As usual, it was packed and noisy, filled with the sounds of children crying, mothers scolding them, and officers barking orders.

Inside the visitors' center, each of Rikers' jails has its own waiting area. Elaine found the sign for OBCC—the Otis Bantum Correctional Center—and she joined its line. When she got to the front, she showed her Medicaid card to the officer. It was the only form of ID she had.

"What's the inmate's book and case number?" he asked.

She said she did not know, and so the officer sent her to an information desk across the room. She joined the back of another line. After a few minutes, she got to the front and an officer scribbled Jamel's number on a scrap of paper. She returned to the OBCC waiting area.

This time, the guard at the front handed her a card with Jamel's name and the time: 12:58 p.m. Soon she and several other women were escorted out the rear door of the waiting area and onto another bus. A guard drove them around the island, stopping in the back of Jamel's jail.

Once inside, Elaine followed orders. She stuck out one hand so a guard could stamp it with invisible ink. She dropped Tenéa's Winnie-the-Pooh diaper bag on the conveyor belt, at the mouth of the metal detector. She stood still while a guard waved a wand over her body. She slid a quarter in a metal locker and stuffed her earrings, parka, and diaper bag inside. Then she sat down in a seat near the front of the waiting room.

In prison, she had felt like she was always waiting to get home, and now that she was home, she still seemed to spend most of her time waiting—for her parole officer, for her welfare caseworker, for permission to see her husband. Seated in this jail waiting room, trapped in the slow grind of yet another bureaucracy, she tried not to become frustrated and angry.

To pass the time, she bounced her granddaughter on her lap. "Te-naaay-a!" she sang. "Te-naaay-a!" The attention did little to improve the baby's mood. Every few minutes, Tenéa spit her pacifier onto the floor.

Nothing about this waiting room was comfortable: hard plastic chairs, children's piercing cries, secondhand smoke from the cigarette of the guard behind the front desk. A poster in the middle of the room warned visitors about smuggling in razor blades. It showed photos of prisoners' faces immediately after they had been slashed, blood still oozing from their wounds. THIS IS WHAT HAPPENS TO YOUR LOVED ONES WHEN CONTRABAND IS SMUGGLED IN THROUGH VISITS the sign said. Next to four pictures of visitors with their wrists cuffed behind their backs, it stated THIS IS WHAT HAPPENS WHEN YOU GET CAUGHT.

Elaine watched the guard at the front of the room set down her cigarette and pick up the telephone. After listening for a moment, the officer called out several names. Women, young and old, lined up along the wall of metal lockers. They did not wait for anyone to give them instructions. Instead, they loosened their belts and untied their shoelaces. Everyone knew the drill. To get through the metal detector and enter the visiting room, they would have to remove their belts and slip off their shoes.

Elaine was not sure exactly how long she had been here, but it felt like half an hour. She considered approaching the guard at the front to find out how much longer she'd have to wait.

On a previous visit to Rikers, she had asked this same question. "Did you hear me call his name?" a guard had shouted. "All right, then. We didn't call it. Have a seat." After years of being yelled at by women and men in uniforms, she did not think she could take much more. This afternoon, she stayed in her seat and kept her mouth closed. She did not want her parole officer to hear she had tussled with a jail guard.

This was the future that she had tried so hard to prevent during all those years she was locked up. She had lectured Jamel about selling drugs every chance she got: over the phone, in her letters, whenever he visited her. Even punching him in the mouth when he was twelve had not brought him to his senses. She had known all along what would happen if her efforts failed: Someday she'd be doing what she was doing right now, spending hours in jail, waiting for the chance to see him.

Inside Bedford Hills, stories about prisoners' children becoming prisoners are common. Many of the boys and girls Elaine had watched grow up in the visiting room later became inmates themselves. Compared to some of her fellow prisoners, Elaine considered herself fortunate. "At least I only have one child in prison," she would say. "Some women I know—all of their children are locked up."

Finally, the officer at the front desk shouted, "Paschall!"

Elaine stood and joined the line of visitors next to the row of lockers. When she got to the front, a guard told her to remove Tenéa's Baby Minnie cap. Hats are not allowed.

"No one told me that," Elaine said.

"This is my steady post," the guard said. "I'll tell you what you can bring in."

Silently, Elaine plodded back to her locker, then returned to the end of the line. A few minutes later, she made it past the metal detector.

An officer whisked her into a large open room filled with tables of visitors and prisoners. They continued through this room and into another, more interior visiting room. Here, each prisoner was locked inside a metal cage with their visitors. The officer gestured toward a cage at the back.

By now, she knew that this was the visiting area for inmates confined in the Bing, the most notorious part of Rikers Island. Prisoners who break Rikers' rules are sent to the Bing, a high-security discipline unit where they are locked in a cell for twenty-three hours a day. The Bing is the Rikers equivalent of the Special Housing Unit at Bedford Hills, where she'd been sent after her fistfight with Michelle Plaza. She did not know exactly why Jamel had been sent to the Bing, but she figured he had probably gotten into yet another fight. Whenever he was on Rikers Island, he spent most of his days locked in the Bing.

According to the clock on the wall in this room, it was 2:30 p.m. She had been on Rikers Island for nearly two hours. Staring through the cage's steel bars, she watched one young man after another enter the waiting area through a door across the room.

Soon she saw her son. "Maaaaaaaa!" he shouted as soon as he saw her.

He walked into the cage, waited for a guard to unlock his cuffs, and then he wrapped his muscular arms around her. While mother and son hugged, the guard locked their cage door.

Elaine still thought of Jamel as the short, skinny boy who had smiled at her all those years from the Polaroids on her cell walls. But, of course, that boy no longer existed. Now Jamel was twenty-three years old, six-foot-two, and weighed 200 pounds. He had recently started shaving his head to hide a bald spot.

At the moment, he wore the jail's visiting room attire—an orange cotton jumpsuit—plus a pair of Versace glasses, white tube socks, and Tommy Hilfiger sandals. He also wore the standard Rikers Island scar. An enemy had sliced him across the cheek with a razor blade, leaving a cut that had required twelve stitches.

He sat down in a chair facing her, took both of her hands in his, and looked into her eyes. "How have you been?" he asked.

"I'm all right," she said.

She handed Tenéa to him. He had never met Tenéa before, and as soon as he held her, she started to cry. Elaine took Tenéa back and rocked her gently. "Are you scared of the orange jumpsuit?" she asked her.

"I heard you on the radio," Jamel said. "I was listening, and I had a couple people listen also."

Elaine had spoken recently on WBAI about the Rockefeller drug laws. "Did you hear me talk about you?" she asked.

"I caught a little bit of it, but my batteries were really going."

Since leaving prison, Elaine had tracked down Jamel's lawyer, studied his indictment, and learned the basic details of his case. Prosecutors had accused him and forty-one other people of participating in one of the city's largest drug gangs. The indictment identified Jamel as a "worker" in the gang. Like most of the other defendants, he had been charged with conspiracy. The indictment accused him of two incidents of drug dealing—a 1994 cocaine sale and a 1995 heroin sale—both of which he'd already served time for. But since "conspiring" with one or more people to sell narcotics is a different crime from selling them, he faced another possible prison term.

Now Jamel was in the same predicament she had been in almost seventeen years earlier, when she was locked up in the Albany County Jail and had spent every day trying to decide if she should go to trial. Jamel, too, had been charged with an A-1 felony. If he went to trial and lost, he would receive at least 15-to-life.

The prosecutors had offered him a deal: three years to life in exchange for a guilty plea. At the moment, he was holding out, hoping for something better.

"I don't want you to go to trial," Elaine said.

"Don't worry," he said. "I know what I'm doing. I'm just bluffing. I'm not going to jump out a window." By now, he knew that going to trial on an A-1 felony was like committing suicide.

"I hope you know what you're doing," she said.

Whenever Elaine spoke, Jamel leaned forward and listened closely. He was quiet, polite, deferential. There was no hint of the fierce temper that the Bing guards knew well. Here on Rikers Island, Elaine's lengthy imprisonment gave her a certain authority in the eyes of her younger son. She could tell that he was proud of her for surviving such a long prison sentence with her dignity intact.

"Why didn't you bring Little Mel?" he asked. Elaine had tried to track down Little Mel by calling the home of Cassandra, Little Mel's mother. The call had not gone well. Apparently, Cassandra's mother was not a fan of Jamel.

"You gotta come home and deal with your own shit," Elaine said.

As usual, there were too many topics to cover and not enough time. They talked about Apache, Satara, Danae, and Jamel's assorted girlfriends. He told her about the rap songs he had been writing. They even briefly discussed Assata Shakur and the Soledad Brothers—prison radicals Jamel said he had been reading about. She studied his fingernails for clues to his state of mind; it was the same tactic she had employed when he was a child. She noticed that his nails were freshly bitten, just like hers.

She was determined not to become teary in front of him, and so she left many things unsaid. She did not tell him about how she had cried earlier on the subway, on the way to come see him. She did not mention how unhappy she was in Apartment 13B. Just as her children had hidden their problems from her when they came to Bedford Hills, now she tried not to burden him with problems he couldn't fix.

Elaine did not admit it aloud, but she hated being on Rikers Island. She loved her son, of course, but she despised everything about this place—the guards, the rules, the rudeness, the waiting. Being back inside a jail made her tense and stressed; she felt like she was back at Bedford Hills all over again. Finally getting out of prison and then going straight to jail to visit your child—this, she thought, was not exactly freedom.

It wasn't just the visible reminders of prison that bothered her. For her, being on Rikers Island meant remembering the biggest mistakes of her life, then feeling guilty about them all over again. If she had never carried drugs to Albany, then turned down a plea offer and gone to trial, maybe she would not be sitting here right now, locked inside a cage with her son.

"Ma, you don't need to be coming here," he said. "You've already done enough time."

"Of course I'm going to come visit you," she said. "I know what it's like when people say they're going to come visit and they don't."

These visits were an investment in the future—the only way Elaine could think of to try to stop her son from spending many more years behind bars. She felt sick whenever she thought about him being locked inside a cell by himself for twenty-three hours a day. She thought he should be spending his days earning a paycheck or a degree, not more Bing time. At that moment, she had no way of knowing when Jamel might next come home; she hoped she would not have to wait too long.

Shortly after 3:30 p.m. a guard approached the cage. They knew what this meant: Their one-hour visit was over. Jamel stood and put his hands behind his back. No tears. No tantrums. No clinging to her leg. A guard snapped a pair of cuffs on his wrists, then led him out of the cage.

As the guard whisked him toward the exit, Jamel shouted over his shoulder. "I love you, Ma!" Apparently, he did not care that everyone in this visiting room could hear him. "I love you!"

"I love you, too," she yelled. "Now, you behave!"

CHAPTER 23

Elaine wanted to find a job, and so she did what most people do: She asked everyone she knew if they had heard of any openings. While this strategy works for many people, Elaine was at a huge disadvantage. She didn't know a lot of people in the city anymore, and most of the people she did know were unemployed. Littleboy would have helped her, but he was in federal prison with a twelve-year sentence for distributing angel dust. Nate was still in prison, too. Two of her brothers were dead. The other two were locked up. And neither of her sisters had a job.

Elaine could think of only four people she knew who had full-time jobs: Lora Tucker, who now worked at a drug-treatment clinic; Shyan's wife, who delivered mail; Charlie Boo, the former numbers runner from the Wagner Houses, who had become a security guard; and another family friend, who worked for the phone company. Elaine called them all, but nobody knew of any available jobs.

Her best job lead came from Charles Grodin, who told her to call HELP USA, a social service agency where he was a board member. Elaine went for an interview and took a urine test, but then she did not hear anything.

Even if someone had called her, she might not have known about it. There was only one phone in her family's apartment, and messages were often forgotten. Any prospective employer who tried to reach her by mail would also have a difficult time, too, since the mailbox in the building's lobby was broken.

Meanwhile, Elaine had heard that the two women who had left Bedford Hills with her both had jobs already. Jan Warren was a secretary at a law firm, a position she had obtained with the help of a professor she met while in prison. Arlene Oberg worked for HELP USA. The news that Jan and Arlene had found jobs before her upset Elaine. She could not help wondering if race was a factor, if these women had found jobs more easily because they were white.

Six weeks after leaving prison, Elaine went to South Forty, an employment agency for former prisoners, located on Eighth Avenue, just a few blocks north of Penn Station. When Elaine arrived shortly before 10:00 a.m., there were already six men in the waiting room. A banner above the receptionist's window announced THE SOUTH 40 CORPORATION: AN AVENUE FROM PRISON TO SOCIETY. She added her name to the sign-in sheet, then picked a seat next to the magazine rack, which held both *Vanity Fair* and *Corrections Today*.

An hour later, she met George Lino, whose job title was "vocational specialist." She was impressed with his outfit: navy suit, sky-blue shirt, freshly buffed black boots. And she noticed that he moved with a sense of purpose, striding through the office's cubicles. He seemed like the sort of man who got things done—exactly what she needed. And she liked the way he introduced himself. "I'm an ex-offender," he said. "I did seven years, from age seventeen to twenty-three."

George was now twenty-nine and had spent the last few years helping other ex-prisoners land jobs. Elaine handed him a copy of the three-page résumé she had prepared before leaving Bedford Hills. It listed her GED, her associate's degree, and fourteen prison jobs. It also cited sixteen certificate courses she had taken, including Basic Legal Research and Microsoft Word 6.0.

"You've got a lot of skills," George said, flipping through the résumé. "You could do a lot of things. But I need to know: Where do you want to go? What do you want to do?"

"Counseling," Elaine said. "I could do that. I enjoy speaking. I speak out about the Rockefeller drug laws. Also, I'm fascinated by computers. I need something I can grow in. I don't want something I'm stuck in. I'm tired of being stuck."

"Let's say we get you into counseling, because it's not easy to get into the computer field without any serious computer background."

In recent months, George and his coworkers had found jobs for ex-prisoners as janitors, dishwashers, cooks, phone dispatchers, and limousine drivers. Elaine's education gave her an advantage over most ex-prisoners. George figured he could get her a counseling job that paid $18,000 to $20,000 a year. If she'd had a bachelor's degree, he probably could have gotten her $25,000 to $30,000 a year.

Elaine was pleased that George did not view her as a future janitor or McDonald's order taker, because she certainly did not see herself toiling in such minimum-wage jobs. After she had appeared on WBAI, the host had told her about a friend who needed somebody to clean their house. "Baby, I am not a maid," Elaine had said. "I didn't get out of prison after sixteen years to clean toilets."

George informed her that a recruiter from a large social service agency was coming to South Forty in a few hours to conduct a group interview. "Do you have time to go home and change?" he asked.

Elaine glanced down at her clothes. This morning, Satara had helped her get dressed, picking out an outfit from her own wardrobe. Not surprisingly, Elaine looked like a twenty-year-old ready to go out dancing on a Saturday night. She wore blue flare-bottom pants, a matching blue shirt, and black platform boots with Velcro buckles.

"I gotta change?" Elaine asked. "What do I wear?"

"Do you have any suits or skirts?" George asked.

"No," she said.

George handed her a referral for Dress for Success, a nearby non-profit agency that gives away used business clothes to women entering the workforce. Elaine left. An hour later, she returned wearing a bright red double-breasted jacket, a matching skirt, nude nylons, a fake pearl necklace, and black lace-up pumps. It was the uniform of a corporate employee, albeit one who was slightly larger than she. The suit jacket was loose and baggy; the skirt hung several inches below her knees.

Elaine spent the afternoon in a group interview with the recruiter from the social service agency. George had told her that the agency needed counselors, but it turned out the only job openings were for custodians. Elaine did not raise her hand and lobby for one of these positions. With George's help, she thought she could do better.

The next morning, Elaine returned to South Forty at 9:00 a.m. for an all-day workshop about job hunting. She did not think she needed this class, but George had told her she had to attend. She walked into the classroom and sat down in the second row. Nearly every chair was taken, and almost all the other students were male.

The teacher distributed manila envelopes. "This envelope is for documents," she said. "Birth certificates, ID with a picture, release papers, rap sheet, letter from a P.O., dispositions from the courts, and any proof of your ex-offender status."

Before South Forty's counselors could help anyone find a job, she explained, they needed some paperwork. The students pulled crumpled slips of paper from their pockets.

"I got a copy of my bail receipt," one man said.

"Okay," the teacher said. "That'll work."

"I don't have anything," said the young man seated behind Elaine. "I had everything in my wallet. They took my wallet. My ID is on the island. My Social Security card is on the island."

This predicament is common. Many people leave jail with no proof of their identity. As a result, they cannot get a job or a Medicaid card. In order to begin rebuilding their lives, they first have to spend days shuttling from one city agency to another, trying to get the necessary paperwork. Elaine had left prison better prepared than some; she did not have her birth certificate, but she did possess a Social Security card.

She opened her pocketbook and sifted through its contents. Usually, she carried so much paperwork that her purse resembled a filing cabinet but this day she'd left most of her papers at home. She pulled out a phone bill, her parole release paper, and a copy of a *Times Union* story about her clemency. She dropped them all in an envelope and passed it to the front.

Next, the teacher handed out a two-page standardized form with questions about one's education, past jobs, and crimes. She explained that South Forty's counselors use this form to prepare résumés, and she told the students to write down everything they had done: GED classes, college classes, vocational training.

Most of the students stared at the form without writing. The prospect of fitting their complicated lives into all these boxes and lines seemed to overwhelm them. Elaine was a couple of steps ahead of the other students, since she had already drafted a résumé. Still, she followed directions and filled out the form.

The teacher urged everyone to be honest about their crimes. "If you have a robbery on your record, they can't send you to a bank to work," she explained.

A woman raised her hand. "Tell me it's not true that if you have a felony conviction, you can't be a home health attendant," she said.

"I don't know," the teacher said, "but we'll find out."

Rules vary state by state, but people with a felony record are often prohibited from obtaining jobs in medicine, nursing, and education. Six states ban ex-inmates from all government jobs. In New York, former prisoners may be barred from becoming barbers, paramedics, firefighters, check cashiers, sanitation workers, real estate brokers, and taxi drivers.

Elaine did not ask any questions, but she listened. A few other students appeared to be paying attention, too. The rest slouched in their chairs, looking bored and unhappy, as if the only reason they were here was that their parole officer had told them they had to be. One man in the back fell asleep.

After the lunch break, a new teacher arrived and handed out stapled packets. "GETTING AND KEEPING A JOB!" read the first page. The interview pointers on these pages might have seemed obvious to most people seeking a job, but not to all the students in this room.

Present a positive attitude.
Show enthusiasm; do not go in looking or acting like the "walking wounded."
Be well groomed, neat, and clean.
Go to the interview alone.
When you sit down, use good posture.
Do not chew gum or smoke.
Avoid using expressions such as "Uh, well, you know what I mean."
Be courteous and pleasant during the interview.
Smile frequently; people like others who smile and do so sincerely.

Another handout informed the students about "What you should NEVER do at an interview."

Bad-mouth a previous employer.
Exaggerate your skills.
Tell lies about your background.
Get argumentative with the interviewer.
Be rude or aggressive.

At the time, New York's economy was thriving. But even during good times, it was not easy for an ex-prisoner to find a job. Only 41 percent of New York's parolees were employed. This meant there were about 27,000 parolees in the state without a job. And as any parole officer knows, a parolee without a job is much more likely to return to prison.

The challenge for the teacher of this class was to boost the students' self-esteem enough so that they could stride confidently into an interview, while also being realistic about their employment prospects. "I'm not going to say everyone is going to get a ten- to fifteen-dollar-an-hour job," the teacher explained. "Because not everyone has the skills to get a ten-to fifteen-dollar an hour job. Please be patient. We have jobs for cashiers, McDonald's jobs, maintenance, plumbing, counseling jobs, some jobs in law firms."

A young man seated behind Elaine raised his hand. "What if your résumé looks like this?" he asked. He held up a blank piece of paper. "I've never had a job before."

"Everyone in this room has had some experience," the teacher said. "Don't ever say you didn't."

"I bagged groceries," another student said.

The young man with the empty résumé pondered the teacher's words. Maybe he had never had a job with a weekly paycheck, but he had been working for years. Selling drugs on the corner was not easy.

"If you were hustling," he said, "you can do anything."

A man in the front row shouted, "That's called 'marketing pharmaceuticals.'"

Elaine laughed, and so did all the other students. Apparently, there were many former drug dealers in this class.

Elaine had held a job every year she was at Bedford Hills, but many prisoners do not work. Some have no desire to work; others want to work, but there are not enough jobs to go around. Even if a prisoner does land a job, there is no guarantee that he or she will possess marketable skills when released. Pushing a broom around a cell block or scooping food onto trays in the mess hall does not prepare one for anything more than minimum-wage work.

Meanwhile, prison living can be the worst sort of training for future employment. Not surprisingly, many inmates grow so used to being in an institution—of being told when to eat, when to sleep, when to go to the toilet—that they lose all their ambition and initiative, precisely the qualities they will need to get a job once they are set free. Every now and then, ex-prisoners entered this building on Eighth Avenue, stepped off the elevator, walked toward the front door of South Forty's office, and then stopped. Instead of trying to open the door, which is unlocked, they waited patiently for someone to buzz them in.

Elaine dropped in to see George Lino at South Forty several times over the next two weeks. These visits reminded him that she was still unemployed, and he usually made a few calls for her while she sat next to his desk. One afternoon, he slipped on his headset and dialed the Fortune Society, another nonprofit organization that helps ex-prisoners.

"Peggy, I know we haven't talked in awhile," he said. "I'm calling because I have a very impressive young lady, Elaine Bartlett, here. Maybe you recognize the name. She has good presentation skills. She's got sixteen years of peer counseling inside the institution. She knows what she wants to do. You know I only send you the best."

Peggy didn't have any job openings, so George called another employer. This time, he said he had a job candidate who was "totally excellent," then went on to describe her. "You could not find a better person. Good writing skills. Good presentation. She's been speaking out. She's got certificates and trainings up the wazoo."

This employer did not have any jobs, either. George promised Elaine that he would keep looking.

These visits to South Forty never lasted long, but they always made Elaine feel better. She liked George's sales pitch and his aggressive style. When he was not too busy, they talked about people they both knew—women from Bedford Hills whom he had helped get jobs. Sometimes she talked to him about her troubles with her daughters, and he offered advice. "Family members can be your worst allies," he said.

To Elaine, George was not only her job counselor but also a tutor about life on the outside. The city's tabloids were full of examples of felons who had failed—prisoners who had been released, committed another crime, and returned to jail. George was one of the very few people she knew who had accomplished the goal she had set for herself: making a successful transition from prison to the free world. He was, she told him, "a very together brother."

Even with George's help, Elaine was still unemployed at the end of March, two months after she left prison. The $1,500 she had received from Cassandra was gone. A few of Jamel's friends had stopped by the apartment and given her envelopes with two or three hundred dollars in cash. She hadn't asked where the money had come from; she was just glad that Jamel was looking out for her. But now, that money was nearly gone, too. She needed to find a job fast.

CHAPTER 24

Elaine thought that all those years of smoking crack and living on the streets had warped Sabrina's sense of how to behave. Her sister used words like *pussy* and *bitch* in front of the children. She scratched her crotch in front of everyone. She spent hours at a stretch in the bathroom, drinking coffee, smoking cigarettes, eating an entire meal, even falling asleep on the toilet, all with her pants around her ankles.

At night, she paced the apartment's narrow hall, moaning and raving. Sometimes, she pushed the door to the back bedroom open, shook Elaine awake, and asked for a cigarette. If Elaine did not have one—or if she refused to wake up—Sabrina would leave the apartment, bang on the neighbor's door and beg them for a cigarette.

Early one morning, Sabrina pulled the refrigerator door open. "Who ate my cheese?" she hollered. She slammed the door shut. "Who ate my cheese?"

Her shouting woke Elaine and everybody else in the apartment. At first, Elaine ignored her. She did not want another reason to be mad at Sabrina. She was already angry at her for so many reasons, it was hard to remember them all. For becoming a crack addict. For going to jail. For not taking care of her own children. For not taking better care of their mother. She blamed her sister for the locks on the bedroom doors, for eroding the family's sense of trust, for transforming their home into a prison.

"Who ate my cheese?" Sabrina shouted.

Elaine had not taken the cheese, but she wanted her sister to stop hollering. "I ate your cheese!" she yelled.

Like many Bartlett family arguments, this one quickly escalated into an all-out war, laying bare resentments that had been pent up for years. Just as Elaine blamed Sabrina for the sorry state of their family, Sabrina blamed her for being gone all these years.

"You stupid ass!" Sabrina shouted. "You went to jail. You hurt Mommy. You're the one that broke her heart by going to jail!"

Elaine's first instinct was to slam her fist into her sister's face. She carried so much rage inside her all the time that she was always looking for a way to release it. Now she had the opportunity, but she knew that if she started pummeling Sabrina, she would not be able to stop. There would be sixteen years of pain and frustration behind every one of her punches. When she punched Sabrina, she would also be punching George Deets, Judge Clyne, and everyone else who had enraged her over the years.

Elaine had been struggling to control her temper ever since she had moved in there. Most days, she succeeded, but not always. One day, she had slapped Satara. Another day, she had punched Danae in the chest so hard, she fell down. If she now attacked Sabrina, she knew she would win the fistfight. But in the end, she knew she would lose, too. One phone call from Sabrina to the cops or her parole officer, and she would be arrested. To Elaine, there seemed only one option in order to avoid going back to jail: She would have to leave.

At the moment, Satara was in the bathroom. Elaine marched down the corridor and stopped outside the door. "You know, once I leave, that's it," she said. "The sad thing is, everyone's going to have a mother, but you and Nay-nay aren't."

"She doesn't need her mother," Sabrina said. "She ain't had one for sixteen years."

Elaine turned to her sister. "Every time I talk to my child, you have something negative to say," she said. "You don't want to see these kids do any better because you're miserable about what you did to your own life."

For weeks, Elaine had been telling Satara to pull herself together and stop moping around the apartment. She wanted Satara to get a job or go back to school, and she wanted her to go out with her friends and have fun. But whenever Elaine yelled at Satara for watching soap operas or lying around the apartment with her boyfriend, Sabrina defended Satara. To get Satara to listen to her, Elaine felt like she had to battle Sabrina, too.

In Elaine's opinion, Sabrina was part of the reason Satara had become so isolated and depressed. After all, Sabrina was the same way. She rarely left the apartment, except to go to a methadone clinic in Harlem. To get there, she rode two buses, even though the subway was much faster. But Sabrina preferred the bus. Whenever she stood on a subway platform and saw a train rushing toward her, she felt the urge to leap in front of it. In the afternoons, she retreated to the living room, where she would watch soap operas or sit in the dark and talk to her dead mother.

The way Elaine saw this morning's argument, it was not about a piece of cheese, but about the future of the Bartlett family. It was about whether or not Satara and everyone else would realize their potential and become self-sufficient. It was about whether the next generation of Bartletts would become productive members of society, or end up in prison or strung out on drugs.

Elaine stomped back down the hall to Satara's bedroom. She got dressed, then began packing. She grabbed her skirt suit, her used pumps, and her résumés, and she stuffed them into plastic bags. She got the garbage can she had bought for the kitchen, washed it out, shoved the rest of her belongings in it, then put it in a corner of Satara's room. She would have to come back for it later.

She hunted for the plastic water bottle she used as a bank and dumped the contents onto the bed. Her dollar bills had disappeared long ago, so she counted the quarters and dimes. She slid her coins into her pocket and headed for the door. By now, the apartment had become eerily quiet.

"All my life, I always put my family before me, but this is the first time I'm putting Elaine before anybody," she said, loudly enough for Satara to hear through the bathroom door.

The dream of living with her children again had sustained Elaine through sixteen years of prison. But over the last fifty-five days, ever since she'd moved in here, she'd felt even more depressed than she had when she was at Bedford. She had vowed never to abandon her children again, but now she felt she had no choice. She picked up her plastic bags and walked out.

Elaine's youngest sister, Michelle, had moved uptown to Harlem five years earlier. At the time, she was thirty years old and had a husband and five young children. They moved into an apartment with five bedrooms and two bathrooms. The rooms were modest, but there was just enough space for the seven of them. By now, however, the apartment held eleven people: Michelle, her husband Pervis, and their five children, who ranged in age from seven to eighteen; their eldest daughter's one-month-old son; and three of Sabrina's children, ages six, eight, and ten.

Unlike 13B, Michelle's apartment was neat and well furnished. Framed pictures of Malcolm X and Martin Luther King, Jr., greeted visitors walking in the front door. The living room was just that—a living room, not a makeshift bedroom. It had a stereo, a big-screen television, and a computer. Polaroids of Shyan and Donjuan in their prison greens decorated one wall. In the hallway, Michelle had hung Donjuan's prison art: images of Mickey Mouse and Betty Boop that he had painted for his nieces and nephews.

Of the five Bartlett siblings who were still alive, Michelle was the only one who had never gone to jail. At age seventeen, she had married Pervis Marcus, her boyfriend from Corona. Now she was thirty-five and still married to Pervis. For almost fifteen years, he had been supporting the family by working as a deliveryman at various grocery stores. At the moment, he had a job at a supermarket in the East Village. Michelle, who had once worked as a nurse, was now a full-time mother.

After Elaine had gone to prison and Sabrina started getting high, Michelle had helped their mother hold the family together. Michelle had raised her children, helped raise her sisters' children, took care of Yvonne during her final years, and worked two jobs—one at the Board of Elections and another at a local medical center.

Now Michelle got up at 6:00 every morning to get her and Sabrina's children ready for school. Then, all day long, visitors paraded in and out of her apartment: a nurse, a home health aide, a tutor. Recently, Sabrina's eight-year-old son had been diagnosed with HIV; he had likely contracted the virus from her before he was born. In addition to caring for an apartment full of children, Michelle was managing his health care, too.

In some ways, Michelle was more like Yvonne than any of Yvonne's other children. Michelle weighed more than 300 pounds, had been diagnosed with diabetes, and now here she was, raising an apartment full of children. Ever since Yvonne's death, Michelle had taken on the role of matriarch. She organized the family's holiday parties, and she was often the most boisterous participant, initiating the dance contests and water-gun fights. If anyone showed up with a bottle of Bacardi, she would inevitably get drunk.

Elaine was not eager to move in with her youngest sister, but she was running out of options. It was either Michelle's apartment or a homeless shelter. After storming out of Apartment 13B, she arrived at Michelle's building in a livery cab, her plastic bags on the seat beside her. The ride from the Lower East Side cost twenty-five dollars. She did not have enough to pay the driver, so Michelle's husband had to loan her the money.

The first few days in Michelle's home went surprisingly well. Elaine's nieces and nephews were excited about the arrival of an aunt they barely knew. Her older nieces gave her fashion tips, loaned her their clothes, and advised her to shave her legs. Every time she reached for the knob on the front door, the children wanted to know when she was coming back. To dissuade her from going out, the younger ones slipped on her shoes and strutted around the apartment.

Elaine felt relieved to be out of 13B, but there was no privacy or quiet here, either. She shared a bed with her fourteen-year-old niece and a few dozen stuffed animals. Relaxing was nearly impossible, at least as long as Michelle was home. With so many children to take care of, Michelle screamed all the time, starting a few minutes after she woke and continuing late into the evening. She yelled so much that she was often hoarse. Whenever Michelle got especially loud, Elaine put her hand over Michelle's mouth. As soon as she removed her hand, Michelle would start shouting again.

The more time Elaine spent in her sister's presence, the more annoyed she became. Over the years, tensions had built up between them. Elaine was mad at Michelle because she'd heard Michelle had been bad-mouthing her in front of her children while she was away. Michelle was angry at Elaine for getting arrested in the first place, then refusing to accept the prosecutor's offer of 5-to-life. "You put all that heartache on your mother," Michelle told her during one fight. "You could've taken the five years and been home."

To Elaine, it seemed that Michelle did not treat her with the respect an older sister deserved. Michelle, too, thought she did not receive enough respect. She thought Elaine treated her as if she were still a teenager—not a thirty-five-year-old woman with five children and one grandchild.

Tensions were already simmering on the day that Michelle told Elaine she was going to the store to buy bread, then returned a few hours later with Star's son. Elaine thought Michelle had purposely deceived her. She hadn't just gone to the store; to get Star's son, she must have gone to Apartment 13B. Elaine imagined Michelle down there talking about her with Satara, Star, and Sabrina, criticizing her behavior and meddling in her relationships.

Elaine had been at Michelle's only four days, and already she felt a sense of uncontrollable anger.

"I'm leaving," Elaine said.

"What's wrong with you?" Michelle asked. "Why are you leaving?"

"Fuck you," Elaine said.

Elaine walked out the door. Weeks later, looking back on this day, she would have trouble explaining exactly why she decided to leave. Maybe just because she could. After so many years of being trapped in prison, she did not ever want to feel trapped again.

Elaine had spent many hours walking around Harlem during the days she stayed with Michelle. The Harlem she remembered had been full of bars and liquor stores, barbershops and numbers spots. Now the beauty parlor where she had worked was gone. Small's Paradise, the legendary nightclub where she and Nate had danced together, had shut down long ago. The Apollo was still there, but many of the new businesses on 125th Street had names she had never heard of: Starbucks, Old Navy, Rite Aid.

Once-deserted apartment buildings had been renovated and now cost more than anyone she knew could afford. As a child, she had sat at the counter at Sylvia's, eating slices of cake with her friends. The counter was still there, but now Sylvia's was three times its original size, and there were buses packed with tourists pulling up to its doors. Even some of the street names had changed. Lenox Avenue was no longer Lenox Avenue; now it was Malcolm X Boulevard.

It was after midnight when Elaine stormed out of Michelle's apartment. Being outdoors at this hour was a parole violation, but she was not worried about Camacho catching her. At the moment, she had more pressing problems. She headed south, walking alone down Eighth Avenue. Except for a few drug dealers on the corners, the streets were empty. Walking outside usually made her feel better, but on this night, she knew walking would not bring her any solace. She needed a place to rest.

Every few blocks, she stopped at a pay phone to call Apache, but she always got his voice mail. She tried a few more people, too: Shyan's wife in Queens, a cousin in the Bronx, Nate's brother Ronald. The only person she found was Ronald, but Elaine did not ask him for help. Ronald had been released from prison two years earlier and now lived in Harlem with his grandmother, who was nearly ninety.

"I'm just going to take a walk," Elaine told him. "I'm sorry I bothered you."

"Be careful, girl," Ronald said.

At 125th Street, she descended the stairs to the A train. At this hour, the subway platform was nearly empty. She rode the A train to Canal Street, then got out. She had left Michelle's with four dollars. After a $1.50 subway ride and many phone calls, her money was nearly gone. If she walked out of the station, she would not be able to afford to go back in and get on the train.

By then it was almost 3:00 a.m. Elaine slid a quarter in a pay phone and called Lora Tucker.

"You're the last person I wanted to call," Elaine said.

"Come to my house," Lora said. "You don't have to apologize."

Elaine got back on the A train and rode it all the way to the Rockaway Boulevard stop in Howard Beach, Queens. It was a long ride; she passed twenty-two stops. When she finally arrived, it was after 4:00 a.m. She searched for a pay phone that worked and called Lora again.

Five minutes later, Lora arrived in her car, wearing her pajamas, moccasins, and a winter coat. Back at her apartment, Lora poured a glass of apple juice for Elaine. The two women sat at the kitchen table and talked until the sun rose and it was time for Lora to go to work.

A few days after her release from prison, Elaine had picked out birthday presents for Danae and Satara. Both of her daughters had been born in March, and she wanted to make sure she did not run out of money before she got their gifts. She bought each of them a gold bracelet, which she gave to them a few weeks before their actual birthdays.

When Danae's birthday arrived—on March 13—Elaine heard that her other family was throwing a party for her. Nobody invited Elaine.

Nonetheless, Elaine gave Danae twenty dollars to buy a cake. She would've bought the cake herself, but she was not sure what flavor Danae liked. Later, she found out that Danae had bought a strawberry cake. "I never would have guessed that," Elaine said.

March 27 was Satara's birthday, and it was the day after Elaine left Michelle's apartment. Elaine wanted to take both daughters to the movies to celebrate, but she did not have enough money. After she left Lora's house, she went to Danae's school, and told an administrator that Danae needed to be excused because of "family problems."

Elaine spent the afternoon with Satara and Danae, hanging out in front of their building, 950 East Fourth Walk, inside the Wald Houses. Danae brought a radio; Satara brought her daughter, Tenéa. Everyone pooled their money so they could buy fried chicken and soda at a take-out place on Avenue D. Then they sat on a wooden bench together, laying out the food on napkins. This birthday picnic was one of the very few times Elaine had been alone with both of her daughters since leaving prison. She should have felt happy, but she didn't.

"Ma, why are you crying?" Danae asked.

"If y'all don't want to live with me and be with me, just let me know," Elaine said. "Here I am, riding the train all night, all the way to Howard Beach, feeling like a homeless person."

"I don't know why you're riding the train all night," Danae said. "You have a place to sleep—950."

"What are you talking about?" Elaine said. "You don't even sleep at 950."

No matter how hard Elaine tried, the reality of her post-prison life had not come close to matching her expectations. Every assumption she had held had been turned on its head. She was free, but she did not feel free. Her family members felt like strangers. Her children's home did not feel like a home. In prison, she'd created a niche for herself: college student, drug-law activist, "Ma" to dozens of prisoners. The whole time, all she'd really wanted to was to be a mom to her own children. But now, on the outside, there seemed to be no place for her.

CHAPTER 25

Elaine usually made an effort to look presentable, if not professional, when she went to South Forty to see George. But on the morning of April 11, she showed up looking as bad as she had on her worst days in prison. Raccoon eyes. No make-up. Peeling nail polish. Gray roots. She looked as if she had not slept in weeks. She had not even bothered to brush her hair; instead, she had just stuck a plastic clip in it.

Five days earlier, George had sent her on her first job interview: for the position of case manager at a nonprofit agency. Now she settled into the chair next to his desk to hear the post-interview verdict.

"Miss Lasson feels you did really well," George said. "You looked fantastic. The only thing is, she said you came very, very early."

"The more I waited, the nervouser I got," Elaine said.

She had indeed arrived very early—two hours before her scheduled interview. In the agency's waiting room, she had tried to make herself inconspicuous by hiding behind a copy of the *Daily News*. The prospect of being grilled by a stranger had made her very tense. Just the idea of being interviewed was enough to trigger flashbacks to her first parole hearing, when she had become angry and flustered, then was later rejected.

After her interview, George had told her that she should write a thank-you note. By now, she was living in her sister Michelle's apartment once again. Over the weekend, while a television blared and her young nephews raced up and down the hall, she had written the note. In the midst of so much chaos, such social niceties seemed absurd. But if this was what she had to do to get a job, she would play by the rules.

George had told her to bring him the note, and now she opened her pocketbook and stuck one hand inside. It was not hard to tell that she was having a bad morning. Her eyes were moist. She blinked hard to stop her tears.

"All the people who are supposed to be helping me aren't doing anything," she said. "I'm fed up."

"Talk to me," he said.

She carried in her purse a book with plastic sleeves, which contained several dozen business cards. These were the people she had met since leaving prison: state legislators, reporters, activists. Almost everyone had nodded sympathetically when she'd told them her story. Many had even promised to help. But, despite nearly three months of effort, she was still broke and unemployed.

She explained to George that she'd had a second interview for a job at HELP USA several days earlier but had not yet heard back. She had also called the Women's Prison Association for help, she said, but had had no luck.

"This whole thing is a joke," she said. "They say they're going to get back to you, but they never do."

George could see that Elaine's situation was urgent. What was the point of finding her a job if personal crises derailed her—if they kept her from being punctual and focused? He slipped on his headset and picked up a directory of single-room-occupancy hotels, known as SROs. These hotels are the city's cheapest form of temporary housing. Tenants pay by the week for the bare necessities—a cot, a shared bathroom, an electrical outlet.

"I'm calling because I need help," he said. "I have a client by the name of Elaine Bartlett. Does that ring a bell for you? She's not a drug user or mentally ill. I'm looking for an SRO setting." He paused. "You have to pay two hundred and fifteen dollars a week?" Too expensive. He hung up.

He called two more SROs, but soon he was distracted by his ringing phone. He glanced at Elaine's thank-you letter. She had written it in pencil on lined school paper. Her lefty handwriting was so slanted that it was almost illegible.

George asked his assistant, Walter Dunn, to type the note. Then he handed the SRO directory to Elaine and found her an empty desk in an adjacent office.

While Walter typed, Elaine sat a few feet away, flipping through the directory. She quickly saw that many of the SROs listed were for a specific population: HIV-positive, mentally-ill, drug-addicted.

"Maybe I should tell them I have psychological problems," she muttered.

Walter overheard her and started a conversation. He revealed that he had been a prisoner, too, albeit for a short period of time at a minimum-security camp. Elaine told him that she had been released from prison at the end of January.

"Where did you expect to be in April?" he asked.

"By now I expected to be in a household with my children," she said. "If not comfortable, at least getting up every day happy to be home, enjoying life, and making plans for my future."

"How did you come up with your timetable? Is it totally arbitrary? Was it based on someone else's experience?"

"It was based on me knowing I was coming home to teenagers. I thought they had it together more than they did. I was going on what they'd been showing me, but evidently all that got lost."

"It sounds like you're disappointed."

"Yeah, I'm disappointed." She lifted a paper cup of coffee to her lips, drained the last drops, and tossed it in the trash.

"Try lowering your expectations a little bit, so you're not caught up in that frustration," he said.

"I just got to remove myself from everybody," she said. "I don't feel like anybody is on my level, or sees things the way I see things. The only one who understands me is my son. I've got to get away. I've got to go. If I stay any longer, it's not going to be pretty. I am in this predicament and I have no choice but to put up with their nonsense. My patience is wearing thin. I don't have patience for nonsense. Don't tell me I don't have control over my life and can't make things different, when I haven't had control over my life for sixteen years. If that's the case, I should've stayed in jail."

She picked up the SRO directory and walked out to find George. When she saw that his chair was empty, she sat down. Just like she had seen George do, she slipped on his headset and dialed the number of an SRO.

"I'm calling because I have a client here," she said. "This woman has been through a great deal. She's done sixteen years, and she got clemency from the governor. And I'm really trying to find her some housing, because her housing situation is dysfunctional. She's been going on job interviews, and employers are very impressed with her. She should have a job by next week."

The person she had called asked who she was. She paused. "My name is Diana Ortiz," she said. "I'm from South Forty."

Elaine figured she would have more luck if she posed as a caseworker, not a homeless ex-con. She was hardly the first person to lie in the hopes of finding housing. The shortage of inexpensive housing in New York City is so severe that it is easier for former prisoners to find a job than a place to live. Some even pretend to be addicts just so they can get into a residential drug program and have a safe place to sleep.

George returned. Since he was not a housing expert, he said, he was going to send her to somebody who was. He made a couple of calls and finagled her an appointment later that day at the Women's Prison Association.

There, Elaine told her story to a caseworker, who booked her a room for ten nights at the YMCA in Greenpoint, Brooklyn. Elaine was not too excited. The only YMCA she knew was on 135th Street in Harlem, where she had taken swimming lessons as a child. That was not the sort of place she wanted to sleep.

The caseworker thought she would like this Y, however. "Most of the ladies we send there don't want to leave," she said.

As Elaine walked out of the Women's Prison Association, she saw a familiar face: Tiffany Collins. Tiffany had been a prisoner at Bedford Hills for almost as long as Elaine had. Now she worked as a counselor there. She greeted Elaine with a hug and asked her where she was staying.

"Why don't you go to Providence House?" Tiffany asked. Providence House is a network of seven shelters started by Sister Elaine Roulet, who works at Bedford Hills. Many women stay at Providence House after leaving Bedford. "Why don't you put your pride to the side, Elaine?"

"It's all I've got. It's what got me through sixteen years," Elaine said. "Why should I go there? Why can't I have a room in the Y and then straight from there move into an apartment?"

"I think Providence House has better linkages. It's a better place, a better environment. Are you working?"

"No."

"Who's helping you?"

"South Forty." Elaine paused. "Things aren't going well. It's either leave or kill everybody, so I'm going to leave."

"Do you have toothpaste? Soap?"

"No. They didn't give me anything."

Tiffany opened a supply closet and pulled out a few items. A package of crackers, a bar of soap, a stick of deodorant, two tubes of toothpaste, a can of fruit.

"I need my own space," Elaine said. "I'm not going to Providence House."

"I understand."

There was another reason, too, that Elaine did not want to go there. Her long, torturous battle for clemency had left her with a grudge against many officials at Bedford Hills, including Sister Elaine, who she believed had some clout in the clemency process.

"If they'd helped me, do you think I'd have been doing sixteen years for four ounces of cocaine?" Elaine asked. "I could've got clemency after ten years."

"You're being so angry," Tiffany said. "It's okay to be angry, but don't let it hold you back."

Elaine boarded the G train, a subway line she had never ridden on before, to get to Greenpoint, a neighborhood she had never heard of. In this immigrant neighborhood, almost every store had a sign in the window that said OTWARTE, which is Polish for "open." Greenpoint's quiet streets and freestanding homes reminded Elaine of Corona, Queens.

After ten minutes of wandering around with a map, she found the YMCA. The man behind the front desk handed her a key to room 313. Sliding it in her door, she discovered a small room with a double bed, a lamp, a color TV, a desk, a mirror, an ashtray, white towels, two bars of soap, and a plastic cup. The only downside was the view: a police station across the street.

"It's not bad," Elaine said. "I could get used to it."

She had been dreaming of taking a vacation ever since she had left prison. Usually, she imagined herself in Jamaica, sipping a piña colada and lying on white sand next to an incredibly attractive man. This YMCA seemed an unlikely spot for a holiday, but for the moment, it would have to do. At least she would be able to stay here for free, and her caseworker had promised a stipend of ten dollars a day—enough for two meals, if she planned carefully.

Over the next few days, she transformed room 313 into a temporary home, retrieving her clothes from Michelle's apartment and placing them in her dresser drawers. She turned the windowsill into a kitchen cupboard, lining it with cranberry juice, Apple Jacks, and cans of sliced peaches.

At this YMCA, the bathroom was down the hall. Elaine bought a pack of paper toilet seat covers and a small bottle of bleach. Prison had given her a fierce paranoia about germs; at Bedford Hills, she had never let her bottom touch any toilet seat. "Ma, you're home now," Satara had told her after she moved into 13B. "You can sit on the toilet." Now that she was living at a YMCA, she clung to her old habit. She refused even to get near the communal toilet here until she had first wiped it with bleach.

Elaine knew only two or three people in Brooklyn, and none of them lived in Greenpoint. One day, she did see somebody she recognized: Katie, a former Bedford Hills inmate, who was also staying at the Y. Katie had been in and out of prison for years, usually for stealing bank account numbers or running some other financial scam. Elaine spoke to her briefly, then kept walking. She figured that hanging out with this particular woman could take her straight back to prison.

For an hour or two each day, Elaine sat in the phone booth in the stairwell, her pockets full of quarters. She called just about everyone she knew: Apache, Lora, George, Officer Camacho. She did not bother calling her sisters or daughters—"my so-called family"—to tell them where she had gone. She wanted them to worry about her, at least for a few days.

At the YMCA, Elaine finally had a chance to rest. It was the first time she'd had any privacy or quiet since leaving prison. It was also the first time she had slept alone. But soon the solitude began to feel uncomfortable. She hadn't liked the chaos of her family's apartments, but she didn't like absolute silence, either. Prison had never been this quiet. And she did not like spending so many hours by herself. At Bedford Hills, she had always been surrounded by people.

Now she felt lonely nearly all the time. Some days, she stayed in her room for hours, lying on her bed, sobbing. She barely recognized herself when she glanced in the mirror. The circles around her eyes were so dark that she looked as if someone had punched her in the face. To stop her tears, she forced herself to leave her room and go shopping. She could not afford much, but she did buy a few items she thought she'd need once she got a job: a curling iron, a blow-dryer, some stockings.

Like many women at Bedford Hills, Elaine had always imagined that the first thing she would do when she got out was have sex. "I can't wait to get home and have a man touch me," she would say. "He ain't got to love me, just love me for that moment." But now that she was back in the city, her libido had vanished. She was too upset about her family to think much about men. As for Nate, she had spoken to him on the phone several times, but she had not yet gone to see him; she was still waiting for permission from her parole officer.

One evening, a man approached her in the hallway outside her room. "Excuse me," he said. "What's your name? I've been meaning to ask you out for a while, because I always see you on the phone."

The man barely came up to her shoulder. He told her his name, but she quickly forgot it. In her mind, she dubbed him "Shorty."

That evening, Shorty and three of his friends invited her to a neighborhood bar. When the bartender asked her what she wanted to drink, she was not sure what to say. After all, she had not been in a bar since 1983. She hesitated for a few seconds, then asked for the only drink she could think of: a piña colada.

Not long after they sat down, Shorty told Elaine that he liked her.

"You don't even know anything about me," she said.

"Well, I like what I see," he said. "You might be the woman I've been looking for all my life."

"Yeah, right," she said. "That's what they all say."

"Tell me about yourself," he said.

She rolled her eyes. "You don't even want to know," she said. "We're not going to go there."

"I'll be your shoulder to cry on," he said.

"Your little shoulders couldn't handle my cries right now."

"I'll be a good friend to you."

"Yeah, right."

"Are you married?"

She did not answer.

"You hesitated," he said. "I know you're married."

"Something like that."

"Where do you live?"

"In Manhattan."

"What are you doing at the Y?"

She paused. "It's a long story."

What was she supposed to say? She was not in the mood to tell her life story to a group of strangers. She leaned forward and sipped her piña colada through a straw. To her, it tasted terrible. She had never been a big drinker. Maybe by now, she had lost her taste for liquor altogether.

Soon she decided she'd had enough of Shorty and his friends. Despite the men's protestations, she headed for the door, claiming that she had to get up early.

"I'm a nine-to-five girl," she said. "What can I say?"

"Can I come by your room?" Shorty asked.

"No, I don't have visitors."

A few hours later, just after midnight, she woke to the sound of fingers tapping on her door. She cracked it open and discovered a drunken Shorty.

"Oh, I'm sorry," he said. "Did I wake you?"

"You've got the wrong woman, buddy," she said. She shut the door and returned to bed.

CHAPTER 26

Anybody who has lived on the Lower East Side for many years knows the story of 8 East Third Street. From the 1960s to the 1980s, this seven-story building was home to the notorious Third Street Men's Shelter, then the central intake center for homeless men in New York City. More than 1,500 men passed through every day. Prostitutes were regular visitors. Shelter employees were arrested for selling drugs. The sidewalk in front reeked of urine. Neighbors referred to it as the "Black Hole of Calcutta."

A social service organization known as Project Renewal took over the building in 1991, transforming it into a residential drug-treatment program. The program has two hundred residents—men who are trying to get clean from drugs, usually heroin or crack. Now the building enjoys a much better reputation. The only people gathering on the sidewalk in front are employees taking a cigarette break.

Addicts in the throes of detox, sweating and shaking, stumble into 8 East Third Street all the time. These men wear their life stories on their bodies: jailhouse tattoos, razor-blade scars, gunshot holes, amputated limbs. Some come because they want to get clean. Others come because their parole officer told them they had to or they would be sent back to jail. Many of them have been sleeping on park benches or in subway cars because they have nowhere else to go.

In the beginning of May, Elaine went there, too. George from South Forty sent her to 8 East Third Street for a job interview. She met first with two assistant directors. Afterward, she went back for a second interview, this time with Donald Myers, the director. At the end of the interview, Myers asked, "Do you have any questions?"

"Yeah," Elaine said. "When can I start working?"

Her blunt, self-assured manner appealed to Myers. It took a certain type of woman to be able to handle working with the men who resided here. "While she didn't have any experience in the field, I felt she had a lot of potential," Myers said. "She's not easily intimidated. She's open and teachable. And she asks a lot of questions." In early May, Myers hired her to be a "residential aide."

Many former prisoners lie about their criminal records to get jobs, then live in constant fear that their boss will find out the truth. There are many ways the truth can leak out: a criminal background check, a visit from a parole officer, a phone call from an angry relative. Being outed at her job was one worry Elaine didn't have. Because South Forty had sent her, Myers knew that she had spent time in prison. As its name suggests, Project Renewal believes in second chances. Many of its employees are former addicts who have graduated from its drug program.

Elaine's job duties included answering phones, enforcing curfews, and inspecting the men's lockers. Though these tasks were not difficult, she soon discovered that the job could be very grueling. She worked in a small, crowded office called Operations, where the phone rang constantly. Men paraded through all day long. Everybody wanted something: a pass to leave the building, a cigarette, their pills, permission to go to the toilet, a few minutes of attention. When they didn't get their way, they got mad. "It's like raising a house full of kids," Elaine said.

Her new job gave her a schedule and a routine. Five days a week, Tuesday through Saturday, she worked from 4:00 p.m. to midnight. The schedule technically violated her parole—her curfew was still

9:00 p.m.—but Officer Camacho gave her permission to work at night.

The job paid $18,000 a year, or a little more than nine dollars an hour. It was not much by Manhattan standards, though it was considerably more than minimum wage. And she did not plan to stay at nine dollars an hour forever. Before too long, she expected, she would win a promotion and a raise.

Going to work usually improved her mood. Few women worked at this drug program, and those who did received plenty of attention. Coworkers and clients flirted with Elaine all day long. For Mother's Day, one male coworker gave her a heart-shaped bottle of Victoria's Secret perfume and a plastic rose that lighted up when she squeezed the stem.

Some days, Elaine's new workplace reminded her of Bedford Hills. All the residents had to wear an ID card attached to their shirt. Prison lingo was common. Men referred to the dining room as a "mess hall" and the small park next door as "the yard." When somebody left the program for good, it was known as "breaking out."

Like prison, this drug program has myriad rules: The men can make only one phone call during their first fifteen days. Employees screen their packages and test their urine for drugs. The men are assigned beds, and on weekdays the lights go out at 10:00 p.m. Unlike prison, though, the front door here is unlocked. The men can quit the program and leave at any time.

Though Elaine was a staff member, she empathized with the residents. On days when she had to search for contraband—drugs, knives, cell phones—she felt as if she were back at Bedford Hills, this time as a guard. When the men balked at the rules and at being told what to do, Elaine understood how they felt. She did not really want anyone telling her what to do, either.

Project Renewal's employees bantered with each other all day long, mocking one another in a playful, friendly manner. Elaine joked with them, too, but her words often had an extra-sharp edge, making her sound angry and defensive.

When Robert Turner, an assistant director, gave her directions, she asked, "Who runs your house? You or your wife?"

"I do," he said.

"Good," she said. "Because you don't run me. Listen, I'm not your wife. No one is controlling me."

In another office, Elaine's attitude might have gotten her fired. But Turner did not show any anger. Instead, he just said, "I'm not messing with you, Elaine."

Like many of the employees here, Turner was an ex-prisoner, too. He had spent eleven years behind bars, including five for selling drugs to an undercover agent. Nearly thirty years had passed since his last arrest and he now wore a suit to work, but he hadn't forgotten what it felt like to come home from prison.

Not long after she started working at Project Renewal, Elaine was transferred around the corner to Kenton Hall, the agency's operation on the Bowery. This five-story building was a last stop for men who passed through the program on East Third Street. If they remained drug-free for several months, they were moved to Kenton Hall for a short stay before leaving the program altogether. Elaine's new schedule was Monday to Friday, 8:00 a.m. to 4:00 p.m.

By now, she had left the YMCA and was back in Apartment 13B. From there, it took her only fifteen minutes to walk to work. To get up in the morning, she relied on her internal body clock, or on Tenéa, who would wriggle next to her. Some days, she overslept. On her first day at Kenton Hall, she showed up thirty minutes late.

A few days later, she woke up at 6:00 a.m.—two hours before her shift started. It should have been plenty of time. But when she walked down the hallway to the bathroom, she discovered she could not open the door. Sabrina's legs were blocking it.

"Sabrina, get out!" Elaine shouted. "I have to go to work!"

Sabrina did not move. Elaine waited awhile, then rummaged around the kitchen for a plastic grocery bag. She shouted at her sister a few more times, but Sabrina did not come out. Finally, Elaine pulled up her nightshirt, opened the plastic bag, and peed in it.

Elaine thought she would have to take a birdbath in the kitchen sink, too, washing herself with a wet towel, the way she had done in prison. But Sabrina eventually emerged, and Elaine hurried into the shower. By the time she walked into Kenton Hall, it was 9:00 a.m. When the supervisor asked her why she was an hour late, all she said was, "Family troubles."

Arriving for work on time might seem like a simple matter, but for people who have just left prison, it is not. In prison, inmates don't have to structure their days or create their own routine. The guards tell them when to go to sleep, and then wake them up in the morning. Inside prison, showing up late for work does not carry the same penalties it does on the outside. At Bedford Hills, a prisoner could be tardy every day and never lose her job.

Elaine had trouble with Project Renewal's dress code, too. One day, she showed up wearing a short denim dress without a slip. The outfit was deemed too risqué. She was sent out to buy a more modest skirt. Another day, a Wednesday, she showed up wearing jeans. A supervisor informed her that employees were permitted to wear jeans only on Fridays. The concept of "dress-down Fridays" was new to Elaine; in prison, everyone wore their state greens every day.

David Hickman, Elaine's boss at Kenton Hall, was a decade older than she and had been working at Project Renewal for nine years. When he gave her instructions about how to answer the telephone or take messages, she sometimes interrupted.

"Shut up," he would say. "Be quiet and listen."

Being told to "shut up" reminded her of the way that some guards at Bedford Hills had spoken to her, and the way that some of her coworkers talked to the addicts here.

"I'm not in recovery," she said. "I'm am employee. Let's not forget that. I'm not going to have you talking to me like that, acting like a male chauvinist pig. You're not going to be pushing my buttons for seven hours a day."

"Don't forget who's the boss," he said.

"Just because you're my boss doesn't mean I have to tolerate abuse," she replied.

When Elaine recounted these spats later, she sometimes blamed

Hickman. Other times, she blamed herself. "I think I've got a problem with authority," she said one day. A few weeks later, she wondered aloud how all the tensions in her family life might be affecting her job performance. "I guess not being happy on the inside is starting to come out," she said. "You can only fake something for so long."

It took only a few weeks before Elaine became very popular with the men who lived at Project Renewal. When she found chips or soda hidden in their lockers, she was supposed to confiscate them, but usually she just pretended she hadn't seen anything. She was supposed to enforce the fifteen-minute limit on phone calls, but she usually let the men talk much longer. And she started bringing an extra pack of Newports to work so she could hand out cigarettes to whoever asked, though she knew she wasn't supposed to.

While some of her coworkers talked down to the recovering addicts, she never did. Instead, she tried to boost their self-esteem. "You gotta be strong," she would say. "You can't give up. Everything you're going through is for a reason. It molds us and creates us and makes us who we have become today."

Every day, she asked dozens of men how they were doing and then listened to their problems. This was not part of her job description, but she enjoyed trying to help everyone she could. After all, she had played this same role for years inside Bedford Hills.

She treated all the men as if they were her children—even when they were older than she—and she gave plenty of unsolicited advice: "Pull your pants up. They're hanging too low." "Do something with that hair, or get it cut off." "Stay out of trouble." "Be good."

"All right, Ma," the men would say.

Whenever she grabbed her coat and pocketbook at the end of a shift, she sparked a minor frenzy. The cries of the building's residents followed her as she walked down the stairs and out the front door.

"Miss B, are you leaving?" they'd ask. "When are you coming back?"

"I gave you eight hours already," she'd say. "You want the whole twenty-four hours? I'm trying to have a life. See y'all tomorrow."

Most of the men who lived at 8 East Third Street did not know that Elaine had just come home from prison. Then, one Thursday morning, she saw a few of them in the waiting room at the parole office. "Hey, Miss B!" they called across the room. It would only be a matter of hours, she knew, until everyone at her job found out about her past.

Soon the basic facts of her story—her sixteen years in prison and the governor's decision to grant her clemency—traveled along Project Renewal's grapevine. The news that she had survived so many years behind bars earned her added respect from the recovering addicts. Many of them had done time, too, but few had been locked up for as long as she had. To them, she was a role model—a real-life example of someone who had made it, who had lifted herself up from the bottom of society and found her place in the workforce. For her part, Elaine hardly considered herself a success, at least not yet—not until she found an apartment where she could live comfortably with all her children.

CHAPTER 27

Elaine wanted to see at least one of her children go to college, and Danae was her best hope. She was the only one still in school; at the moment, she was a student at P.S. 169 on East Twelfth Street. Several years earlier, Danae had convinced Apache to start a basketball team for girls, and now she played guard on a team that he coached. Apache had told Elaine that if Danae worked harder—if she spent less time smoking marijuana and more time practicing basketball—she could have a shot at a college scholarship.

During her first months out of prison, Elaine visited Danae's school almost every week. She met with the principal and learned that Danae had decent grades but that she often misbehaved. She also found out that Danae was in a special school for kids with learning and behavioral problems. This fact bothered Elaine; she thought Danae belonged in another, better school. She took her to the district office and applied for a transfer. They were told the wait would be several weeks.

One day that spring, Elaine stopped by Danae's school to see if she wanted to go to lunch. As Elaine rounded a corner, she heard a familiar voice. "Get the fuck out of my face!" There was Danae, screaming at a teacher. Elaine wanted to grab Danae and smack her, but instead she suppressed this urge and just walked out of the building.

"She's out of control," Elaine said later. "She's very disrespectful. She's in school, acting like an animal. And basically, she's been doing what she wants to do for so long that she don't care about nobody right now but Danae."

It was obvious that getting Danae to graduate from high school— much less go to college—would require an extraordinary amount of effort. In some ways, Danae reminded Elaine of herself as a teenager; she had a temper, a stubborn streak, and a love of marijuana. But Elaine certainly did not want Danae to make the same sort of mistake she'd made. Whenever Elaine crossed Avenue D, she checked to make sure Danae was not hanging out with the drug dealers on the corner.

Although Elaine kept trying to convince Danae to move home, she still lived with her friend's family. Her refusal to live at 13B upset Elaine; she felt like Danae preferred someone else's mother over her. Danae's attitude in her presence only reinforced these feelings. When Elaine showed up at Danae's basketball games, Danae's friends flocked to her, hugging her and calling her "Ma." Danae, meanwhile, pretended not to see her. She acted the same way whenever she visited Apartment 13B. She would see Elaine in the kitchen or the hall, then walk by her without saying hello.

Danae did not have any memories of Elaine before she went to prison. She only knew her mother as an inmate in a green uniform, seated at a table in a visiting room. "Basically, with my daughters, everything they know about me is from the visits and whatever they have heard the family say around them," Elaine explained. "And you know how family is. When they get mad, they're liable to say anything. That don't mean it's true, but it was said. And children, they listen, even when they're playing and you think they're not listening, they're listening."

There was one person Elaine thought Danae had spent too much time listening to: her sister Michelle. After she left prison, Elaine discovered that Danae did not believe Nate was her father. Michelle had told Danae that her real father was Littleboy. Elaine insisted that this was impossible, but Danae was not sure. About Littleboy, she said, "I look just like him, with big-ass lips. I look like him more than I do Nathan." The fact that Danae doubted her infuriated Elaine. She blamed Michelle for sowing seeds of confusion in Danae's mind, undermining her relationship with her youngest child.

By the spring, Elaine had found Danae a slot in another school—Martin Luther King, Jr., High School on the West Side. Michelle's name was listed as a contact in Danae's student file, and at the end of May, a school administrator called her to say that Danae had been skipping school. Michelle went downtown to talk to Danae, and when Elaine heard the news, she tracked down Danae, too.

Elaine found Danae and Michelle seated on a bench together in front of 950 East Fourth Walk. The sight of Michelle talking to her daughter enraged Elaine. Now that she was home, Elaine thought she should be playing the role of Danae's mother, not Michelle.

"I go through all this to get you in school, and you don't go anyway!" Elaine shouted. Then she raised her left arm and punched Danae in the face.

Danae spun around and lunged toward Elaine. Michelle held Danae back.

"What did you do that for?" Michelle yelled. "That's just going to make your kids hate you if you keep doing that."

"You turned my kids against me!" Elaine shouted.

Danae rubbed her cheek. "I wish my grandmother would have never left me here with this," she said. "I want to die, too." Glancing toward the sky, she said, "Grandma, take me with you."

"Stop saying that," Michelle said. "I'm here for you. She ain't going to put her hands on you no more."

Elaine watched Michelle lead Danae down the project's asphalt path. To Elaine, it seemed Danae never listened to her when she spoke. She thought that punching her might wake her up. "I know violence is not the answer," Elaine said later, "but the way kids are today and how disrespectful they are, they need to be knocked on their ass. That's the bottom line. They ain't got no respect."

CHAPTER 28

The last Sunday in June turned out to be the perfect summer day: nearly ninety degrees, a bright blue sky, no clouds. Lora Tucker suggested to Elaine that they go out to lunch at Dojo restaurant on St. Marks Place in the East Village. At 2:00 p.m., they were seated at one of Dojo's outdoor tables, their sandals resting atop a rug of plastic grass. On the table in front of them was a pack of Newports, an ashtray, a lighter, a plate of fried calamari, and two virgin piña coladas.

Lora had picked Dojo because it is inexpensive and because its outdoor tables are prime spots for people-watching. There is never a shortage of passersby on St. Marks Place, and today it was especially crowded. Many of the men strolling down the sidewalk wore shorts but no shirt. Whenever an especially attractive man passed by, Elaine and Lora turned to check out his backside.

Elaine wore what she called her "hoochie mama" outfit: a thin black skirt that barely reached midthigh and a matching tie-on top that covered only her front. The outfit hid maybe 5 or 10 percent of her ample body, and its message was obvious: Look at me! Or, better yet: Flirt with me! After so many years of drab prison uniforms—of feeling invisible and unsexy—this skimpy outfit announced that Elaine Bartlett was back.

Lora wore a pair of shorts and a T-shirt with a pink triangle, in honor of that day's Gay Pride parade. The rest of her outfit was a tribute to their friendship. Elaine had helped her pick out the cow-bone beads that decorated her dreadlocks. The sandals she wore were a recent gift from Elaine. And the black angel pin attached to her T-shirt was just like the one she had given Elaine on the day she left prison.

Since that day, Elaine and Lora's friendship had flourished. They spoke on the phone several times a week, listening to each other's worries and giving each other advice late into the night. Sometimes they talked about politics and the latest Rockefeller drug law reform efforts. Other times they talked about work and family. Most of the time, though, they talked about men.

The warm weather seemed to have awakened Elaine's libido. Lately, she had been conducting an experiment of sorts, trying to figure out how much sex appeal she still possessed. Finding boyfriends had been easy when she was twenty-six, but what about at forty-two? During all those years in prison, it had been impossible to know whether she still possessed the ability to turn a man's head when she walked down the street.

So far, she'd been pleased with the response she'd received, and, of course, the hoochie mama outfit helped. But even when she was not wearing it, she had no trouble meeting men. She met them everywhere: on the street, in a bodega, at her job. She flirted and collected phone numbers, but so far, she had not found anyone she really liked.

After everyone at her job found out that she had recently left prison, Elaine got even more attention. "All of them are looking at the fact that this woman has been away for sixteen years," she said. "Her husband's in prison and no man is calling for her. They're tripping over themselves to see who gets it first."

Lora glanced up from her piña colada, a look of amusement on her face.

At the moment, Lora had a boyfriend. His name was John, and he, too, was a former prisoner, though he had been free for ten years. Recently, the subject of Elaine's sex life in prison had come up during their conversations. John did not believe Elaine had been celibate at Bedford Hills.

"John said, 'You're telling me, she just laid back for sixteen years?' " Lora said. "I told him, 'I don't care what she did.' "

"Tell him I did what I had to do to survive," Elaine said. "I hope you flipped the script on him: 'Excuse me. Weren't you in for ten years? Don't tell me you were celibate.' "

Elaine offered no more details about her past sex life, and Lora let the subject drop.

In recent months, Elaine had been busy trying to catch up on all the new trends she'd missed. Recently, she had learned about thongs. Before she went to prison, she had never heard of them. And inside prison, everyone had to wear state-issued underwear. But now it seemed that every other woman walking down St. Marks Place had a thong strap peeking out above her waistband.

The topic had even surfaced one day while Elaine was talking to one of her coworkers. "He asked me, 'Do you wear thongs?' " Elaine told Lora. "I said, 'No, I haven't tried them.' "

Elaine grinned as she recalled the conversation. "He said, 'I'm going to buy you a pair.' I told him, 'If you buy me some thongs, buy seven, and the bras to go with it. If you want me to wear 'em, give me a week's supply.' "

She paused, lifting her cigarette to her lips. Lora stared at her without speaking.

"That's how you gotta do it," Elaine explained. "I grew up around men, my brothers. I know how to handle them niggers."

Even though she had been locked up since the mid-1980s, Elaine talked about men as if she were an authority on the subject. According to her, flirting and dating were part of an elaborate power game, in which the underlying question was always the same: "What can you do for me?" In their phone conversations, she had told Lora that she wanted a man who would wine and dine her, treat her like a queen and spoil her with gifts. She said she was holding out for someone who could take her to Jamaica. "The first nigger who gets me is going to have me on the white sand," she'd said. "I want to see prints on the sand."

She had been fantasizing about a trip to Jamaica ever since she had seen *How Stella Got Her Groove Back* at Bedford Hills. She loved the story line: a forty-year-old woman, played by Angela Bassett, travels to Jamaica and falls in love with Winston, a stunningly attractive man who is half her age.

Elaine had convinced a guard to smuggle in a copy of the movie for her. Every Saturday afternoon, after she was done watching *Soul Train* on the television in the dayroom, she had popped the tape into the VCR.

"Not *Stella* again, Elaine," the other women would say.

"Oh yes," Elaine would respond. "You know I need my energy to keep me going."

Since leaving prison, her romantic life had not come close to matching her dreams. None of the men she had met looked anything like Taye Diggs, the actor who played Winston. And none was able to whisk her off on vacation. They were all married or broke, or both. Until she found a man who could take her to the Caribbean, she made do with going to a nail salon and getting palm trees painted on her fake nails. "That's as close to Jamaica as I'm going to get," she would say.

Lora had told Elaine that her expectations about men were completely unrealistic. With so many black men behind bars nowadays, she explained, the pickings were slim. And in Lora's opinion, Elaine's "treat me like a queen" approach to men was dated. "You can't expect a guy to do all that," Lora would tell her. "The way it is in this day and age, guys are looking for what they can take from you."

A waitress walked over and set down lunch: a hamburger for Elaine and a turkey burger for Lora. Over the next half hour, they talked about Elaine's children, the Gay Pride parade, Lora's job, Lora's parents, the institution of marriage, and the upcoming basketball tournament at Rucker Park.

Eventually, Elaine returned to her favorite subject. She announced that the day before she had met a man in the bodega near her job. He wore a Panama hat, a silk shirt, and six or seven gold rings. They talked for a few minutes, just long enough for him to give her his beeper number.

"He looked all right," Elaine said. "He's not tall."

"You don't want someone who's tall, dark, and handsome," Lora said.

"I don't know what type of man I'm looking for," Elaine said. "Maybe I'll try a variety."

"Get the variety pack," Lora said.

Elaine borrowed a cell phone and called Project Renewal. She did not have to work today, but she wanted to find out if a certain coworker was working. Eight East Third Street was just a few blocks away. If he was there, she wanted to drop by. Maybe he had already bought her those thongs and bras.

"Don't you know when you wear a thong, you don't wear a bra?" Lora said.

"Why not?" Elaine asked.

"Why are you going to wear a bra when you're only wearing a string up your behind and everything else is hanging out?"

While Elaine pondered these words, Lora reached into her bag and pulled out a paper fan. As it turned out, her coworker was not in. Elaine clicked off the cell phone.

Lora reached across the table and fanned Elaine. "I've been tickled ever since you walked out," Lora said. "Who would've thought? We've known each other since you were behind the walls, and no one ever thought we'd be friends. Everyone was warning me, 'You have to keep these boundaries.' I'm just tickled."

The possibility of a friendship had never occurred to either of them when they'd first met. Elaine thought Lora was prissy and naïve—yet another do-gooder who had come into Bedford Hills with grandiose ideas about helping the less fortunate. For her part, Lora had thought Elaine was too wary and too weary ever to open up to her. Inside Bedford Hills, their relationship had been defined by an enormous power imbalance: Elaine needed Lora's help if she ever hoped to get out of prison early. For Lora, it was impossible to discern Elaine's true character while she was locked up. The only way Lora could truly know Elaine was to wait and see how she acted after her release.

Now, in some ways, Lora felt more comfortable with Elaine than with many of her other friends. Elaine was tough and blunt, sweet and funny. And if Elaine could survive sixteen years in a maximum-security prison without losing her mind, then certainly Lora could conquer her own demons, which at the moment included writer's block.

Two years earlier, Lora had been a regular on the city's spoken-word circuit, reading her poems at open-mike events nearly every weekend. After she was diagnosed with AIDS, she had stopped writing. Now she rummaged through her bag and pulled out a poem she had just finished, "Silver Ribbons." The title referred to the spirals of razor-wire circling the fences at Bedford Hills.

" 'Silver ribbons/strung through/metal mesh of restrained dreams. Shining blades of fear/boxed tightly/neat/Gifts/No one cares to open/ No one cares to keep . . .' " Lora read.

She continued for almost a minute, and Elaine listened intently. For Lora, this impromptu reading marked a pivotal moment. "Silver Ribbons" was the first poem she had written in two years. When she finished, Elaine clapped loudly.

A smile spread across Lora's face. "Come in that outfit to one of my poetry readings," she said.

By now, the two women had finished their burgers and their piña coladas. They pushed back their chairs and headed down the block toward Lora's car. To get home, Elaine would have to walk another ten blocks.

"Do you want a lift, or do you want to strut?" Lora asked. "You've got to remember to pull down your skirt because you're showing a lot of leg."

"No, I'm not," Elaine said, hiking her skirt up a little bit more, enough to make Lora laugh. The two women hugged, and then Elaine turned around and strutted down the street.

CHAPTER 29

Most twenty-six-year-old men would not be too thrilled about sharing a bedroom with their mother, but Apache did not complain. After Elaine had left the YMCA and returned to Apartment 13B, she'd moved into Apache's room. She had decided not to sleep in Satara's room because she wanted to give Satara a chance to spend time alone with her boyfriend. This way, Elaine thought she could minimize tensions.

At the moment, Apache's bedroom was also the de facto headquarters for Exodus, a basketball club he had started a few years earlier. It now had seven teams, which played in tournaments around the city. Game schedules hung from the wall above Apache's bed. Copies of *Slam*, the basketball magazine, covered the milk crate that doubled as a night table. The room was not much larger than the king-size bed it held, and Elaine's arrival made it even more crowded. She hung her clothes from the curtain rods and slept next to Apache at night.

Her stay at the YMCA had helped clear her head, but soon she felt like things were fuzzy once again, as if she was losing sight of her goals. Compared to the highly structured world of Bedford Hills, life in this apartment was complete chaos. Most days, no one went to sleep before midnight. The phone rang round the clock. At night, the number of friends and boyfriends crashing here pushed the apartment's population to ten or more.

Elaine hated coming home from work, exhausted after another eight-hour shift, and walking into a dirty apartment reeking of marijuana. "You've got a household full of teenagers," she explained. "Everybody comes up here to smoke reefer because now it's a hangout. They got the boyfriends, they're coming in there laying up, smoking reefer, and they're laying up on filth. I mean, they might sweep the room out, but the dirt pile is right there. They ain't even going to pick it up and put it in the garbage."

The apartment's clutter might have bothered her less if everybody worked, but she was the only one with a full-time job. Some nights after walking home from Project Renewal, she sat on the bench in front of the building, staring at the sky. You're free, Elaine, she would tell herself. At least things aren't as bad as they were. Usually, these thoughts were enough to get her off the bench and into the building's elevator. But once she got upstairs, she usually felt depressed once again. Sometimes, on her days off from work, she retreated to Apache's room, locked the door behind her, and slept all afternoon.

As soon as Elaine had moved into this apartment, she had searched it for signs of Yvonne. She had discovered a stack of old photographs that Sabrina had collected, and she found one antique doll from her mother's collection: a black girl wearing a green coat with fur trim. But she had found nothing else. She was particularly upset that she could not locate the one picture she had ever seen of Ronald, the man she thought was her father. Yvonne had always kept it on the wall in her home: a photograph of a large white man in a bathtub, his chest covered with hair. Elaine remembered the picture well.

In prison, Elaine had spent much of her time thinking about her childhood, trying to make sense of all the things she had seen and heard. There had been so many lies and half-truths passed around that she did not know what to believe. She remembered watching Ronald die, but she didn't know what the cause of death had been. And she still didn't know why she'd been sent to Mount Loretto. She had always wanted to interrogate her mother, but Yvonne did not like to talk about the past. And if Yvonne did not like to talk about something, there was nothing anyone could do to get her to open up.

Whenever anyone asked Elaine who her father was, she said his name was Ronald Winslow Bartlett. This is what Yvonne had told her. The two men Yvonne had been with in the late 1950s—Frank Bartlett and Ronald Windsor—had become one person in the minds of her children. Several months after she left prison, Elaine obtained a copy of her birth certificate. Next to the space for her father, she saw the name Fred Bartlett. "Who's Fred Bartlett?" Elaine asked her family. Nobody knew. And now that Yvonne was gone, Elaine doubted she would ever learn the answer.

Elaine often summed up life on the outside with a single word: *ridiculous*. The 9:00 p.m. curfew imposed on parolees was "ridiculous." Having to wait six months for permission to visit her husband in prison was "ridiculous." Of all the rules governing her new life, there was one she found particularly "ridiculous": the ban on former prisoners living in public housing.

The city's Housing Authority prohibits people with criminal records from living in its housing projects. Elaine learned about this rule during her first week home, when she asked the building's manager if her family could transfer to a larger apartment. "You've got a felony conviction," the manager said. "You're not even supposed to be here. Be thankful you're here and be quiet."

Elaine found her predicament very confusing. "The governor gave me clemency, they paroled me to the projects, and then they tell me I can't live in the projects," she said later. "They're crazy. They tell me not to make a stink, but the governor released me to that address. They knew where they were releasing me to. You're contradicting yourself. Why would you release me to a project apartment when you know I have a felony conviction?"

New York City has the nation's largest public housing system, with 345 projects, which contain a total of 181,000 apartments. An estimated 600,000 people live in public housing. Nobody knows for sure exactly how many have criminal records, but the number is undoubtedly high. Despite the Housing Authority's determination to weed out criminals, parolees move into its projects every week.

The state Division of Parole knows where its parolees live, but it has not made a practice of giving these addresses to the city Housing Authority. It is easy to imagine what would happen if the parole agency did share this information: Parolees would be evicted, and the city's homeless shelters would be even more swamped.

Parole officials certainly do not want this to happen, since it would only make their job more difficult. A parolee with a stable home is easier to keep tabs on—and less likely to return to jail—than a parolee who is sleeping in a shelter.

The rules banning felons from public housing grew out of the anger and frustration of tenants. Their complaints were many: crack vials crunching beneath their feet, gunshots waking them at night, children terrified to leave their homes. In 1988, Congress passed the Anti-Drug Abuse Act, which permitted local housing authorities to evict an entire family if anyone engaged in "drug-related criminal activity."

Congress strengthened this ban with new legislation twice in the 1990s. And in 1996, President Bill Clinton announced an initiative, known as One Strike and You're Out, to expedite the evictions of drug dealers.

Meanwhile, in New York City, the Housing Authority had been aggressively enforcing this ban for years. When the Housing Authority learned that a tenant had been arrested, the tenant lost the lease. And when a tenant applied for a transfer and a background check revealed a criminal record, they, too, were evicted. Though many former prisoners lived in the projects undetected, the agency's rule was enforced often enough to make any resident with a rap sheet nervous.

The Housing Authority oversees not only the city's projects but also a voucher program, known as Section 8, which subsidizes rental payments to private landlords. Three months after leaving prison,

Elaine applied for both—a rental voucher and a project apartment—in the hopes of obtaining one or the other. In June, she received a letter informing her she had been rejected for Section 8.

Her felony record did not eliminate her; the Housing Authority did not even conduct a background check. They had so few vouchers that they gave priority to only a select group: domestic violence victims, residents of homeless shelters, and people in the witness-protection program. Elaine did not know it at the time, but the agency had stopped accepting new applications for vouchers in 1994.

Elaine was equally unsuccessful in her efforts to obtain a Housing Authority apartment. According to the agency's rules, somebody convicted of an A-level felony (or a Class B or C felony) can get an apartment only after finishing parole and then waiting an additional six years.

Even if Elaine had managed to convince somebody at the Housing Authority to add her name to its list, the wait for an apartment would have been at least a year and a half, and maybe much longer. Some would-be residents wait ten years to get a project apartment. At the time, the waiting list had 130,000 names.

Caseworkers at the Women's Prison Association advised Elaine that the fastest way to get an apartment would be to enter the city's shelter system, since homeless people are given special priority. Elaine knew other ex-prisoners who had gone this route, including one woman who had been in the shelter system with her children for nearly three years. To Elaine, this scenario sounded like a nightmare.

As a short-term solution, a caseworker found Elaine an opening at an SRO in Brooklyn. Elaine refused even to visit. "I don't want a room," she said. "I want a home."

Elaine knew virtually nothing about apartment hunting in New York City, but she knew what type of home she wanted: a place large enough for her and all her children, preferably a three- or four-bedroom apartment. She wasn't sure if she could convince both daughters to live with her, but she wanted to try. "I need a home to create a family," she said.

Finding an affordable apartment in New York City is difficult for anyone. For somebody with a small salary, who does not qualify for subsidized housing, it is virtually impossible. The fastest way for Elaine to get her own place would have been to scale down her ambitions and strike out on her own, searching for a cheap studio instead of a three- or four-bedroom apartment.

Many people advised her to do this. Elaine, however, refused even to consider leaving her family. "I can't just walk away, because the love I have for them is what kept me going the sixteen years that I was incarcerated," she said. "It's easy for people to say, 'Walk away. They're teenagers now.' They might be teenagers, but they're still my babies."

Elaine wanted to stay on the Lower East Side, close to her job, but the prices in the neighborhood were well out of her reach. The neighborhood was no longer an open-air drug market. Drug dealers still hung out on Avenue D, but there were far fewer of them. An aggressive police effort had pushed many dealers indoors.

While the Lower East Side had once been synonymous with junkies and shooting galleries, it was now dotted with expensive restaurants and renovated apartment buildings. Gentrification had elevated rents so high that many neighborhood residents had already fled to the outer boroughs in search of housing they could afford. Studio apartments on the Lower East Side rent for at least $1,000 a month. Three-bedroom apartments can cost at least $3,000 a month.

Whenever Elaine walked around the Lower East Side, she scanned the windows of apartment buildings for signs of vacancies. One day, when Apache walked her to work, they passed a building that was being renovated.

"I wonder what they're going to be," Elaine said. "Apartments or shelters?"

"It'll probably be expensive," Apache said. "You'll probably have to start robbing banks or something."

One reason for the dearth of inexpensive apartments involves the state's budget priorities. In 1968, New York State set up the Urban Development Corporation to build housing for poor people. Under Governor Mario Cuomo, this public agency did indeed build a great deal of housing for the poor, but not the type of housing that the

UDC's creators had intended. Most of this housing was in the form of prisons located in rural towns in upstate New York. Between 1984 and 1989, the UDC issued about $1 billion in bonds. More than 80 percent of that money, or $819 million, went toward building prisons.

The Rockefeller drug laws had created an enormous need for more prison beds. During his three terms in office, from 1983 to 1995, Governor Cuomo presided over one of the largest expansions of a prison system in U.S. history. He more than doubled the size of New York's prison system, opening four maximum-security prisons, twenty-five medium-security prisons, and three minimum-security prisons. The cost of this construction, including interest, was close to $7 billion.

Whenever the temperature outside rose during the summer of 2000, so did the tensions inside Apartment 13B. The fan in Apache's room barely worked, and the air conditioner in the living room was broken, too. Even when Elaine opened every window, it was impossible to get much of a breeze because of the apartment's layout: Each room was attached to a long windowless hall. The summer heat became a new source of stress and friction, turning 13B into a tinderbox, ready to explode with only the slightest provocation.

For Elaine, there seemed to be no way out, or at least no immediate solution to her predicament. Together, she and Apache devised a temporary plan: Switch bedrooms with Satara, who still had the largest room in the apartment. This room had long belonged to Apache; he had agreed to give it to Satara before their mother came home only because he thought she would stay in there. Now he decided it was time to reclaim the room. He knew Satara would not give it up easily, however. "It's going to be a battle royal," he predicted.

Indeed, when Satara and Sabrina's daughter Star heard about this plan, they sat down with Apache and Elaine in order to try to dissuade them. A shouting match erupted, and soon it became clear that this fight was about much more than who got which room; it was about who was in charge.

This apartment had two lease holders: Star and Satara. Elaine was not even supposed to be living here; if the building manager had wanted to, he could've evicted her and the entire family. Elaine knew all of this, but as far as she was concerned, she was the oldest Bartlett living here and that meant that she was the boss.

One morning in early July, she and Apache decided to implement their plan. After explaining it to Satara, they pushed Apache's bed and dresser into the corridor and piled Elaine's outfits on top. Satara sat on her bed in the back bedroom, looking extremely unhappy. "I'm not moving," she said. Elaine ignored her and kept mopping the floor of Apache's now-empty room.

A few minutes later, at 11:40 a.m., somebody pounded on the front door. Glancing down the corridor, Elaine saw two police officers.

"We got a call about a domestic dispute," an officer said.

Elaine did not know who had called the cops; maybe it had been Satara's boyfriend. There was no time to interrogate him, however. Elaine headed down the hall toward the front door.

"I just got out of prison after sixteen years," she said. "Governor Pataki sent me to this address. So if there's a problem with that, tell him. File a report, because something has to be done." She gestured around the apartment—at the bare bulbs, the dirty ceiling, the cluttered foyer. "I'm a mother coming home after all these years," she said. "Would you want your children living like this?"

Satara followed the officers out of the apartment. Depending on what her daughter told them, Elaine knew that her life could become much more difficult.

Eventually, the cops left and Satara returned. Apache pulled her into the back bedroom and closed the door.

"I can't believe you let your man call the cops on your mother!" he shouted.

"What did I ever do to warrant this?" Elaine yelled at her. "There's nothing but negativity in this house. You should want something better for you and Tenéa. I didn't come home to put my hands on you and your sister, but y'all don't know what I've been through in the last sixteen years."

Satara stared at her feet. She said nothing. If this incident had occurred a few months earlier, Elaine might have smacked Satara. But on this day, she did not hit anyone. Punching Danae in the face recently had only strained their relationship further. In recent weeks, Elaine had vowed to try harder to contain her rage.

She picked up the telephone and called Officer Camacho. Rule 6 of her Conditions of Release stated, "I will notify my parole officer immediately anytime I am in contact with or arrested by any law-enforcement agency." Elaine knew that once she told him that the police had come to her house, he would start keeping closer tabs on her. This was the last thing she wanted. The more closely a parole officer is watching, the more likely he is to catch his parolee breaking a rule. Elaine wanted Satara to understand this, and to realize that one call to the cops could undo everyone's efforts to free her.

A few days later, Elaine found a crumpled copy of the police report in Satara's bedroom. Under "Victim," she saw Satara's name; under "Suspect," she saw her own. The description of the incident was succinct: "Both parties involved in verbal altercation over bedrooms. Settled w/o incident." Skimming the one-page report, Elaine felt more sad than angry. This pink piece of paper was just another reminder of how tense relations with her family were, and how far they all still had to go.

CHAPTER 30

Nathan Brooks walked into the prison visiting room shortly before 10:00 a.m. on a Sunday in mid-July. He had taken his time getting ready this morning—showering, ironing his shirt, getting dressed—because he knew Choo Choo wouldn't mind waiting. Choo Choo, a childhood friend, was the only person who came to see him. The two were so close that they called each other brothers.

Nate approached the guard at the front desk. "Where's my brother?" he asked.

"Do you have a wife?" the officer asked.

"Yeah."

The officer pointed across the room. "She's over there."

Nate glanced across the room and saw Elaine seated alone at a table in the back, next to a wall of windows. A giant grin spread across his face. Finally, she had come to see him. This was the moment he had been fantasizing about for months, ever since he'd read in the newspaper about her clemency campaign. In every scenario he had imagined, she jumped up, sprinted toward him, and threw herself into his arms.

He hurried toward her. When he reached her table, she did not bother to stand and greet him.

"What took you so long?" she asked, looking up from her chair.

"Can I get some love after all these years?" he asked.

"No," she said. "I'm mad. You took too long to come down. If you take too long like that again, I'm not coming anymore."

Nate waited a couple of moments, but Elaine stayed seated. He bent down and hugged her around the shoulders. Then he sat next to her.

He could see that her hair was still long and brown, just like it had been in 1984. She had put on some pounds, and her eyes looked puffy and stressed. She looked older, he thought, but still beautiful. And he could tell that she had dressed up for their visit. She wore a long, loose-fitting black-and-white dress.

Elaine, for her part, could see that Nate was in excellent shape, muscular and trim from years of prison-yard workouts. He had a shiny bald pate and a neatly trimmed beard; his Afro had disappeared long ago. The wrinkles around his brown eyes gave away his age, but he still looked great. Even in his prison greens, even at age forty, she thought he looked better than any of the men she had met recently.

Nate did not have to ask Elaine why she was angry. He knew. It had little to do with her one-hour wait this morning and everything to do with a letter he had sent her a few weeks before she left Bedford Hills. In that letter, he had told her for the first time that he had married somebody else five years earlier.

Elaine had known that other women visited him, but she certainly did not think he had remarried. When he sent her divorce papers several years ago, she had just stuffed them under her bed. Afterward, he kept writing to her every few days, just like he had before. He never mentioned a new wife. After all these years, she still thought of Nate as her husband.

"Look me in the eyes and tell me what happened," she said. "Don't make no excuses. Just stick to the facts."

"She had cancer and was getting ready to die," he said. "So I asked her, 'Did she want to get married?'"

"C'mon, there's more to it than that. Be a man about it. Just come out and tell me you had feelings for her."

"Yeah, I had feelings for her. Because she was there at a time when I was real vulnerable. I don't know why you wouldn't be happy for me. I'd be happy for you in a situation like that."

After Judge Clyne had sentenced him and Elaine, Nate had been taken to the state prison in Elmira. There, in the visiting room, he had met the sister of another prisoner's girlfriend. She lived in the Bronx, 225 miles away, but she began to visit Nate regularly. When he was transferred to Green Haven, she followed him. Eventually, after nine years of visiting-room dates, they got married and applied for a conjugal visit. Before their first overnight visit, however, she became very ill. She died before she could visit him again.

Once Elaine heard Nate admit the truth about his other relationship, telling the story without any excuses or evasions, she felt slightly less angry. In her heart, however, she still did not forgive him. Maybe that would change with time. Maybe not.

Together, Elaine and Nate sauntered over to the row of vending machines that lined the wall of the visiting room. A strip of yellow tape on the floor about ten feet in front of the machines reminds prisoners that they cannot use the machines themselves. Cash is contraband in prison; getting caught with a dollar bill could get a prisoner sent to solitary confinement.

Nate watched while Elaine bought lunch, sliding a handful of coins into the machines. One bag of popcorn, one bottle of water, three packs of pancakes, one fish sandwich, one chicken sandwich. On a table by the window, they laid down paper napkins and spread out their picnic.

By now, she had already said enough on the phone for him to know that she was unhappy in Apartment 13B. "It's a disgrace," she said. "I don't even want to tell you about it."

"Go ahead and tell me," he said. "I want to go through the same things you have to go through in life. That's what friends are for, partners, husband and wife."

She revealed a few details about how the apartment was filthy, how there was always laundry piled up in the front hall, how Sabrina kept breaking the toilet seats, how instead of buying new rolls of toilet paper when it ran out, everyone just used napkins.

"Why don't you fix that place up?" he asked.

"There's no fixing it up," she said. "I tried that already."

Back in the early 1980s, when they shared the same apartment, Elaine had always been the more volatile one. Whenever Nate angered her—when he stayed out all night, or when she discovered a hotel key in his pocket—she would start swinging her fists. He would grab her arms and try to calm her. If that failed, he would leave the apartment until she cooled off. Now, with him still in prison, she had no one around to confide in and help her control her temper.

On the phone, she had already told him a little bit about Danae acting up in school, cursing out a teacher, and refusing to move home. Now she told him about their latest fight. "I punched Nay-nay in the mouth," she said.

"Why don't you sit down and talk to her?" he asked. "If you hit her, you're going to make her resent you more."

"She is never going to forgive us."

"Why not?"

"She said we abandoned her when she was small."

"As time goes on, she'll heal from that. They have a right to feel angry because we weren't in their life when they were small—taking them to school, waiting for the school bus, picking them up, being at their school plays."

During his years in prison, Nate had received one letter from Satara, but none from Danae. He knew very little about their day-to-day lives, but he still thought about them all the time and kept photos of them in his cell. The civilians he knew who worked at the prison often talked about their own children, about attending basketball games and soccer matches. Listening to their stories, Nate thought about the events in his own daughters' lives that he was missing, all the travails of childhood and adolescence they were enduring without him.

Just as she had inspected Jamel's nails in the visiting room at Rikers Island, now Elaine decided to examine Nate, searching for clues to secrets not yet shared. On the outside of his pinkie finger, she discovered a circular bump.

"Where did you get that scar from?" she asked.

"This is from writing you so much," he said. "That's what the doctor told me."

Besides the callus on his finger, she found only one other curious mark, a scar on the back of one leg from a welding accident long ago.

"Are you finished examining me?" he asked. "What are you inspecting me for? Are you the doctor now?"

He moved his chair around so that he was sitting across from her. Leaning forward, he kissed her face, pressing his lips against her eyelids, her forehead, her cheeks, her mouth. He thought she kissed better now than she used to, but he didn't ask if she had been practicing. The way her body responded to his, he could tell that she needed to be held.

He wrapped his arms around her, never forgetting to keep his butt firmly glued to his chair. It was an awkward embrace, but he knew the rules. NO LAP SITTING/ONE CHAIR PER PERSON read the sign on the officer's desk. Whenever a guard walked by, he let go of her for a moment, just long enough to avoid a reprimand.

"If I get out, we're going to do all the things we never did," he said. "I want to go on a cruise, see the world."

He often preceded talk about the future with the word *if*. He had been in prison too long to assume that he would leave alive. Over the years, he had known quite a few men who had died inside these walls. Five years earlier, a prisoner had killed himself at Green Haven. He'd heard about another man who had been stabbed in the yard a few days before he was supposed to go home.

"After everything we've been through, there's nothing we can't endure," he said.

"We have been through a lot, Nate, haven't we?" she said.

"You're damn right."

Nate led Elaine out of the visiting room and into a small yard dotted with wooden picnic tables. This was the spot where every prison couple came to kiss and grope each other, away from the guards' gaze.

They strolled hand in hand around the perimeter of the yard—a well-worn path than ran next to a metal fence and alongside the cell block used for inmates in protective custody. Trees loomed in the distance, visible above the concrete wall, as if beckoning the prisoners to come join them in the free world. For Nate and Elaine, it was almost like taking a walk in the park, if they shut their eyes and the caged men stopped howling for a moment.

They posed for a few Polaroids in front of a brick wall, next to the door to the visiting room. Before the visit, Elaine had paid two dollars apiece for ten pictures. As the photographer peered through the camera, Nate lifted Elaine's dress to check out her legs.

Until recently, he'd had the job of visiting-room photographer. It was an extremely desirable position, since it allowed access to dozens of prospective girlfriends—all the women who came up to see their brothers or cousins or friends. But when Nate heard Elaine was going home, he had quit his job. He figured she would visit him often, and he wanted to make sure he would be free to see her.

She sat down on a picnic bench in the yard and he lay next to her, his head resting in her lap. She pulled a Newport from her pack.

"You're still smoking?" he asked. "Why are you smoking? You don't got to smoke. Are you stressed?"

She smoked half the cigarette, then stubbed it out. If not for his influence, he thought, she would have smoked three or four.

He liked to give her advice. He told her to stop eating so much junk food and drinking so much coffee. And he told her he had a plan about her love handles. "I'll be your trainer and we'll get rid of them," he said. In the past, he had clipped articles about parenting and mailed them to her. Recently, he had skimmed *Essence* magazine and checked out the latest hairstyles for her. "When I come home, I'm going to take you to the beauty parlor and you're going to cut it," he said.

Eventually, Nate and Elaine returned to their table inside the visiting room. Reaching into the bag of popcorn, he pulled out a handful and began feeding it to her piece by piece. Their conversation swerved from one topic to the next, from the Rockefeller drug laws, to Green Haven's gangs, to Satara and Danae. There were, of course, too many things to talk about and never enough time.

Soon they returned to the one subject that neither of them could forget: the crime that had sent them both to prison.

"Why weren't you man enough to stop me?" she asked.

"Why didn't you listen to me?" he replied.

It was the same exchange they had been having for years, and it always went around and around, without any resolution.

Nate had spent thousands of hours analyzing the past, remembering every event and every mistake that had led to his 25-to-life sentence. What if he had not gone to Albany with her? What if he had thrown George Deets out of the apartment that night? What if he had never moved in with her in the first place? Trying to make sense of the past meant sifting through hundreds of similar questions. Eventually, all of this searching led him back to the beginning—to that first night they had spent together.

"Out of all the dudes, why me?" he asked.

"It was your lips," she said.

"My lips? That's what attracted you to me? You could've had anybody you wanted, and, y'know, just let me be."

"No, I wanted you."

"Yeah, right. You were lucky my mother was living next door to you, or you would've been history. You wouldn't have seen me no more."

"I would've found you."

"You wouldn't have found me. There's a lot of females still looking."

Over the years, Nate had run into several men at Green Haven whom he knew from Harlem. When he told them he was doing 25-to-life for a drug sale, they were always shocked. "Not you!" they said. "Nate, what happened?" Almost no one did that much time for a drug crime, unless he was running a cartel. And these neighborhood acquaintances knew that Nate had never been anything more than a small-time seller. After they heard his story, they always asked the same question: "And you still love her?"

"Yeah," Nate would tell them. "I still love her. She's got my kids.

And to tell you the truth, she was my first love. I ain't gonna lie. She was my first love, meaning a real woman. I had other females, but they were just females I met when I went to a club or a disco. Not like where you have your key and you go home and you've got your woman and your kids. That was kind of big for me at a young age. That's why I say she was my first real love."

By now, Nate had been in prison for almost seventeen years—nearly three times as long as he and Elaine had been together in the outside world. Another man would have stopped talking to his girlfriend if she got him arrested and sent to prison. But Nate had done just the opposite. Loving Elaine had become something of a full-time job for him, between writing her lengthy letters, calling her on the phone, telling his friends about her, and fantasizing about the future. Their relationship helped him cope; loving her was a way to keep himself from descending into bitterness. Now that most of his family had died, all he really had left was her and their children.

"Do you want to get married again?" he asked. It was the same question he had already asked her many times on the phone.

"All right," she said.

"Do you want me to get on my knees?"

"Naw, you don't have to."

Getting married once again was the only way they would be able to spend time alone with each other. Only married couples could apply for a conjugal visit, which consisted of a weekend together inside a trailer on the prison's grounds.

"If the shoe was on the other foot, if I was in jail for you, I would probably want to kill you," she said. "You sure you don't want to get me in the trailer and kill me? It's one thing to go to jail for something you did. It's another thing to go because you're in love. That's a hell of a love."

"As much as I loved my mother, I would've never done this much time for her," he said. "So I got to love you twice as much."

They talked so much, they forgot to eat, and soon the guards announced the end of visiting hours. It was 2:30 p.m., less than five hours after their reunion began. There was still plenty of food—an untouched sandwich, a half-eaten bag of popcorn. They stood and hugged each other tightly. Turning his mouth to her ear, he whispered, "I want to go home with you."

She could feel these seven words in every part of her body, like a pain shooting through her, fueled not by pity so much as by memory. She knew exactly how powerless and frustrated and defeated he felt. In some ways, they knew each other better than anyone else. They had both endured the sort of pain and sadness that is impossible to describe. They both knew what it felt like to lose a mother while stuck behind bars, then arrive at her funeral in handcuffs.

He did not ask her when she would come back to see him, and she made no promises. Perhaps the future would hold a prison wedding and trailer visits, too. She did not want to spend any more days in prison, but she also did not want to be away from him. Whatever happened, she knew she could not erase him from her heart. Being with him in the visiting room—feeling his beard scratching against her cheeks, his fingers stroking her hair—she was the happiest she had been since the day she left Bedford Hills.

After a few more minutes, they pulled themselves apart and headed in opposite directions. He joined the line of prisoners on the ramp leading toward the cell blocks. She stood with the other inmates' relatives, next to the officer's desk. They gazed at each other across the room, her waving, him blowing kisses. Tomorrow, she vowed, she would visit him again.

CHAPTER 31

Elaine had always told herself that as soon as she was released from prison, she would resume Yvonne's tradition of cooking huge holiday meals. July Fourth and Labor Day passed without her taking charge; her sister Michelle organized those family events. But as Thanksgiving approached, Elaine finally felt ready to have the sort of party Yvonne used to throw. For her, this Thanksgiving would mark the end of a seventeen-year wait. When she had gone to Albany in 1983, expecting to earn $2,500, she had planned to use part of that money to buy food for Thanksgiving.

Now, before she could make any preparations, she had to raise funds for the feast. Elaine turned to Gary Williams, her newest suitor. "I'm sure I can get him for fifty or one hundred dollars," she said. She had no qualms about asking him or any other friends for money; after all, whenever she had extra money, she loaned or gave it to just about anybody who asked. When she told Gary about her Thanksgiving plans, he handed her $200. Apache gave her another $200, and Elaine dipped into her meager savings.

Elaine had met Gary a few months earlier through a friend at her job. Gary, too, had recently come home from prison; he'd spent four years locked up for selling crack. Hanging out with him constituted a parole violation, but this did not deter Elaine. Gary was thirty-five years old, eight years younger than she. Elaine liked him because she felt like he understood her plight. After all, he had almost as many problems as she did. His wife was in the hospital, and he was taking care of her elderly mother and her two children.

In the late summer, Elaine had gone back to Green Haven five times to see Nate. Every visit had cost her nearly $100, including the van ride, snacks, and Polaroids, plus a contribution to his commissary account. As the months passed, her visits became less frequent. Her shortage of money was part of the reason, but there was also another reason. In her heart, she still had not forgiven Nate for lying to her all those years about marrying somebody else. She rarely talked about this betrayal, but it upset her whenever she thought about it.

A few weeks before Thanksgiving, she decided she would cook her meal in Apartment 13B—instead of at Michelle's home—in order to make sure that Sabrina was included. Celebrating Thanksgiving in this apartment would require buying not only food but also a table and chairs, as well as pots and pans. At K-mart, she found a table and four chairs for $159. She sent Sabrina's daughter Star to the store to buy bathroom supplies: a foam toilet seat, an aqua rug, and a plastic shower curtain decorated with aqua fish.

By Thanksgiving day, Apartment 13B did indeed look better than usual. The sheet in the living room doorway was gone. There was no stroller packed with dirty laundry blocking the hall. There were no half-eaten cartons of Chinese takeout littering the kitchen. The aroma of roast turkey filled the apartment and wafted into the building's hallway. Platters, bowls, pans, and foil tins covered every surface, including the new kitchen table, two card tables, the kitchen counter, the windowsill, and the top of the refrigerator.

There was enough food for fifty people: two turkeys, two ducks, roast beef, roast pork, a ham decorated with cherries and pineapple, a giant platter of shrimp with cocktail sauce, green salad, potato salad, macaroni salad, macaroni and cheese, stuffing, rice, yams, collard greens, turnips, and sliced tomatoes. There were also eight sweet potato pies and five peach cobblers, all made but still needing to be baked once the oven was free.

To prepare this feast, Elaine, Satara, and Apache had stayed up cooking until 5:00 a.m. At 12:30 p.m. on Thanksgiving Day, Elaine stood next to the stove, checking on a pot of turnips. Apache was asleep in his room. Satara slumped in a chair in the kitchen, looking as if she, too, might doze off.

Cooking this meal had taken all night, in part because the oven was just one foot wide. Only one dish fit inside at a time. By now, Elaine was expert at cooking with a tiny stove; she had been doing it for years at Bedford Hills. At the moment, she was baking a sponge cake on the stove top, using an old prison method: She had poured the batter into a cookie tin, then placed it atop a pan filled with boiling water.

A rottweiler puppy sprinted from the back bedroom into the kitchen and began licking grease off the front of the oven. Two months earlier, Lora and her boyfriend had given Elaine this puppy as a present for her forty-third birthday. Elaine had named her Kyra. Parole rules stipulated that she could not own a rottweiler. If Camacho ever asked about the dog, she planned to say that it belonged to one of her children.

She reached down, grabbed Kyra around the collar, and led her next door to give her a bath. Fifteen minutes later, she returned, carrying the wet dog wrapped in a towel.

"You've got some nerve to hold that damn dog like a baby," Sabrina said.

As soon as Elaine let go of the dog, she scurried toward the chair in the living room where Sabrina sat. "Get the hell out of here!" Sabrina said.

Elaine picked up the dog. "This is my baby," she said.

"Everybody's got to have somebody," said Sabrina, rolling her eyes. "I've got me."

Elaine fetched a plastic comb, then began working on Sabrina's tangled hair. Today, Sabrina seemed a little better than usual—more animated and less depressed. She wore a red T-shirt and a pair of light blue pajama bottoms decorated with pink stars and purple moons. On her lower right leg she had a white bandage. Recently, she had gone to the hospital with an abscess on the side of her leg. After several days, she had discharged herself, walking about a mile back to the apartment, dressed only in hospital pajamas and slippers.

At 2:00 p.m., Elaine headed into the bathroom to take a shower. The dog followed. When Elaine reappeared, she was wearing black knee-high boots, white nylons held up by garters, a black hip-hugging skirt, a sparkly silver top, and a gray zip-up sweater with fake fur around the hood and wrists.

"My mother looks like a cross between *Charlie's Angels* and Glenn Close in *101 Dalmatians*," said Apache, who had just woken up.

He slipped on an oven mitt and checked the turkey. The night before, he had employed a trick he had learned from Yvonne: He'd talked to the birds. "You're pretty," he had whispered. "You're going to be beautiful." His words seemed to have worked. The turkeys did indeed look tasty.

"Sabrina, come out!" Elaine shouted at the bathroom door. "C'mon, y'all! We're getting ready to eat."

Elaine had to be at work by 4:00 p.m., so she had decided to serve dinner early, just before 3:00 p.m. She picked up a knife and sliced a leg off the turkey, then squatted down and placed it on the floor. "Happy Thanksgiving, baby," she said. Sabrina stopped ladling food onto her plate long enough to look over at the dog gnawing on the turkey leg.

"When I come back," Sabrina said, "I want to come back as a dog."

"We didn't bless the food," Apache said.

"We're all here," Elaine said. "That's a blessing."

Gesturing to the dog, Apache asked, "Do you want me to get that rat a soda?"

"No," Elaine said.

She piled food onto paper plates for Apache, Satara, and Tenéa. And she filled a large metal tin with dinner for the dog. By now, there were sixteen people inside Apartment 13B, including assorted friends and relatives.

At 3:15 p.m., Gary walked in. He wore a tan suit with a handkerchief tucked in the breast pocket, a diamond on a chain around his neck, a gold hoop in one ear, and a wedding ring.

"Go ahead," Elaine said. "Wash your hands and take your coat off."

While Elaine prepared him a plate, Gary pointed a disposable camera at her. "I just took a picture of your butt," he said, flashing a mischievous grin. Elaine shot him a look of annoyance, but it was easy to see she was only pretending.

There was not enough room for everyone to sit down, so they scattered around the apartment. Most people balanced paper plates on their laps or in their palms. Elaine ate in the living room. Apache stood by the stove. Satara sat on a chair in the apartment's hallway, next to an unplugged television and a laundry basket full of plastic toys. Sabrina ate alone at the kitchen table, then fell asleep in the living room in front of *One Life to Live*.

Elaine served seconds to whoever wanted them, then covered the tins and plates with foil. There was enough food left over for at least forty people. Elaine had expected her sister Michelle to come down from Harlem with ten or so family members, but there was no sign of them. She had been hoping Danae would come, too.

"Tara," Elaine shouted down the hall. "Call Nay-nay and ask her if she thinks she could find her way over here and spend a little time with her mother before I have to go to work."

By 3:45 p.m., Danae had still not arrived. Elaine picked up the phone and dialed Project Renewal. "Gordon, this is Bartlett," she said. "I'll be there. So if I'm not there right at four, don't panic."

Elaine turned to one of Danae's friends. "Did you call Nay-nay?" she asked.

"Yeah," the friend reported. "She's asleep."

Elaine did not grab the phone and call Danae herself. She did not stomp over to her daughter's other home. She felt hurt that Danae had not shown up, but there was no point in getting angry anymore. "By the time she gets here," Elaine said. "I'll be gone."

It was nearly the end of her first Thanksgiving since leaving prison, and the event had not come close to resembling the family dinners she remembered from childhood. The dishes were the same, but nothing else felt familiar or festive. Even with all this food—even with "Happy Thanksgiving" napkins and a new kitchen curtain decorated with cows, pigs, and ducks—something was not quite right. Nobody bickered, but nobody laughed, either.

All the hours of cleaning and cooking could not mask the misery that permeated this apartment. If Yvonne had still been alive, she would have been able to lure everybody here. But Michelle and her family were missing, and so was Danae. Jamel, at least, had a good excuse. He was in Mt. McGregor prison, north of Albany, where he had recently begun a 2-to-4-year sentence. And Nate, of course, was still at Green Haven, where he had just started year eighteen.

Elaine had done all she could to make the holiday a success, and now there was no time to ponder how it had all turned out. She had a job to get to. At 4:15 p.m., she headed down the corridor to the back bedroom. When she returned, she wore a long winter coat and the same black knit hat that she had worn on the morning she left Bedford Hills.

"Bye," she said. "I gotta go."

She walked out the apartment door and headed for the elevator. Gary, carrying her scarf and pocketbook, followed close behind.

CHAPTER 32

Two days before New Year's Eve, Elaine sat beside Gary in the front seat of his wife's Nissan, riding north on the FDR Drive. Suddenly, she felt the car swerve to the left. Her body slammed against the passenger door. Through the windshield, she saw they were heading straight toward the guardrail. The next thing she knew, she was on her back in the rear of an ambulance, the sound of sirens in her ears.

The ambulance took her to New York–Presbyterian Hospital on East Sixty-eighth Street. The first relative to arrive at the hospital was Danae. As soon as she saw Elaine, she began sobbing uncontrollably. Michelle and her husband showed up next. When Michelle saw Elaine, she too became hysterical. Elaine's face was swollen, bloody, almost unrecognizable. Her front teeth were gone.

"It's all right, Michelle," Elaine said. "I can still move my mouth."

"Don't say it's all right," Michelle said. "You haven't seen a mirror yet."

Gary walked into the room. He was a little rumpled, but otherwise he looked fine. "What the fuck happened?" Michelle shouted at him. "Why don't your face look like hers?"

A look of terror crossed Gary's face.

"If you don't get the fuck out of here, I'm going to beat the shit out of you!"

"Calm down, Michelle," Elaine mumbled.

"I finally get my sister home after sixteen years, just to have you almost kill her?" Michelle hollered. "Get your retarded ass out of here!"

Gary disappeared. Meanwhile, other people arrived: Lora, Apache, his friend Spider. Slowly, they managed to piece together the story of Elaine's accident: Gary had lost control of the car, swerving across a lane and smashing into a guardrail. The collision had deployed Elaine's air bag, and now everyone could see the results.

"It's going to take you a while to recover from that," Pervis, Michelle's husband, said. "You're pretty messed up there, girl."

"I look all right," Elaine insisted.

Michelle held up a mirror so Elaine could see her face. "Oh, my God," Elaine said. "I ain't all right."

Later that night, Elaine's family took her to Michelle's apartment. Elaine spent the next few days drinking liquids and popping painkillers. Her face was so swollen that her nieces and nephews dubbed her "Elephant Man." A doctor told her that she had fractured several facial bones.

While in prison, she had dreamed of spending her first New Year's Eve in Times Square, blowing on a horn and watching the ball drop. Instead, she passed the hours on Michelle's sofa, staring at the television, watching other people celebrating in Times Square. She held a piña colada in one hand. With her other hand, she pressed an ice pack against her face.

The next week, Elaine had several appointments with doctors, but she had nobody to take her to them. So she went by herself, riding the subway alone, carrying a backpack stuffed with medical documents. She had Oxford Health insurance through her job, but it never occurred to her to show her insurance card to the doctors she visited. She was not even sure exactly how health insurance worked.

The only good thing that came out of this accident was the possibility of a payday. Jerome Marks, a retired judge who had become an anti–Rockefeller drug law activist, called Elaine to check on her. After hearing the story of her crash, he suggested she sue the car's owner. He even steered her to one of his lawyer friends. Until he called, she had not known she could bring a lawsuit.

By mid-January, Elaine's face looked much better, though she still did not have any front teeth. She had used up one week of her vacation and one week of sick leave. If she didn't go back to work soon, she would have to go on disability, and her income would shrink substantially. She returned to Project Renewal in the third week of January. When she walked into the lobby, the residents crowded around her and applauded.

A few days later, Elaine moved from Michelle's apartment back downtown to the Wald Houses. Several hours after she arrived, Sabrina became sick. She swayed back and forth, sliding in and out of consciousness. Elaine did not know exactly what was wrong, but she thought maybe the abscess on Sabrina's leg had become infected. She called 911, and Sabrina spent the next two weeks in Beth Israel.

One evening in early February, a few days after Sabrina returned home, she seemed more incoherent than usual. She threw Kool-Aid all over the living room, then defecated in the hall. Elaine thought Sabrina was having a bad reaction to the anti-HIV meds she had just started taking. Elaine dialed 911 again, then rode in the ambulance with Sabrina to the hospital.

It was nearly 3:00 a.m. by the time Elaine returned to the apartment, cleaned up the mess, and went to bed. Five hours later, she walked into work. After her shift ended, she returned to Beth Israel to check on Sabrina. A doctor told Elaine that Sabrina had been poisoned. He said she might have ingested antifreeze. Drinking antifreeze might seem an odd way to attempt suicide, but it is not uncommon.

Elaine did not believe the doctor. "We don't have a car," she said. "Where did she get antifreeze? She hasn't been anywhere except the methadone clinic. And we didn't find anything when we cleaned up her room. If she had anything, we would have found it in her pockets."

Apparently, there was evidence of ethylene glycol, the chemical in antifreeze, in Sabrina's blood. This same chemical is also found in detergents and cleaning supplies. To Elaine, the idea that Sabrina had tried to kill herself by drinking a poisonous liquid made no sense. Elaine thought that if Sabrina really wanted to end her life, she would have done something more extreme. "She would have jumped off a bridge," Elaine said, "or thrown herself in front of a bus."

That night, when Elaine got back to the apartment, she told the rest of the family that Sabrina's situation was dire. "Hope for the best and prepare for the worst," she said. When Elaine returned to the hospital the next night, she brought along Sabrina's daughter Star, Satara, and Satara's boyfriend. Sabrina was now in the Respiratory Isolation Unit. On their way to her room, they walked by several half-covered patients, their wasted bodies visible behind glass doors.

The halls in this part of the hospital were so quiet that the only sound was the nurses' rubber soles padding down the corridor. Sabrina had been given a room of her own with a sliding glass door. A white sheet covered her body. Only her face and the soles of her feet were visible. Elaine slid on a surgical mask, pulled the door open, and walked inside. Satara took a mask, too, then hesitated for a few moments before joining her. Sabrina's daughter and Satara's boyfriend stayed outside the room.

After all those years Elaine had spent fighting to get her life back, now here she was with her younger sister, who seemed determined to end her own. Sabrina's eyes were closed. The only part of her that moved was her chest, the crisp white sheet rising and falling with each breath. She was in a coma, and nobody knew for certain if she would ever come out of it. Elaine stood next to the bed, her fingers wrapped around Sabrina's. With her other hand, she reached up and smoothed her sister's hair.

CHAPTER 33

Elaine attended ten anti–Rockefeller drug law events during her first year out of prison. The largest was a 3,000-person march at the state capitol in Albany. Perhaps the most memorable was a one-day bus trip to Washington, D.C., organized by Randy Credico. Elaine and a few dozen activists attended a hearing in a Senate office building, then went to an event at Howard University School of Law. At 9:00 p.m., they made one final stop—at a liquor store, where Randy picked up a jug of cheap wine—and then they all headed home on a bus.

After an hour or two, it became apparent that the bus driver did not know his way back to New York. He got lost in Pennsylvania, then again in Delaware. The longer the ride took, the worse the bus smelled. The driver had cranked up the heat, and the odor of everyone's sweat filled the air. Every time somebody opened the door to get to the toilet in the back, the stench of urine and feces drifted out. Finally, the bus arrived in Manhattan just before 5:00 a.m. The ride had taken twice as long as it should have.

Elaine had to be at work in three hours, but she did not complain. Despite all the logistical snafus, her faith in Randy had not flagged.

After all, she thought, if not for him and his rallies, she would still be in prison.

In some ways, Elaine needed Randy just as much as he needed her. When everything else in her life seemed to be going wrong, anti–drug law events gave her a sense of purpose. By showing up and giving speeches at his rallies, she felt as if she was accomplishing something.

On the last day of February, Elaine left the apartment shortly after 11:00 a.m. The temperature was only thirty degrees, and a strong wind made the air feel ten degrees colder. It was the sort of day when most people stayed indoors, but Elaine had a rally to get to.

She walked over to Avenue D, wearing a short black skirt with a slit in the back. Her dog had chewed up her only pair of panty hose and now she needed a new pair. She strode into a bodega and found the panty hose near the front, next to the Sunny Delight. She bought one pair, then walked out and flagged down a taxi going south.

Sitting in the backseat, she ripped open the package, hung the hose around her neck, and tugged on both ends. Then she slid off her boots and lifted her skirt. "I know they made these cabs smaller," she said, wiggling into the nylons, her knees banging the seat in front of her. "You ain't got no damn room in them." By the time she got both of her legs jammed into the hose, the taxi had crossed the Williamsburg Bridge and was zipping along the Brooklyn-Queens Expressway.

Randy had decided to stage this day's protest in front of the Queens County Courthouse because it held the office of Richard A. Brown. Brown was the district attorney of Queens. In recent weeks, he had been defending the Rockefeller drug laws in the media on behalf of the state's prosecutors.

Elaine's taxi pulled up in front of the courthouse at 12:30 p.m., a half hour after the rally was scheduled to start. A crowd of sixty people huddled together on a sidewalk, surrounded by wooden police barricades. It was a surprisingly large turnout for such a cold and windy day.

Elaine recognized some of the people. There was Tony Papa, the former prisoner who had helped Randy start these rallies; Grandpa Al Lewis, who wore green wool pants and puffed on a cigar; and, of course, Randy himself, who was wearing only a thin suit and a yellow tie.

Elaine scanned the crowd, searching for Donna Charles. At Bedford Hills, Donna had been one of her closest friends. Finally, the governor had granted Donna's request for clemency, and she had been released a month earlier. Elaine had spoken to her on the telephone, but she had not seen her yet.

Randy stood at one end of the crowd, a microphone in one hand. "How many people know who Richard Brown is?" he asked. Nobody raised a hand. "Mr. Brown runs against nobody," he hollered toward the courthouse. "He's not accountable to anybody. Well, four years from now, you will be held accountable. We're going to be out here once a week for the next four years!"

Randy actually had no intention of staging weekly protests here, criticizing the district attorney. But he never let the facts get in the way of one of his anti-prosecutor rants. "We are going to show the skeletons in the closet!" he yelled. "We know where they're buried: Attica! Green Haven! Wende!"

Eight cops stood nearby, and a few courthouse employees watched from the building's steps. From a distance, this rally did not look very impressive: just a smattering of shivering people clutching well-worn posters. But the real purpose of this event had less to do with drawing a big crowd and more to do with getting media attention. And, indeed, there were a few reporters and photographers milling around.

"You are a fraud, and this is a fraudulent prosecution of the laws! Ninety-five percent are blacks and Latinos!" Randy shouted toward the district attorney's office. "Come out here and face your accusers! You're going to hear a lot of stories today. We're going to bring up Elaine Bartlett, who did sixteen years in prison. Sixteen years! She'll tell you about the Rockefeller drug laws."

"C'mon, Elaine!" one woman shouted.

Elaine made her way to the front of the crowd, carrying a poster with a photo of Nate. A few days ago, she had received a new set of front teeth, replacing the ones that had been knocked out in her car crash. Now she was feeling more confident than she had in a while. Randy handed her the microphone.

"Good afternoon, everybody," she said. "I'm a mother of four children. At the age of twenty-six, I agreed to deliver a package for a friend. When I got arrested, my friend got arrested with his friend, me, and my husband. Me and my husband went to jail. I was sentenced to twenty to life. First offender, never been in trouble before, never had any dealings with the law, never had a traffic ticket or anything.

"But the judge gave me twenty to life. My children were ten, six, three, and one. No one cared about them or what was going to happen to them. I was lucky enough to have a mother that stepped up and raised them, to prevent them from going to foster care. But how many mothers are in prison and their children have to go through the foster care system? In foster care, kids get abused, misused, or mistreated. No one cares about that."

. Elaine never had a prepared speech with her when she attended these rallies. She liked to speak, she said, "straight from the heart." At this rally, most of her sentences resembled ones she had uttered at earlier events. What had changed over the months was her tone. As she became more comfortable with a microphone in her hand, she spoke longer and louder, with more confidence and more outrage.

"Y'all spend all this money to send us to prison, instead of putting it back into the communities," she said. "They could have educated me. They could have had me doing community service, working with young kids, so they wouldn't have to go through what I went through. The fact is, they'd rather warehouse us and treat us like cattle and spend that money on building more prisons. You're building more prisons because you're creating jobs for people living upstate. What about us? What about us that are coming out of these communities and coming back? You have just as much drugs out here now as you did sixteen years ago, when I went to jail."

"More!" someone shouted from the crowd. "More!"

"And even more," she continued. "You talk about drug enforcement. You talk about you need all this money to prevent the drugs coming here. We're not the ones bringing them to this country. We're not the ones putting them out here on these streets. We're not the ones that are educated enough to be in these laboratories with these chemicals, coming up with crack cocaine and everything else you come up with."

Another ex-prisoner might have been nervous about publicly criticizing the government while still on parole, but Elaine wasn't. "I thank Pataki for giving me clemency and giving everyone else that has received clemency," she said. "But that's not enough. We want more. We want you to change these laws. Do away with these Rockefeller laws, because the only thing you are doing is destroying families. The only thing you're doing is incarcerating our kids, as well as us. When I was in front of that judge, he made it seem like I was the last thing on this earth. He made it seem like I had no life. Like I was nobody.

"When we do come out, our struggle still goes on because now we are labeled. No matter where we go, we have to carry this with us. If you have a felony conviction, you can't even get public housing now because it's against the law to be in the projects with a felony conviction. So what are we going to do? Where are we supposed to live? And where are we supposed to go? Are we supposed to carry these burdens for the rest of our lives?

"The Rockefeller laws—what are they really about? What is prison really about? You talk about rehabilitation. Rehabilitation comes from within the individual, because there is no rehabilitation in prison. We're looked at as a number. For sixteen years, I was looked at as 84-G-0068. That's not who I am, and that's not who I plan to be."

Elaine paused. She took a breath. "And with that," she said, "I'll give the mike to Grandpa."

"Yeaaaaah!" The sound of gloved hands clapping rose from the crowd.

Elaine's smile was so wide, she appeared to be glowing. After sixteen years of being told she was a felon, a number, a menace to society, it felt great to see friends and strangers applauding her. And after sixteen years of feeling silenced, it felt good to know that so many people cared what she had to say.

For her, rallies like this one were always an ego boost. No longer was she just another criminal who had tried to make money illegally. Here, she was considered a victim of overly punitive laws, a survivor, even a celebrity. These rallies had enabled her to reinvent herself in a way that made her feel proud: Now she considered herself a political activist.

All those years she'd spent in prison, reading and rereading her trial transcript, fuming about George Deets, her crime had seemed like the ultimate tragedy. But now she no longer felt as if her years behind bars had been a total waste. By giving speeches at events like this one, she had transformed the story of her crime and punishment into a political tool, one that she could now use to help others win their freedom.

These rallies were a necessary form of therapy for Elaine, a way to release her rage without using her fists. They were also about revenge. These anti–drug law events—and the media coverage they sparked— were her way to strike back at everyone: Judge Clyne, George Deets, the state police, the guards who had shown her disrespect, the prison administrators who had underestimated her.

Each newspaper article in which she was quoted sent a message back to Bedford Hills. It didn't matter if only one or two people read it. Word would get around. Everyone would hear that Elaine Bartlett was thriving.

It was too cold and too windy to stay outdoors for long, and by 12:45 p.m. nearly all the journalists had left. A volunteer collected the posters in a garbage bag. Just as Elaine was considering leaving, she noticed a woman walking toward her, dreadlocks piled atop her head. "I'm going to kick your behind!" Elaine shouted at her. When she got closer, the two women embraced. Finally, her friend Donna Charles had arrived.

"You look terrific," Randy said.

"I was all the way over by Sutphin Boulevard," Donna said. She had gone to the wrong courthouse, wandered around looking for the rally, finally reached Randy on his cell phone, then got back on the train.

"Look at you!" Elaine said.

"Elaine, I don't believe it," Donna said. "I was on the subway, looking stupid. But I said, I'm going to get there."

"There's a diner over there," said Randy, whose lips were nearly blue. "We've got to keep moving. I can't stand here any longer."

Elaine linked her arm around Donna's and the two women followed the rest of the crowd. Here they were, in the middle of Queens, far from Bedford Hills, no longer wearing their prison greens. Giggling together and leaning against one another, they looked like sisters, as if they had known each other forever. It was a reunion that had existed for many years only in their imaginations.

"Coconut, did you ever think we'd be crossing the street together?" Elaine asked. "All those years of walking up and down that same damn hill."

After all they had endured, the act of marching arm in arm across a freezing boulevard felt like a triumph. Inside the diner, they settled into chairs at a table near the back.

"Oh Lainey, oh my God," Donna said. "Who would have believed this?"

"I know," Elaine said.

On a borrowed cell phone, Elaine called Project Renewal. She asked a coworker to search in her desk drawer for a piece of paper with a phone number. The number belonged to her newest suitor, who she hoped would drive her back to Manhattan.

"You got to see this one," Elaine said. "This one is a Muslim."

"When you met him?" Donna asked.

"About two weeks ago."

"Been hanging with him ever since?"

"No, I ain't been hanging with him since. There's several. He can't get all of mine."

"C'mon, who do you think you're talking to?"

Elaine assured Donna that the answer to her unasked question was no; she was not having sex with anyone. "Not yet," Elaine said. "I'm not. I'm not. I haven't found the one that I want to say, 'Take it off.' " Both women erupted in laughter.

Their lives were similar enough that Elaine could imagine how Donna's first days out of prison had gone. Like Elaine, Donna had a son behind bars. And like Elaine, Donna was a new grandmother. Her twenty-year-old daughter had a twenty-month-old son. Elaine knew the whole family. Her children had grown up with Donna's children in the visiting room at Bedford Hills.

"I went to my P.O., and she said I can't go see my son," Donna said. "It's kind of rough. I've been crying a lot. When you get out here, it's not like people say it is. Everyone just says, 'Don't worry. You're going to be out. You're going to be all right.' "

"It ain't like that, but you'll be all right," Elaine said. "You got a résumé, right?"

"Yeah."

"Give me a copy of your résumé."

"I thought you told me to go to South Forty."

"I was going to send you to South Forty, but I'm going to see if I can get you in here."

"Where you're at?"

"Yeah. I'm going to see what I can do."

At the moment, Donna was living at the Providence House in Richmond Hill, Queens. Elaine thought they should move into a place together with their children.

"You know, I'm getting ready to get a house," Elaine said. "I'm looking for one. The money they want me to spend on a three- to four-bedroom apartment, I might as well get a two- or three-family house and rent one floor out."

"I got to get a job first," Donna said. "I can't pay rent without a job."

A waitress set down a grilled cheese sandwich in front of Donna. She gave Elaine a cup of cream of turkey soup. Finally, they were eating a meal together some place other than a prison mess hall.

Thirteen months had passed since Elaine left Bedford Hills, and she still cared what the women there thought of her. Nine weeks earlier, *The Village Voice* had published a lengthy article about all she had endured during her first year out of prison. She did not mail the story to her friends at Bedford Hills, but she knew they would all read it.

"One day, everybody was talking about the article, and they said it was in the library," Donna said. "I couldn't get it. But one day I finally got the whole newspaper. That night, I went upstairs, took my shower, went in my room, and laid down in bed. Elaine, when I read that article, I thought, Oh, my God! I can't deal with Elaine out there struggling."

Elaine had received many letters from her friends in prison during her first months home, but she had not replied to any of them. "Everybody was saying, 'Why isn't Elaine writing?'" Donna said. "And I said, 'Listen, we don't know how tough it is out there. We can't sit here and say she's not writing. You don't know until you get there. When she got there, maybe it was so hectic, she couldn't do anything.'"

"After the article came out, what did they say then?" Elaine asked.

"Then they said, 'Oh, my God,' That's when I got scared. I said, 'Oh shit.' Everybody's telling me, 'You're going to be all right. You're going to be all right.' But I said, 'Elaine is telling the real deal here. This is the real deal.' To tell you the truth, I got scared. I said, 'My God. That's what I'm going out there to?'"

Donna explained that she had been happy on her first night home—she had gone out to dinner at McDonald's and had a Big Mac and large fries—but that ever since she had been depressed and overwhelmed. Trekking to the parole office. Trying to obtain an ID card. Baby-sitting for her daughter. Looking for a job.

Elaine told Donna about her first months home, too, about going on job interviews and traveling to Rikers Island. She explained that Jamel had pleaded guilty in exchange for a 2-to-4-year sentence and was now upstate in Mt. McGregor prison.

"I think they have board at Mt. McGregor today," Elaine said. "If they have a board, he goes to the board today. So we'll wait and see what happens."

If the parole board approved Jamel's release, he would finally be coming home. It would be the best news Elaine had heard since she found out that she had received clemency. She did not have to explain all of this, however. Donna understood.

What does freedom look like? Four hundred days after leaving prison, Elaine was still sharing a bed with Apache. She now had a small wardrobe, but she had to keep it in plastic bags, since there was no room in his closet. She had received a promotion at work, but she still earned less than $20,000 a year. To save money, she often ate just one meal a day, and carried a Hershey bar in her purse to nibble on when she was hungry.

The biggest news story of the last year was the presidential election and the Florida recount, which had dragged on for weeks. Technically Elaine was free, but she still could not vote. In New York State, everyone who is in prison or on parole is denied the right to vote. It did not matter that Elaine knew more about politics than most people. She still had to watch the presidential election from the sidelines.

Elaine had made it through her first year on parole without getting sent back to jail, but she still had at least two more years to go. In some ways, she was doing much better than the average parolee: She had held a job for nine months and had never failed a drug test. She was still supervised by Officer Camacho, and they continued to have a good relationship. Nevertheless, the possibility that she could go back to jail never strayed far from her thoughts.

On a recent morning, Officer Camacho had gone to Apartment 13B and discovered a young man in the doorway, standing in a cloud of marijuana smoke, a blunt in one hand. He was the boyfriend of Sabrina's daughter. At the time, Elaine was not home. Camacho later told her there had been so much smoke that he thought he was going to get a buzz. He could have ordered her to move immediately, but he knew she had nowhere to go. "I hope you're not smoking with those kids," he said. "You need to get out of there."

Like most parolees, she did not follow all of parole's rules all the time. Sometimes she stayed out past curfew. And she had skipped a few parole appointments. Camacho had not locked her up for these lapses, but she knew that another parole officer might have.

The only good thing about not having moved anywhere yet was that she had not had to switch parole officers. Recently, however, Camacho had told her he was going to be promoted. She had heard enough horror stories about other parole officers to be nervous about whom she might get next.

She still spoke to Nate regularly on the telephone, but she had not been back to Green Haven to see him in several months. And she still had not decided whether to remarry him. Meanwhile, flirting with other men was no longer as much fun as it once had been. Her relationship with Gary had fizzled after their car accident. And she was not too excited about the Muslim man who had been calling recently. She had been home for more than a year, and so far, she had not met anyone who came close to matching her prison fantasies. "Men were better in my mind," she said.

Elaine had a few friends at her job, and she sometimes saw Lora Tucker. Most of the time, though, she felt very alone, as if she were surrounded by people who could not possibly understand her. In her purse, she carried letters from friends at Bedford Hills. She also carried around the piece of cloth from Betty Tyson's prison coat, which Betty had given her several years before as a goodbye gift.

The only people Elaine knew who could empathize with her were other women from Bedford Hills, but she did not want to hang out with too many of them. Socializing with ex-prisoners violated parole's rules, and even if it had not, she had no desire to sit around and talk about the past. Seeing Donna at the rally had lifted her spirits for a few hours, but it did not erase her loneliness.

Elaine wondered if she would ever recover from her years in prison, if she would ever be able to rid herself of her frustration and anger, sadness and guilt. Maybe she could paper over them with successes—her own apartment, another promotion, a few more nice outfits—but she worried that these accomplishments were only temporary morale boosts, that they would never really erase all the pain inside her.

Every week or so, Elaine went to see her sister Sabrina in the hospital. The sight of her, immobile and attached to a machine, was so upsetting that Elaine had stopped going to visit her alone. Some nights, Elaine found being in Apartment 13B equally depressing. Her frayed relations with her daughters, especially Danae, felt like yet another form of punishment, one that she knew she could not easily escape.

Ever since she'd left prison, she had been trying to undo some of the damage her absence had caused. Progress was slow, if it came at all, and usually she just felt frustrated. "After being away for sixteen years, you come home and you're a complete stranger to your family," she said. "They love you, but they're angry with you at the same time because of everything they went through in those sixteen years and you weren't there. You can't get the birthdays back. You can't get the graduations back. You can't get the nights they laid up crying, wanting mommy, and she was nowhere to be found. You can't get them years back. No matter what you do in life, you can never go back."

PART FOUR

A Second Homecoming
2001–2003

Apartment 13B was more crowded than usual on the morning of Tuesday, April 3. Satara stood in front of the stove, flipping pancakes. Elaine sat at the kitchen table. Danae and two friends waited in the living room, their book bags on the floor. "I thought he'd be here by now," Elaine said. Every time she heard a noise in the building's hallway, her head snapped toward the front door. "Where is that boy?" she asked. "He's got us all waiting on him."

At the end of February, the parole board had approved Jamel's release from prison. Not long afterward, he had been moved to Edgecombe, a work-release facility in Washington Heights, at the northern end of Manhattan. Prison officials had transferred him closer to home in order to ease his transition back into the world. During the day, prisoners in work-release facilities are allowed out so they can look for a job.

Jamel had told his family that today he would be allowed to leave, but it was nearly 10:00 a.m. and he had not yet appeared. "I don't know what happened, unless they didn't let him out," Elaine said. "I bet he's tight right now."

For the last several weeks, Jamel's homecoming had been the talk of the apartment. Everyone was excited about his return from prison, but not everyone was optimistic about his prospects of staying out. "He's going to come out and do right," Elaine often said, prompting Satara to roll her eyes. Satara had already seen Jamel come home from jail many times, then go right back. For years, she had been hearing stories about him—about his crimes, his temper, his brawls with jail guards.

"You don't know your son," Satara said, a spatula in one hand. "When you hear stories about him, you probably say in your head, 'He didn't do that.'"

"How do you know what I think?" Elaine asked.

Satara paused. "You were probably like that yourself," she said.

Elaine whirled around and glared at Satara. Her daughter's words felt like a smack across the face. Nobody said anything for a moment or two.

Danae walked into the kitchen. "You're lucky Mommy came home and saved your ass," she said to Satara. "You were one step from the dungeon." To make her point, Danae rattled off the evidence: A year ago, Satara hadn't been combing her hair, hadn't gotten dressed every morning, rarely smiled. Ever since their mother returned from prison, Satara had undergone a transformation.

"You look much better," Danae said.

"I look the same," Satara said. "I always had my hair done."

"You look much better," Elaine and Danae said in unison.

Apache entered the kitchen. "You used to walk around here like the mummy," he said, referring to Satara's past habit of keeping a sheet wrapped around her all day. Danae took a couple of stiff-legged steps and started everyone laughing.

No one had dared joke about Satara's depression a year ago. But now that she no longer moped around the apartment all day, her past travails were fair game. Now she had a job as a supermarket cashier, and she had been socializing more often with her friends. She was still quiet, but she was much less withdrawn than she had been. Elaine considered the improvement in Satara's spirits to be her own greatest achievement since leaving prison. Nobody was going to give Elaine a prize or a paycheck for this, but at least Danae and Apache knew what she had accomplished.

By 10:30 a.m., the kitchen and living room were packed with people: Elaine, Danae, Satara, Tenéa, Apache, and three of Danae's friends. The only people missing were Sabrina's daughter Star and her son. It was difficult to imagine they were sleeping through all the noise. Elaine thought her niece was probably not happy about yet another person moving in.

"Did Mel say he was coming here first?" Danae asked.

"Yeah," Elaine said. "Where do you think he went?"

"To get some butt first," Danae said. "Because if I was in there, that's what I would be doing."

"That's a possibility," Elaine said.

Shortly after 11:00 a.m., Elaine called Jamel's girlfriend, Tisha, who lived in Queens. According to her, Jamel was getting out the following day, not this morning. The mix-up was blamed on a guard who had ordered him to stay at the prison and do chores. Another inmate had called Tisha and told her all this an hour earlier. She had tried to call Elaine, but she had not been able to get through. For some reason that nobody could explain, the phone in Apartment 13B could make outgoing calls but could not accept incoming ones.

Elaine returned to the kitchen and passed on the news. "You know he's tight right now," she said.

"You know he probably knocked somebody out," Satara said.

At 8:00 the next morning, Jamel surveyed the Lower East Side from the backseat of his cousin's Jeep Exterior. The street he knew best was Avenue D, where he used to spend hours every day on the corner, selling envelopes of heroin and vials of crack. Now a supermarket, two bodegas, two cleaners, a Chinese take-out place, a fried-chicken take-out place, a pizza parlor, and a dental office lined the block across from the Wald Houses, just north of Houston Street. The avenue was cleaner and quieter than he remembered, but then he had not been here in five and a half years, since the fall of 1995. Jamel, now twenty-four, had been gone since he was eighteen.

The Jeep pulled into the Wald Houses, and Jamel was the first one out, hurrying toward his grandmother's building. There was no time to waste. He had to be back at Edgecombe by 4:00 p.m. His girlfriend, Tisha, and his cousin C. J. , who is Shyan's son, trailed behind.

Jamel wore the standard exit uniform of the state prison system. A plain brown sweatshirt, a couple of sizes too small, stretched tightly across his muscular chest. Dark denim pants hung from his hips, ending before they reached his ankles. White canvas sneakers with rubber soles covered his feet. The outfit had been made by prisoners upstate. Jamel could not wait to take it off.

In the elevator, he pressed the button for the thirteenth floor. The elevator seemed much smaller than he remembered. Since the last time he had lived here, he had grown six inches. Eventually, the elevator door opened, and he could see graffiti, done in red marker, decorating the dingy corridor.

Jamel stepped out of the elevator, turned left, and banged on the door of 13B. Apache appeared.

"What up?" Jamel said. They slapped palms.

"Good to see you, man," Apache said.

Jamel stepped inside and glanced around. The apartment was in far worse shape than the last time he had been there, back when his grandmother was in charge. The kitchen's walls were bare and dirty. The living room was packed with stuff, including a stroller, two plastic storage bins, two televisions, and a six-foot basketball backboard. Today, though, there was no time to worry about the state of this apartment.

"Where's Mommy at?" he asked.

"She's in the back," Apache said.

Jamel headed down the narrow corridor, navigating his way past a child's bicycle, a high chair, two training potties, and a laundry basket filled with toys. At the end of the hall, he pushed open the bedroom door.

That morning, Elaine had awakened at 7:00, discovered that nobody else was up yet, and returned to bed. Jamel found her still in bed, the top of her red nightshirt poking out from beneath a duvet. He dived on top of her and nuzzled his head in her hair.

Word of Jamel's arrival spread quickly. Apache, Satara, and Danae crowded into the room.

"C'mere, Tara," Jamel said. "Look at how big you got!" He picked her up in a bear hug.

"Mel, you're breaking my back," Satara said.

Danae threw her arms around Jamel's neck. "When are you going to be home for real?" she asked. "It's about time. It's been so long!"

For the last few months, Danae had been carrying around a Polaroid of Jamel in the front pocket of her parka. The two of them had always been close. During his years in state prison, she was the only sibling who had traveled across the state to visit him. Ever since she had heard he was coming home, she'd been in a good mood.

"Nay-nay, do you remember the last time you saw me, that time you came up to Wyoming [prison] with Cassandra?" Jamel asked. "Do you remember what you told me?"

"That I wanted to sell drugs," Danae said.

"What did I say?"

"You looked at me all serious and said you were going to kill me."

Four years ago, when Jamel had heard from his friends that Danae was flirting with the idea of selling drugs, he had told Cassandra to bring her to him. Now he was pleased to hear that his visiting room lecture had worked, that Danae had obeyed him. Once he was released for good, he would be able to watch her closely and make sure she didn't repeat his mistakes.

As soon as Jamel heard that he was going to be released, he had started worrying about his wardrobe. "What are you going to get me to wear home?" he had asked his girlfriend Tisha. To make sure she bought him the right items, he had ripped out photos from his favorite hip-hop magazine, *The Source*, and mailed her the pages.

Now he disappeared into the bathroom and turned on the shower. When he reappeared, he wore a brand-new outfit: red sweater, baggy Polo jeans, leather jacket, Timberland boots. The entire outfit had cost nearly $500.

He would have to change back into prison greens at the end of the day, but at least for the moment he felt free. He certainly did not want to be walking the streets with state clothes on his back. In this neighborhood, everyone knew what it meant if a man had on canvas sneakers, dark denim pants, and a sweatshirt without a logo. They would know he had just left prison, and they would assume he was broke.

Jamel tossed his state clothes on top of the garbage bag in the kitchen, then walked out. Elaine, Satara, and Danae followed. Next to a window in the building's hall, Jamel draped a muscular arm around Elaine's shoulders. Satara pointed a disposable camera at them and snapped a picture.

"You didn't smile," Elaine said to Jamel. Indeed, he had struck the standard rap-star pose, glaring at the camera with an expression that advertised his toughness.

"I ain't been smiling," he said.

She reached up and playfully smacked him across the face. "That's for all the times I didn't get to bust you up the side of the head," she said with a smile. "You know you're supposed to be looking for a job."

"I know," he said. "I'm going to stop at a few places and get some paperwork to show them." Returning with tangible evidence of at least a minimal effort to find a job was necessary, he knew, if he wanted to keep the prison officials off his back.

Satara took a few more pictures, and Jamel gave a last round of hugs. When he got to Danae, he shot her a stern look. "You didn't go to school yet?" he asked. "Don't be late."

Jamel wrapped his arms around his mother and bent down to kiss the top of her head. "Ma, I love you," he said. "I'm coming back Friday."

"Make sure you get back on time," Elaine shouted as Jamel joined C. J. and Tisha in the elevator. "Y'all be good."

"I love you," Jamel called out just before the elevator doors closed.

Back inside the apartment, the morning resumed its usual rhythm. Danae grabbed her school bag and left. Satara poured cereal into two bowls, one for herself and one for her daughter. Apache loaded basketball uniforms into the laundry machine, which sat next to the kitchen sink. Elaine scooped up Jamel's discarded clothes, folded them, and stacked them on the stove; she thought maybe one of the men at her job would want them.

According to Satara, Jamel had been putting on an act this morning, pretending to be someone he was not—a peaceful, sweet-tempered boy. "That nigger ain't innocent," Satara said, lifting a spoonful of Corn Pops to her mouth. "He acts like that because she's around. She's rubbing his head like he's six. Wait till he gets out. You're gonna see. His voice never used to be like that. He used to talk really mean. Now he's like, 'Maaaaaaa.'" Imitating her brother, Satara sounded like a small child. "Mel is slick like that," she said. "Don't let him fool you."

"All of you were trying to fool me," Elaine said. "All of you were acting one way when you came to visit me in prison—my little boys and my little girls. When I got home, I saw all your true colors."

This spring promised to be a time of enormous uncertainty for the entire family. As long as Jamel did not break any prison rules, he would be released in two weeks and moving in here. The mood inside the apartment was one of excitement tinged with trepidation. Everybody living here already knew how the return of a family member from prison can tip a household's balance of power, creating all sorts of unexpected drama.

Finally, after many chaotic months, a fragile peace existed. By now, Elaine was less combative and impatient than she had been when she first moved in. Skirmishes with her family were far less frequent. Once Jamel moved in, however, the dynamics in 13B would undoubtedly change once again. And, inevitably, his arrival would bring many more people into the apartment: his parole officer, his friends, Little Mel, Cassandra, Tisha, and various other girls.

Elaine didn't like living here, and she knew Jamel would not like it, either. After so many years spent under the constant watch of prison guards, he would need a room of his own, where he could have a little privacy. But every bed in this apartment already held two or three people. Elaine worried that Jamel would soon start hanging out on Avenue D again unless she could find a new place for them to live. For

Jamel, she thought, this familiar neighborhood could easily become a trap, drawing him back into the world of drugs and fast cash.

On the telephone the day before, he had told her that he might not come see her as soon as he got out. "Boy, don't play with me," she'd said. Now she figured it was a good sign that he had listened to her and stopped in here first. It didn't bother her that he had stayed for less than an hour; soon he would be home for good. And once he moved in, she knew that she'd have yet another responsibility: teaching him how to navigate life on the outside. She hadn't been able to keep him out of prison, but now she was determined to stop him from going back.

CHAPTER 35

Cassandra Rivera started going to Rikers Island in the fall of 1994, when she was fifteen years old. At the time, Jamel was seventeen and locked up in Rikers' adolescent jail. Fifteen-year-olds are not allowed to visit their boyfriends on their own, so Cassandra got a fake school ID, which stated she was sixteen. For the next ten months, she visited Jamel at least once a week. Their relationship became more serious after he was released in the summer of 1995. Within a few weeks, she was pregnant.

By the fall, he was back in jail, and she was making weekly trips to Rikers Island once again. She gave birth to their son, Little Mel, in the spring of 1996, then took him to Rikers Island two weeks later so Jamel could meet him. When Jamel was sent upstate to prison, she followed. Every other weekend, she and Little Mel took an overnight bus across the state to see him. And whenever Jamel said he needed money, she deposited $1,000 into his prison commissary account.

Over the next few years, their relationship became more strained. Visiting Jamel in state prison was much more exhausting and expensive than traveling to Rikers Island. Every year, he would tell her, "I'm coming home next year." But then he did not return home, and eventually she got tired of waiting. In 1999, she got pregnant with another

man's baby. She stopped going to see Jamel, but did not at first explain why. When she was five months pregnant, she finally told him
the truth on the telephone. He cried and shouted, demanding that
she get an abortion. She refused. At the beginning of 2000, she gave
birth to a daughter, whom she named Antonique.

When Cassandra heard that Jamel was finally returning home from
prison, she flew to New York City. At the time, she was staying in
Florida. She had not seen Jamel in nearly two years. A few days after
his release, she showed up at Apartment 13B with both of her children: Little Mel, now four, and Antonique, who had just turned one.
"Oh, my God," Apache said when he saw her. "More drama. Like we
don't have enough."

At first, Cassandra and Jamel appeared to get along. He convinced
her to take him shopping, and she bought him a wallet, underwear,
socks, two outfits, and a pair of Nike sneakers. In the apartment, he
often walked around in a sleeveless undershirt, showing off the results of thousands of hours of prison workouts. "He was so damn
fine," Cassandra said. "Shit. I ain't going to lie. He was so damn fine.
Oh, my God. He was so built up. He was gorgeous. It wasn't even his
face; it was his body. He looked cut up."

On his chest was a crude tattoo he had done himself several years
ago on Rikers Island. He had fashioned a tattoo gun from two needles
and a ballpoint pen, burning the needles onto the pen's end. Then he
dipped the pen into tattoo ink and stabbed himself enough times to
create three overlapping hearts with the names Jamel, Cassandra, and
Little Mel. Cassandra had a tattoo on her chest, too, though hers was
much more professional. It was Jamel's name, written in elegant
script above her heart.

By now, though, the love and devotion that had driven them to get
these tattoos no longer existed, at least not in the same way. Soon
Cassandra and Jamel were fighting all the time. They could not speak
to each other for more than five or ten minutes before somebody was
shouting. Whenever he talked to other women on the phone, she got
angry. Whenever she bent over and her shirt lifted, revealing a new
tattoo, he got angry. He thought that the Arabic word she had tattooed

at the base of her back was the Muslim name of her daughter's father. She denied this, but he didn't believe her. "What do you think I am?" he said. "A damn fool?"

Elaine overheard their arguments and tried not to take sides, but she understood Jamel's anger. "It's one thing to cheat on a lover when they're in prison," she said. "But when you bring a baby, it's a constant reminder."

One morning, less than a week after he was released, Jamel walked into Apartment 13B with his girlfriend Tisha. Cassandra was already there. Tisha walked to the back room, while Jamel entered the bedroom where Cassandra was changing her daughter's diaper. As usual, the two got into an argument.

Soon their verbal fight escalated into a physical one. He smacked her across the cheek. She picked up a telephone and threw it at him, hitting him in the face. In his mind, her decision to hit with the phone meant that now he was free to get the revenge he'd been craving. Or, as he later explained his thinking, "Now I can beat her ass."

He wrapped one hand around her throat, threw her on the floor, and started kicking her. Apache rushed into the room and grabbed Jamel, attempting to pull him off Cassandra. Eventually he convinced Jamel to leave the bedroom.

By now, the fight had drawn the attention of everyone in the apartment: Elaine, Sabrina's daughter Star, Little Mel. Behind the closed door, they could hear Cassandra talking on the telephone. "This guy just beat me up," she said.

"Don't call the cops!" Elaine shouted.

Cassandra had actually called her mother, but she pretended that she had dialed the police.

"You're going back to jail!" she hollered through the door. "I'm going to have you locked up!"

Jamel told Apache that he wanted to get back into the bedroom. "Let me say good-bye to my son," he said. As soon as he got into the room, however, he lunged toward Cassandra and started hitting her in the face. Together, Elaine and Apache pulled him off.

"C'mon, Tisha," Jamel shouted down the corridor. "Let's go."

After Jamel left, Cassandra went to the emergency room at nearby Bellevue Hospital. Her mother met her there and tried to convince her to file a police report. Cassandra refused. She knew all the Bartletts would blame her if she pressed charges and Jamel returned to jail. Anyway, she figured it was only a matter of time until he wound up back behind bars. "He's going to end up doing it to himself," she said. "He's going to dig his own hole."

CHAPTER 36

When Jamel had last gone to state prison, his maximum sentence was four years, or forty-eight months. The parole board had released him early, after twenty months. Though he was no longer locked up he was not exactly free, either. Now he would have to finish his sentence on the outside, reporting regularly to the parole office on West Thirty-first Street.

He was assigned to a female officer, and during his first visit with her, she gave him the usual speech about parole's rules. The one that rankled him most was the 9:00 p.m. curfew.

"C'mon, Ma," he said afterward. "Are they crazy?"

"Don't worry about it," Elaine said. "They do it to everyone."

In New York City, most parolees are required to attend some sort of program: drug treatment, domestic violence counseling, anger-management classes. Elaine's parole officer had not sent her to a program, but Jamel's parole officer did. She told him to go to La Bodega de la Familia, a nonprofit organization located in a storefront on East Third Street, one block from the Wald Houses. La Bodega provides counseling to drug-addicted parolees and their families, in order to improve the odds that they will stay out of jail.

Jamel did not think he needed to go to La Bodega, and, indeed, this may not have been the right place for him. He had gone to prison for selling drugs, but he was not an addict. Nevertheless, Elaine urged him to go. Now every week he had two appointments: one with his parole officer and another with Arturo Smith, a counselor at La Bodega. The meetings with his parole officer were usually brief and formal, while his visits with Arturo were more relaxed.

On his twenty-ninth day out of prison, Jamel learned that he had a new parole officer. He met her and decided immediately that he did not like her. She was more strict and less empathetic than his former officer. He thought she spoke down to him, as if he were a child.

As soon as he got out of the parole office, he called Elaine at her job. "I'm not dealing with that damn woman," he said. "I'm not report-ing back. Parole is just going to have to fuckin' find me."

They both knew what would happen if he stopped reporting to the parole office: Sooner or later, a pack of parole officers would show up at the apartment, snap a pair of cuffs around his wrists, and whisk him back to jail.

"Let me handle this one," Elaine said. "Don't worry about it."

The next day, Jamel had an appointment already set up with his counselor, Arturo, at La Bodega. This time, Elaine and his girlfriend Tisha went with him.

Arturo led the group into a back room and closed the door. Jamel slouched in a chair, jamming his hands into his jeans pockets. Elaine and Tisha sat down on either side of him. Everyone looked glum.

"How are we doing, Jamel?" Arturo asked. "What's wrong?"

"Parole is trying to do something that I'm not liking."

"Which is what?"

"Changing my parole officer to some other lady."

"Miss Russell," Elaine said.

Arturo asked Jamel a few more questions, but soon Elaine cut in. "He's very uncomfortable with her," she said. "I called her yesterday, and she's an idiot. Bottom line. I called her to set up a meeting with me, her, and Jamel. She told me there was no need for us to have a meeting."

Nobody knew why Jamel's case had been switched to a new,

stricter parole officer. To them, it seemed an arbitrary move. In fact, his case had been transferred to the gang unit because of his past involvement with the Dead Men Walking gang.

"She was just telling me what she expects of me," Jamel said. "Basically telling me that I'm in a gang. And she told me to roll my sleeves up and show her my arms and all that. She's telling me that she wants me to cooperate as far as telling her who is selling drugs in the neighborhood."

Jamel had never cooperated with the police when he was in jail, even when it meant he would have received a more lenient sentence. There was no way he was going to become a snitch now. Anyway, everyone knew that ratting out drug dealers was like asking for a death sentence.

"I'm ready not to go back, truthfully speaking," Jamel said.

"Truthfully speaking, you realize you have to go back," Arturo said. "That's a requirement. Free time beats jail time."

"I've got two years left, and I'll do it," Jamel said. "If that's what it comes to, I'll do the two years. That's how I feel about it."

"That's a pretty strong feeling if you'd rather go back to jail," Arturo said.

"It's not that I'd rather go back," Jamel said. "But if there is no other alternative, where I can't change my parole officer, then, yeah, I would rather go back."

Jamel had thought he was free after he left prison, and now, once again, he felt the grip of the criminal justice system tightening around him. To him, it seemed his new parole officer wanted to lock him up—not see him succeed. He thought that as soon as he made his first mistake—as soon as she caught him staying out past 9:00 p.m.—she'd take him back to jail. He did not think he could cope with having her in his life, watching his every move. Dealing with the rules and whims of the parole system was too stressful. To him, there seemed only one solution: avoid parole altogether.

By refusing to return to the parole office, he thought he'd be seizing control over a situation in which he had very little. Rather than waiting around for the parole officer to lock him up, he would just choose that fate for himself. If he went back to prison, at least he would know what to expect. He hated the daily dose of humiliations and deprivations, but at least prison was a familiar place—more familiar than the outside world.

"There's something that can be worked out," Arturo said. "That's what you have to learn now that you're back out. You are empowered now to do things. You don't have to accept situations that you don't agree with. And there's a way of going about changing them without going to extremes."

Several minutes later, Arturo escorted Jamel, Tisha, and Elaine back to the waiting room. Jamel seemed calmer now, but Elaine knew that this was only the beginning, just the first major hurdle. To keep Jamel out of prison, she'd not only have to coax him into obeying parole's rules, but she'd also have to convince him that life on the outside was worth the struggle. This was a job for a mother, a role that she'd been unable to fulfill for most of his life. Jamel seemed appreciative. As they walked down the sidewalk together, he reached over and held her hand.

CHAPTER 37

One day in the spring of 2001, Elaine called her boss's voicemail at 6:45 a.m. "This is Elaine Bartlett," she said. "I'm calling in sick." She was not actually sick, however. She was calling from a bus headed to Albany, where she planned to spend the day lobbying legislators to repeal the Rockefeller laws.

A few weeks later, when she wanted to attend an anti–drug law rally, she left another message. "This is Elaine Bartlett," she said. "I'm not coming in today." No explanation. No feigned cough or other allusions to illness. She knew her supervisor would not be too pleased, but at this point, she no longer cared.

Her enthusiasm for her job had begun to wane after she had been working at Project Renewal for almost a year. While she had once imagined herself rising quickly through the agency's ranks, now she fantasized about quitting. She had grown tired of the low pay, the drudgery, the chaos. She was tired of listening to other people's problems all day, then coming home to an apartment full of many more problems.

By now, Elaine was a case manager. She had earned this promotion after four months on the job. Her duties involved overseeing a case-load of fourteen men, helping them to navigate the welfare system and figure out where to move once they left Project Renewal. She ran group-therapy sessions and continued to spend much of her time counseling residents one-on-one, regardless of whether or not they were actually on her caseload.

Though she had worked full time for a year, she felt like she had little to show for her efforts. She still did not have enough savings to afford a place of her own. Part of the problem was that she earned very little. She brought home $577 every two weeks, or $13,848 a year after taxes. The pay at Project Renewal was so meager that many of her coworkers had a second job.

Elaine's cash woes were compounded by the fact that relatives were constantly asking her for money. When Apache could not raise enough cash to take two girls' basketball teams to a tournament in North Carolina, he turned to her. "What do I look like? Rockefeller?" she asked. After listening to him beg for a few days, she gave him $500. When Satara needed money to go with a friend to Miami—her first-ever trip on an airplane—Elaine gave her $200. When Little Mel's fifth birthday arrived, Elaine threw a party and spent $300 on food and gifts.

Shortly before Easter, she started hearing from her nieces and nephews, who said they needed new sneakers. She thought that her sister Michelle had told the children to call her. "She knows I got a little income tax refund, so now it's like, 'Let's spend Elaine's money,'" Elaine said. Buying new outfits and shoes was a family tradition; Yvonne had always made sure everyone had new clothes to wear on Easter. Eventually, Elaine caved in and bought eight pairs of sneakers.

"It's good to have a big family, but sometimes it's not good," Elaine said. "I'm the one coming home, and everybody is expecting me to take care of them. I feel like I'm in a web and they're pulling me. The top of my head is gray now. I didn't have this much gray in the whole sixteen years." Every few weeks, she vowed to start saying no every time someone asked her for money. "I'm not obligated to do nothing for nobody," she said. "Nobody is sending me no checks. I'm the one working."

Elaine felt as if everyone's hands were in her pocket, and sometimes they literally were. A year earlier, soon after she had started working, one of her paychecks disappeared. She noticed the check was missing from her pocket after she cleaned the bathroom, running the mop around the toilet while Sabrina sat on it. Nobody ever admitted taking the check, but Elaine thought Sabrina had picked her pocket. Over the next few days, she noticed that Sabrina, who was always broke, suddenly seemed to have money. Every time she walked into the apartment, she was carrying bags of candy and cigarettes.

It was not easy for Elaine to stop her personal problems from rippling into her work life. After Jamel came home from prison and her responsibilities increased, she had even more trouble keeping her two worlds separate. Because the phone in 13B did not accept incoming calls, everybody who wanted to talk to her had to call her at her job. Jamel called to vent about his parole officer. Tisha called to fish for information about Jamel's other girlfriends. Sabrina's doctor called to report that she was still in a coma.

Elaine's coworkers did not know about all her family dramas, but they could tell she was often distracted and depressed. And, of course, they knew when she skipped work altogether. In addition to the days she went to political events, Elaine missed a few other days of work that spring, too. She was scheduled to work on Easter, but she never showed up. When she walked into Project Renewal the next morning, her supervisor told her it didn't look good to call in sick on a holiday.

Rumors of a shake-up swept through Project Renewal in mid-June. Two employees were fired. Elaine's boss called her into a meeting and informed her that he was demoting her. She would lose her caseload and her title, and he was sending her back downstairs to Operations. Instead of working 8:00 a.m. to 4:00 p.m., she would be switched back to the less desirable shift of 4:00 p.m. to midnight. She would also have to take a pay cut.

"Okay," Elaine said. She was determined not to show any emotion, not to give her supervisors the satisfaction of knowing they had upset her. It was a skill she had picked up in prison. Never let them know when you are angry or hurt. Never let them see you cry.

Instead, Elaine expressed her displeasure with her clothes. She

knew that employees' attire was a touchy issue; a memo about the office dress code had recently circulated. The day after she was demoted, she walked into work wearing her red skirt suit, the one she
had picked up for free during her first weeks home. The suit was
guaranteed to attract attention; it was baggy, bright, and too formal for
her job. Elaine did not bother putting on panty hose, leaving her hairy
legs visible.

The next day, she wore an oversize white cotton jumper, which she
called her "nurse outfit." It looked like the sort of dress one would
wear to the beach over a bikini. Underneath, Elaine wore a T-shirt
that belonged to one of her children; the logo across the back said
SOHK, for School of Hard Knocks. Because the shirt was so large and
the dress so thin, the letters were visible to anyone who glanced at her
butt. The outfit screamed, I don't care!—about the job, the bosses,
the demotion, the dress code.

Meanwhile, word of Elaine's demotion spread through the building. "Miss B, why are you moving back to Operations?" the residents
asked. "That don't make sense."

"I'll be all right," Elaine said.

She tried to pretend she was fine, but the demotion did upset her.
To make herself feel better, she did the same thing for herself that she
did for the recovering addicts: She gave a pep talk. It's all a test,
Elaine, she told herself. It's got to be a brighter ship coming in. It has
to be.

When she had started working at Project Renewal, she had imagined she would be successful. She thought she might someday become a supervisor, then maybe an assistant director. She'd figured she
would make a good boss; after all, she thought of herself as a leader.
But now, here she was, being kicked back downstairs, demoted to an
entry-level position. She thought about quitting, but she knew she
could not afford to lose her paychecks. Still, she wondered how much
longer she would last.

CHAPTER 38

The phone call Elaine had been dreading finally came one afternoon in late June. Sabrina was dead. "Get out of here," Elaine's supervisor said. "Take a couple days if you need it." Tears started down her cheeks before she even got out the front door. Walking down East Third Street, she began gnawing on her pinkie nail. She crossed an avenue without looking, and a bus nearly ran over her.

She rode the F train to 145th Street, then got out. While she waited on the platform for another train, she saw two men wearing identical cotton outfits: chalk-green shirts and matching shorts. Maybe they had just left prison. Maybe they were on work release. Elaine did not know, and she didn't want to think about prison anymore. She turned her back to them.

A D train arrived, packed with briefcase-toting commuters and people in Yankees caps on their way to the game. When the doors opened, Elaine recognized one former Bedford inmate amid the sea of passengers. "Hey, Elaine," Angie said as she stepped off the train. There was no time to stop and chat, so she spoke quickly. "I just graduated. I'm starting Hunter in the fall." ´

A year ago, Elaine had enrolled at a local college, which had a program to help women continue their education after prison. She had attended two classes, then dropped out. She didn't have enough money for books, and her work schedule and family problems had sapped nearly all her energy. Angie, meanwhile, was heading off to graduate school. As the subway doors closed, Angie blew her a kiss.

Elaine slumped in a seat and began nibbling on her nails. She exhaled loudly. She wrapped her arms around the pocketbook in her lap, trying to make her stomach stop hurting. By the time she got off at 182nd Street, it was nearly 8:00 p.m., almost two hours after she'd left work.

A livery cab took her to the central Bronx and deposited her in the parking lot of St. Barnabas Hospital. She wandered around for ten minutes before she found the nursing home, which was in a separate building from the hospital.

On the fourth floor, she encountered a man with a surgical mask on top of his head; he was standing behind a reception desk.

"I'm here about Sabrina Bartlett," she said.

A look of unease crossed his face. "They took her body to the morgue five minutes ago," he said.

"Was anybody here?"

"I think two people were here."

He gave her directions to the morgue. She went back down in the elevator, out a door, around the side of the building, across the entrance to the parking lot, and into the hospital. There, a security guard told her to take the elevator to the basement. Signs on this floor led to the cafeteria and the mailroom, but none pointed to the morgue.

At this late hour, the halls were empty. Several minutes passed before Elaine could find anyone whom she could ask for directions. When she finally located a custodian, he pointed her to a darkened room, where she discovered a security guard staring at a few surveillance screens. The guard told her that she was in the wrong place. She needed to go back upstairs to the admitting area.

"Unbelievable," she muttered to herself. "They could've told me that."

Eventually, she found the admitting area. This place was deserted, too. Even the chair behind the receptionist's desk was empty. Elaine searched around and found an employee. "I'm here to view my sister's body," she said.

"Have a seat and wait," the woman replied.

Her sister Michelle was the one who had called her at work with the news. Michelle had said she was going to St. Barnabas with a few relatives, but there was no sign of her or anyone else.

The only faces here were those staring out from the wall: dozens of NYPD photos of missing persons tacked to a bulletin board, among them a fourteen-year-old girl and an eighty-five-year-old man with Alzheimer's. In some ways, it seemed, Sabrina's face belonged up there, too. The old Sabrina, the one Elaine had grown up with, had disappeared long ago.

Of Yvonne's seven children, three were now dead and two were still in prison. Only Michelle and Elaine were left to hold together the rest of the family. Before today, however, they had not spoken to each other in nearly a month. The cause of their most recent dispute was difficult to pinpoint, but the heart of the matter was always the same. It was a battle about power and control, about who was going to lead the Bartlett family.

Throughout the spring and early summer, Michelle and Sabrina's daughter Star had handled all the decisions about Sabrina's medical care. Elaine was left out of the loop. Nobody solicited her opinion about whether to let the doctors remove Sabrina's respirator. When Sabrina was transferred from Beth Israel in Manhattan to this hospital in the Bronx, Elaine found out weeks later.

The employee Elaine had spoken to reappeared. "The supervisor said that three sisters and two brothers had already come by and viewed the body for a while," she said. "She's not taking it out again."

Elaine would later learn that Michelle had come here with Star, Star's friend, Sabrina's son Thomas, and Thomas's father. Apparently, nobody had waited for Elaine to show up. She did not explain this to the woman standing in front of her. She did not shout or complain or demand to speak to the supervisor.

"All right," she said.

She turned around and walked toward the exit. Maybe it was better that she had missed the viewing. "I've already seen Sabrina suffer enough," she muttered to herself. "I don't need to see her corpse."

Shortly before 11:00 p.m., after taking a livery cab and two subways, Elaine arrived at the F train station near her job. She made her way through the streets of the East Village, heading back to the Wald Houses. It was a balmy night, and instead of entering her building, she sat on the bench in front. A few teenagers in prom dresses sauntered by.

It was summer once again, her second summer since leaving Bedford Hills. She still hadn't met any men who excited her, and, of course, Nate was still in prison. If she could have been with him right now, feeling his strong arms folded around her, she would have felt a little better. Even talking to him would have helped. But, of course, she couldn't call him.

Not long after she sat down, Jamel emerged from the building, pushing his bicycle.

"Did you hear what happened?" she asked.

"No," he said.

"Sabrina passed. They didn't tell you?"

"No."

He stared down at the ground. "I didn't get to visit her," he whispered. After a few moments, he looked up. "Are you all right?" he asked.

"Yeah," she said.

Jamel lifted himself onto his bike seat and pedaled a few yards.

"Where are you going?" Elaine asked.

He stopped, got off his bike, and leaned it against the fence. Then he sat down on the bench beside her and wrapped his arms tightly around her shoulders. She leaned her head against his chest. When he noticed a tear sliding down her cheek, he lifted his hand and brushed it away.

CHAPTER 39

Jamel met Alfredo Bryan in the mid-1990s, when they were both locked up in the adolescent jail on Rikers Island. Alfredo had been arrested for robbery, Jamel for selling drugs. They discovered they were both related to the same person—the sister of Shyan's wife. Soon they began calling each other "cousin."

Whenever someone would start rapping in the jail's dayroom, Alfredo would go search for Jamel. "I'm going to get my cousin to battle you," he would say. An audience of inmates would listen to the various contenders delivering their rhymes, then pick the best one. In these verbal duels, Jamel was often the winner.

Jamel had been writing rap lyrics since he was twelve, and soon Alfredo was writing songs, too. In 1995, Alfredo was transferred to the state prison system. Jamel went upstate in 1996. Over the next two years, they saw each other many times, in four different prisons.

Alfredo had grown up in the Queensbridge project in Long Island City, and now some of his childhood friends were becoming rap stars. His best friend's brother took the name Havoc and joined up with a teenager named Prodigy to form Mobb Deep. And the teenager he had known as Nasir Jones became Nas, one of the hottest new acts in the business.

Jamel and Alfredo followed the rappers' successes in the pages of hip-hop magazines, and they talked about launching their own rap careers once they got out. Alfredo went home in the fall of 1998. Two years later, he appeared on two major albums, one by Nas and the other by Prodigy. His rap moniker was Littles, and soon Jamel was reading about Littles's rise in the pages of *The Source*.

Meanwhile, Jamel was still in prison, still writing rap lyrics in his cell every night. He wrote about a wide range of topics: watching cartoons, stealing girls from other men, committing crimes, losing family while being locked up. For safekeeping, he mailed his rhymes to his girlfriend Tisha. By the time he left prison, there were more than 500 songs stored in plastic bags in Tisha's apartment.

In his first months out of prison, he attempted to start a rap career. He tracked down a few friends who had a recording studio and tried to convince them to make a tape of him rapping. He carried a mini cassette recorder around in his jacket pocket and spit rhymes into it whenever he felt inspired. And he called Littles every day or two. Sometimes Littles called back; sometimes he didn't. Jamel didn't know it at the time, but Littles was testing him to see how hungry he was.

Whenever Jamel wrote a new song, Elaine took the handwritten lyrics to her job and photocopied them for him. Whenever Lora called the apartment, Elaine put Jamel on the phone so she could hear his latest rhyme. Just as she had reinvented herself as a political activist, Elaine thought maybe Jamel could reinvent himself, too, transforming the troubling experiences of his past into credentials for a new career. After all, professional rapper is one of the few jobs where a felony record can be an asset.

"You've got a brain on you," she told Jamel. "You're gifted with this rapping stuff. You can make it. Do your music and let them see you up there voicing your opinion."

Despite her enthusiasm, she did not actually know how much talent he had. Her musical tastes ran more toward Diana Ross than Tupac Shakur. "His music might be farfetched," she admitted privately, "but if that's what's going to keep him off the streets, then I say go for it."

The rules of parole dictate that parolees find an on-the-books job. Chasing rap stardom does not count. Jamel knew this, of course, but he was not nearly as focused as Elaine had been about looking for work. He was also less qualified. He had stopped going to school in tenth grade. Shortly before leaving prison, he had taken the high school equivalency exam, but he had failed it by one point.

Sometimes he talked about getting a job as a courier, delivering envelopes and packages on foot around the city. Messenger jobs are popular among people who have just left prison because they require few skills and they allow them to be outside all day, moving around—not stuck in an office, with a boss lurking nearby. In fact, Nate's brother Ronald worked as a messenger for *The Village Voice*. Jamel, however, never did become a messenger.

Two months after he left prison, Jamel's parole officer sent him to Greenwich House, a drug program in Greenwich Village. There, Jamel met with a counselor, who told him about a state-run job-training program known as Vocational and Educational Services for Individuals with Disabilities, or VESID. He qualified for this program because the Division of Parole had classified him as a drug addict, and VESID considers addiction a disability. This program pays students to attend classes: to learn data entry, attend culinary school, get a commercial driver's license. Jamel said he wanted to study computers. First, though, he had to show that he had been drug-free for ninety days.

While he waited to see if he was going to get into a data-entry course, he was required to go to Greenwich House twice a week for counseling and to give urine samples. The rest of the time, he wrote songs, worked out at a nearby park, and played *Grand Theft Auto* on the PlayStation 2 attached to the television in the living room. He also hung out with Joanna, a new girlfriend he had recently met.

On a Saturday night near the end of the summer, Lora invited Jamel to the Knitting Factory, a nightclub in downtown Manhattan. That evening, she was hosting an open-mike event for spoken-word poets. Beginning at 6:00 p.m., she stood in the back of a darkened room in the basement, holding a clipboard and sign-up sheet. Twenty people sat in front of her, reclining on sofas and chairs. Small tables were scattered around the room, each holding a tiny white candle and a bottle or two of beer.

Elaine, Jamel, and Joanna arrived at 7:00 p.m., one hour late. In this bohemian scene, Jamel stood out. He wore an oversize football jersey, a terry-cloth headband, baggy jeans, and a pair of Nikes. By now, Lora had nearly run through her list of performers. As soon as the poet at the front finished, she called out Jamel's name.

Surveying the crowd, Jamel decided this was not the type of audience that wanted to hear about shooting rival drug dealers or being chased by the cops. He had only one song that he thought would be appropriate. It was about Baby Regina, Sabrina's daughter, who had died in her crib many years ago.

Jamel grabbed the microphone and held it close to his lips. "First, thanks to my moms and Lora for making this happen," he said, "and to my wife." He paused and looked over toward Joanna, who sat near the front. She smiled back at him. They'd been hanging out together for three months, and he liked to pretend they were married.

That night marked the first time Jamel had performed in front of strangers, outside of a prison. No crinkled notebook paper fluttered nervously in his fingers; unlike the evening's other performers, he was empty-handed.

"This is what I wrote for my little cousin who passed away," he said. "She was, like, four months."

In a strong, steady voice, he began.

> How come she went so fast/ This little baby had no past/ Just plans for the future/ Bright days that didn't last/ I always ask these questions/ Late night before resting/ Mind testing/ Looking for answers in these deep thought sessions/ Baby cousin I'm troubled/ Wanted to tell you that I love you/ But I used to hustle/ Hunting for new ways to bubble/ I was scared to touch you/ Picking you up caused a struggle/ Heart beating I hugged you/ Face-to-face we used to snuggle/ Being caught in a

rapture/ Of life where things don't matter/ Remember I
had to/ Cover my hands to prevent from scratches

I was used to seeing/ Your face when I was creeping/
In the house late night/ Looking to see if you sleeping/
Sometimes I drift from facts/ Wishing you could come
back/ This world's wack/ I peeped that/ Trust me, you
good where you at/ True innocence/ It got me hurting
inside/ There was no meaning/ Made no sense when I
heard that you died/ It gets me tight, cousin/ Wish it
was me/ I ain't fronting/ I'm doing dirt on this earth/ You
ain't never do nothing

Why do the precious go/ Some things are never con-
trolled/ It's just the way that it goes/ Meanings of death
be unknown/ In time I find some answers/ Don't be upset that I ask this/ Did you really wanna stay/ Or be a
part of our pasts/ Yeah, I'm already seeing/ They think
I'm mentally sinking/ When I say you better off/ They
don't be feeling my meanings/ In time I'll teach me
seeds/ Keep 'em focused on needs/ Bless 'em with lessons on sex death money and greed/ Found out how to
treat her/ Make my daughter a leader/ Keep your presence in the future/ Name my baby Regina

The crowd erupted in applause. Elaine, Joanna, and Lora clapped
the hardest, but everyone in the audience was enthusiastic. "All
right!" Elaine shouted. Watching her son, she was filled with pride
and also surprise. She had never heard this rhyme before. Until right
now, she had not known how he'd felt after Baby Regina died.

Now she could see that his rhymes helped him in the same way
that her speeches at rallies helped her. Both of them were trying to
make sense of the tragedies that had shaped their lives, to ease their
pain by talking about it publicly. And, she was pleased to discover, he
did indeed have talent. Maybe he really would find a way to realize his
dream.

CHAPTER 40

Anyone who walked into Apartment 13B could tell that the living room now belonged to Jamel. His possessions were everywhere: Timberland shoe boxes, rap CDs, PlayStation 2 games, unopened condoms. Pictures of Sabrina's children were still taped to the back wall, but the broken sofa and the sheet in the doorway were gone. Jamel slept on the floor, sprawled atop a few quilts, just as he had when he was a child living in this same apartment. Some nights, Danae slept here, too. She liked to spend time with Jamel, and she had seemed much happier ever since he'd come home.

At the moment, Jamel's most frequent visitor was his new girl-friend, Joanna, a spunky twenty-three-year-old from Brooklyn. Jamel had met her through her twin brother, with whom he'd been locked up on Rikers Island. Elaine made an effort to get along with Joanna just as she did with Tisha. "Whatever keeps him off these street corners," Elaine said. "If he didn't have her, there's no telling what he'd be up to by now. Whatever keeps his butt out of trouble."

During his first months out of prison, Jamel spent as many hours as possible having sex, or as he put it, "hitting the walls." Every few weeks, Elaine brought home a bag of condoms from her job and handed it to him. "I hope you're using your Trojans, because that thing is going to fall off," she said. "You're sure making up for lost time." When Satara had gone to Miami, Jamel had taken over her bedroom. Elaine had not chastised him; she had just told him to make sure the sheets were washed before Satara returned.

Besides all his friends on the Lower East Side, Jamel had many friends in Corona, Queens, from the days when he used to hang out there with his uncle Shyan. One of these friends was Dude Massard. Dude was the son of Althea, who still lived on 100th Street, across from the Bartletts' former home. Twenty-five years ago, Althea had taught Elaine about buying high heels and sneaking out at night to go dancing. When Elaine got out of prison, Dude had given her an envelope of cash and a bouquet of flowers.

Elaine liked Dude and the rest of Jamel's friends from Corona, but she knew that if he spent much time with them, he would soon be back in prison. Many of them had felony records. Dude himself had gone to prison for selling drugs and was now on parole. Elaine did not know if he was still selling drugs, but she did know that he was twenty-five years old and driving around the city in a bright yellow Mercedes-Benz.

As the months passed, Jamel spent less time in Queens and more time on the Lower East Side, inside Apartment 13B. Elaine was glad that he had decided to stay close to her. This way, she could keep an eye on him. She knew he would not tell her if he was selling drugs again, so she spied on him. She varied the ways she walked home from work in order to try to catch him on the corner. So far, she had never seen him on Avenue D.

What Elaine really wanted to do was get Jamel out of this neighborhood altogether. She figured it was only a matter of time until he got arrested again, or got shot. She knew that Jamel had more than his share of enemies inside this project—from arguments that dated back to the days before he got locked up. He did not tell her the details of these past disputes, but she worried about his safety all the time. As Elaine put it, "I'm not trying to get a phone call: 'Miss Bartlett, We need you to come down here and identify your son's body.'"

Her fears about Jamel's safety gave her housing hunt an added sense of urgency. She spent much of her free time looking for an apartment. Every Sunday, she bought the *Daily News* and skimmed the real estate section. She had little experience reading listings, however. When she saw the letter *K*—as in $200K—she said, "What does *K* mean?" When she learned that a security deposit of two months' rent was required to a get a certain apartment, she was shocked. "That's highway robbery," she said.

From one of her children's friends, she heard about a three-bedroom, $500-a-month sublet at the Baruch Houses, the public-housing project just south of the Wald Houses. Subletting a project apartment is a violation of the Housing Authority's rules, but some lease holders do it anyway. Elaine visited the apartment and decided she liked it. After a few weeks, however, she heard that the lease-holder had changed his mind.

Near the end of the summer, a troubling rumor swept through the Wald Houses: Housing Authority police planned to go door-to-door, hauling out any resident with a criminal record. Rumors were always rampant in the projects, often fueled more by paranoia than by facts. This particular rumor was not true. Nevertheless, it put both Elaine and Jamel on edge.

"We're getting out of here," Jamel said. "Nobody is putting no fucking handcuffs on me."

"Just hold your head up," Elaine told him. "I'll get you out of here."

Elaine had recently heard about another sublet. This one was in the Breukelen Houses, a project in Canarsie, Brooklyn. She had never been to Canarsie, but she got a ride there so she could check out the place. The two-bedroom apartment was smaller than she wanted, but she was desperate. Even the prospect of a two-train, one-bus commute did not faze her.

The woman who had the lease said she wanted $700 a month. Elaine talked her down to $650. Then she and Jamel pooled their money. He borrowed from a few friends; she dipped into her savings account. Together, they came up with $1,300—two months' rent. The move-in date was scheduled for the Saturday of Labor Day weekend.

Elaine started decorating the apartment in her mind. For months, she had been putting cash down for a big-screen television, which she had on layaway; now she would have a place to put it. When Labor Day weekend arrived, she could not find the woman who held the apartment lease. The weekend was nearly over by the time Elaine heard from her. For reasons she did not explain, she said the apartment was no longer available.

Several days later, an incident inside the Wald Houses reminded Elaine yet again why she needed to get Jamel out of the Lower East Side. She walked out of the back bedroom and into the kitchen, and immediately she could tell that something was wrong. Danae looked teary and shaken. "You better tell your mother," Star said. Danae shot back: "I'm not telling my mother." After eavesdropping for a minute, Elaine figured out that something had happened to Jamel.

She hurried out the apartment door and into the elevator. In front of the building, she found a pack of young men. Everyone was talking about Jamel. "Where's Mel at?" Elaine heard them saying. "Is he all right?" She could not see Jamel, so she followed the group as it moved toward the back of the project. There she spied Jamel, looking dazed and distraught. He was covered in sweat, pacing back and forth.

Elaine did not know it at the time, but there had just been an argument between two groups of boys in the project. Jamel had intervened, trying to play the role of peacemaker, and somebody had pulled out a knife. He had not been cut, but he could've been. Since leaving prison, he had already been shot at twice. Both times he escaped injury. He had not told his mother about either incident.

Elaine did not waste time trying to figure out the details of this latest fight.

"Get upstairs right now!" she shouted.

"Ma, I ain't doing nothing," he said.

She knew he did not want her yelling at him in front of his friends, but at that moment she did not care. The stakes were too high to worry about whether he was embarrassed.

"You ain't going nowhere," Elaine shouted. "You're going to get the hell upstairs and tell me what's going on!"

This latest incident was just another reminder of how easy it was for Jamel to find trouble. By now, Elaine did not need any more reasons to worry. What had happened to Dude was enough of a cautionary tale. Two months earlier, Dude had been at an auto-body shop in Queens, not far from his mother's house. While he waited for work to be done on his family's car, he got into an argument with another man, who was later identified as a parolee and a drug dealer.

The man pointed a gun at Dude and fired at least four times, hitting him in the chest. Dude's father witnessed the shooting and chased his son's assailant down the block. The father was shot once in the arm, but he managed to drag Dude's body into the car and drive to Elmhurst Hospital. By the time they got into the emergency room, Dude was dead. Elaine thought that if Jamel had been hanging out with him that day, he would have been killed, too.

CHAPTER 41

On a Thursday morning in mid-December, Elaine pulled open the door to the parole office and walked in. A sign next to the security guard's desk stated NO PAROLEES BEYOND THIS POINT. She stopped, turned left, and stepped into an elevator. This was the parolee elevator; it only went to the second floor, where it opened into a waiting room. Elaine got off, walked to the front of the room, and added her name to a sign-up sheet.

There were no copies of *Newsweek* or *Vanity Fair* or any other magazine in this waiting room. The only reading material was the large sign hanging near the front:

WAITING AREA RULES

Sign In
Have A Seat
Wait To Be Called
Take Your Hat Off
No Radio Playing
No Walkman Use
No Cell Phone Use

No Loud Talking
No Pets

Elaine sat down and unzipped her winter parka. Underneath, she had on a gray cotton shirt decorated with tiny black polka dots and gold glitter. Her gray slacks were freshly ironed, a crisp crease running down the front. She planned to go straight to work from here. It was now almost 10:00 a.m., and she had to be at Project Renewal by 4:00 p.m. It was impossible to predict how long she would be here, so she usually came early. On a good day, she got out within an hour or two.

She used to know what to expect when she came to this parole office. For seventeen months, she had been on Camacho's caseload. He had been, in many ways, the ideal parole officer. Not because he was a pushover, but because he explained the rules clearly and enforced them consistently. She had felt confident that as long as she kept her job, did not get high, and did not have any contact with the police, she would remain free. With Camacho as her parole officer, parole was an inconvenience, not a source of enormous stress.

Six months earlier, Elaine had checked in with Camacho for what would be their last visit together. That day, a large white man sat in his office, watching him work. Camacho introduced him and explained that he was a parole officer trainee. Elaine settled into the chair next to Camacho's desk.

"Listen, Camacho," she said. "I think I'm going into the shelter system. I can't take it anymore. This playing mom and trying to catch up isn't working. You know, I gotta get high to deal with this daily life."

Camacho looked surprised. "Are you getting high?" he asked.

"You know I am," she said.

"I've got to give you a drug test," he said.

"All right," she said. "Are you sure you want to do that?"

"Yeah."

"Damn, Camacho. Are you trying to violate me?"

Camacho thought she was joking about getting high, but there was only one way to know for certain. He reached into his pocket and pulled out a plastic cup and a dipstick. Elaine had never seen these dipsticks before. This drug test, which provided instant results, was the newest weapon in the agency's battle against parolee drug use.

Elaine went into the bathroom and filled the cup with urine. Afterward, Camacho instructed her on how to test it. She placed the dipstick in the cup, waited several seconds, then removed it. In a tiny window in the middle of the stick, a blue line appeared next to each type of drug: marijuana, cocaine, heroin.

"Elaine, it's negative," Camacho said. "You must not have done enough drugs."

"Better luck next time, buddy," she said.

By now, Elaine figured she had provided enough amusement to keep his trainee entertained for the rest of the day. "We gotta make this fun," she whispered to Camacho as he escorted her back to the waiting room. "We can't make this boring."

Since that afternoon, Elaine had been through two other parole officers. Today, she did not know whom she would see. Her last officer had just transferred to the Bronx.

At 11:30 a.m., an hour and a half after she had signed in, Elaine was still seated in the waiting room, still wondering when her name would be called. In this room, everybody always looked bored. Parolees stared out the window onto West Thirty-first Street. They dozed. They scanned the room, searching for friends and acquaintances. Men who knew one another slapped palms; women hugged and kissed one another on the cheek. Sometimes, Elaine saw a friend here, but not on this particular day.

Soon Jamel walked in. He had recently started taking a data-entry class in a building a few blocks away, as part of the VESID program. He sat down in a chair next to her.

Jamel no longer reported to Officer Russell, whom he had disliked so intensely. Several months earlier, he had somehow managed to get off her caseload; he was not sure exactly how. In recent months, he and Elaine had shared the same parole officer. This was standard practice. When parole officials figure out two parolees live in the same apartment, they usually put them on the same officer's caseload.

At 12:40 p.m., Elaine heard her name. "Bartlett!"

She looked up and saw Officer Russell. Not a good sign. Elaine and Jamel stood and walked over to her.

"I'm not going to see both of you together," Officer Russell said.

"Why can't you see us together?" Elaine asked. "The last P.O. we had in your division was seeing us together."

"I see each parolee individually. Period. That's it," she said. "We will continue this conversation in the office."

Elaine told Jamel to sit back down in the waiting area. Then she started down the hall leading to the officers' report rooms. Russell walked behind her. By now, Elaine was seething. She did not like Russell, and now it looked like this woman was going to be her new parole officer. Elaine thought she had gotten this officer out of her life after Jamel was transferred to someone else's caseload, but here she was once again.

Her animosity toward Officer Russell stemmed not only from Jamel's complaints but from what she had heard from other family members, too. Everybody in the family knew Officer Russell. Nobody liked her style. When Camacho used to stop by the apartment, he stayed in the front foyer, chatted briefly with Elaine, then left. Officer Russell did the opposite; she walked in, strode down the corridor, and inspected each bedroom. After she left, everyone in the apartment complained about her for days, criticizing her gruff manner and accusing her of violating their privacy.

Ana Russell was forty years old, four years younger than Elaine. Unlike Elaine, she had no children and had never been married. Elaine thought that she was West Indian, but in fact she was from Costa Rica. She had moved to New York City when she was fourteen years old.

Elaine would have been surprised to learn that there were a few similarities in their upbringings. Russell had also grown up poor in a large family—one of six siblings raised by a single mother. In the mid-1970s, when Elaine was living in her own apartment in a city housing project in East Harlem, Russell and her family moved into a housing project in Coney Island.

Unlike Elaine, Russell graduated from high school and went on to a four-year private college in Buffalo, where she majored in psychology. By the time Elaine met her, she had been a parole officer for ten years. Occasionally, she recognized a few of the parolees who came into the office because they had grown up in the same building as her. She had little patience for these men, or for anyone else who committed crimes. "I was in the same rough-neck neighborhoods, but just didn't associate with the rough necks," she would say.

By now, Officer Russell already knew a few things about Elaine. She knew Elaine had spent many years in prison for selling drugs. She knew that Elaine lived in a messy, overcrowded apartment. She also knew that Elaine had called her supervisor in the past to complain about how she had treated Jamel when he was still on her caseload.

Officer Russell sat down at her desk and Elaine sat in a chair. Immediately, Elaine began to complain—about her long wait, about how Russell had spoken to her son in the past, about how she was tired of being bounced from one officer to another, about how Russell should see her and Jamel together.

To Officer Russell, it seemed like Elaine thought she was the one in charge. On occasions like this one, Russell relied on a few of her standard lines. "You're sitting on that side of the desk; I'm sitting on this side," Russell said. "So who calls the shots? Be careful how you speak to me."

Elaine did not respond. Officer Russell picked up her pen and continued with her usual routine. "Where do you work?" she asked.

Just like every other parole officer, Russell had to make an entry in Elaine's chrono notes, noting any changes in her life, including her residence or employment status.

"Did you read my chart?" Elaine asked. "Did you take the time to familiarize yourself with my case?"

"Where do you work?" Russell asked.

Elaine did not reply.

"Just answer my question," Russell said. "Where do you work?"

Elaine refused to respond, even though she knew her silence constituted a violation of Parole Rule 5: "I will reply promptly, fully and truthfully to any inquiry of or communication by my Parole Officer or other representative of the Division of Parole."

"There is an interaction that takes place when you make your face-to-face reports," Officer Russell said. "I make the inquiries, and you're obliged to respond truthfully and properly according to the guidelines of your parole." Once more, the officer asked, "Where do you work?"

"If you need to find out anything about me, you can read my record," Elaine said. "I'm not going to tell you a damn thing."

Officer Russell stepped out of the room. Her supervisor was not around, but she returned with another senior parole officer.

"Just answer her question," he said. "That's all."

"I'm not going to answer that," Elaine said. "This woman is disrespecting me."

"How is she disrespecting you?"

"By the way she's talking to me."

"We're going to ask you one more time: 'Where do you work?' "

Elaine did not answer.

"Stand up."

As the senior parole officer watched, Officer Russell pulled out a pair of steel cuffs and locked Elaine's wrists behind her back.

"Are you going to answer the question, or are we going to have to take you in?" he asked.

"Do what you got to do," Elaine said.

She sat back down. Despite her best efforts, her tough veneer was beginning to crumble. Pretending she did not care what happened to her next was, of course, a huge lie. Her legs shook. One foot started to flap.

She watched Officer Russell dump the contents of her pocketbook onto the desk. A pack of Newports, a black book filled with business cards, a pen, an envelope, her Project Renewal ID card, the leather wallet Nate had sent her. Elaine knew that Russell was inspecting her possessions to prepare for taking her into custody.

As Officer Russell walked toward the door, Elaine contemplated kicking her in the shins. Stopping herself required all the energy she could muster. She knew that if she did explode, she would give the officer yet another reason to take her back to jail. And she knew that if

Jamel heard she had been locked up, he would erupt. Then they'd both end up on Rikers Island.

Elaine liked to think of herself not as a parolee but as a political activist. Yet here she was in this drab parole office, dressed in her work clothes, with a pair of cuffs digging into her wrists. In this office, in the eyes of Officer Russell, all she had accomplished seemed to count for nothing. She was just another drug dealer, just another garden-variety criminal. She had thought these days were over—the days of being treated like a number instead of a person—but here she was, still paying for a mistake she had made eighteen years earlier.

On past visits here, she had seen plenty of other parolees seated just as she was now, with their wrists locked behind their backs. She had seen the fingerprint smudges left behind on the office walls by parolees who were ordered to put their hands up so an officer could frisk them before they were cuffed. When she had been on Camacho's caseload, she had never doubted she would leave this building on her own. But this day was different. Now she was getting a taste of the Division of Parole's true power.

She had never heard the term *cuff therapy*, but every parole officer here knew what it meant: snapping a pair of cuffs around a parolee's wrists, then letting the person sit and stew for a while. Cuff therapy was a tactic officers used on parolees who did not comply. Not all officers endorsed this practice, but many did, and for one reason: It worked. Ten or twenty minutes with his arms locked behind his back was usually enough to scare a parolee into submission.

The parole officer who shared this report room with Russell turned to Elaine. "You don't want to go to jail," he said. "Do you really want to be locked up for two weeks? I can tell you are a very proud woman, but don't let your pride get in the way, because right now you're in a no-win situation." The officer's calming words were a standard tactic. Parole officers in the same report room often played the roles of good cop/bad cop in order to get parolees to cool down.

"I understand what you're saying," Elaine said, "but I'm not going to be treated like that, whether I'm on parole or off. So if it means me being dragged downtown, I guess I just have to do it to make a statement."

Officer Russell returned to the room. As the minutes passed, Elaine's stubbornness slowly began to subside. If Elaine had become more belligerent—if she had sworn again or shouted at Russell—she would have spent at least the next fifteen days on Rikers Island. Instead, after about twenty minutes, the senior parole officer returned and unlocked her cuffs.

Officer Russell continued where she had left off. "Where do you work?" she asked.

"Project Renewal," Elaine said.

"Do you bring in pay stubs?"

"No. I don't have to do that. I did that in the beginning."

"Bring in a pay stub next time. What time is your curfew?"

"I don't have a curfew."

"All parolees have a curfew."

Technically, everyone on parole is supposed to obey a curfew, but Camacho had been flexible about this rule. He had given Elaine permission to work at night. If she got off work at midnight and returned to the apartment at 12:45 a.m., he did not threaten her with prison. And if she wanted to spend a night at Lora's house in Queens, he gave her permission.

Officer Russell pulled out a yellow form, which bore the heading SPECIAL CONDITIONS OF RELEASE TO PAROLE SUPERVISION. Just like the handcuffs, this piece of paper was a tangible reminder about who was in charge. In the space below the heading, Russell wrote, "I will abide by a curfew of 12:30 a.m. to 8:00 a.m. when scheduled to work 4:00 p.m. to 12:00 a.m., and on days off Fridays, Saturdays, and Sundays, I will abide by a 9:00 p.m. to 7:00 a.m. curfew inside of my approved residence. . . . Failure to abide by the above-written special condition may result in a violation of my parole."

Watching Officer Russell write these words, Elaine could feel herself getting angry all over again.

"Read this piece of paper," Russell said.

On the bottom of the form was a blank space for a parolee's signature. "Sign this," she told Elaine.

"I'm not signing that," Elaine said. "To sign that means I agree with that, and I don't."

Russell called for the supervisor again. "What now?" he asked.

"She's refusing to sign the paper."

"Just put on the paper that she refused to sign."

For the last ten months, Elaine had been on a once-a-month reporting schedule. She had earned this privilege by following parole's rules for a year. Now Officer Russell told her that she was being put back on a weekly schedule. She would have to report back here again the following Thursday.

Elaine returned to the waiting room. Jamel stood when he saw her, and she held the door open for him. She did not utter a word about what had just transpired. She would wait until after his meeting with Officer Russell to tell him about her own.

Elaine left the parole office, and at 2:45 p.m., she walked into Project Renewal. She was seventy-five minutes early, but she figured she would feel better if she were here, rather than wandering around the streets fuming. She saw Felix Laboy, a friend and coworker, who was also on parole.

"I had a rough day," Felix said.

"I did, too," Elaine replied. "I almost got locked up."

"For what?"

"For not answering where I work at."

"It's got to be more than that."

"I'm dead serious."

Elaine called everyone she could think of who might be able to help: Lora, Randy, Tony. She called Reverend Annie Bovian, who ran the Women's Advocate Ministry in Harlem and had been a frequent visitor to Bedford Hills. She could not reach everyone, but she managed to track down Lora. "Now I won't be able to come to your house on the weekend," Elaine told her. Elaine sounded so upset that Lora offered to drive into Manhattan to visit her at work that evening.

Every time Elaine got a sympathetic ear on the phone, her frustration and fury spilled out. "Can you picture that?" she asked. "Me being back in prison for Christmas? If it wasn't so close to the holidays, I probably would've gone to jail. It makes no damn sense. They act like they don't want to let you go. It's crazy. Two years of straight, good parole with no problems. So, c'mon. What's going on? You're telling me if I earn something and I get switched, they can take it away from me, so what I earned means nothing.

"How do you take a person's case if you don't even review the charts? She's not even trying too hard. She's obviously not reading my chart or any paperwork on me. What are y'all writing in it for if you don't read it? I have no understanding. I'm going to make as much noise as I can, until they get sick of hearing about Elaine Bartlett. I ain't letting it go."

Venting to her friends made her feel a little better. What she really wanted, though, was some sort of recourse. But for a parolee who feels she has been treated disrespectfully, there is really nowhere to go. Any attempt to fight back can easily backfire. If Elaine called the parole office and shouted at a supervisor, she would likely enrage Officer Russell, placing herself in an even more precarious position.

That night, Danae was so distraught she couldn't sleep. She spent the evening outdoors, wandering around in the cold. All she could think about was her mother seated in the parole office, her hands cuffed together. "That crushed me when I heard about it, so I know that must've crushed her," Danae said the next day. "If my mom gets locked up, I don't know what I'll do."

Though she was nineteen years old, Danae's voice sounded like a little girl's. Her mother's near miss at the parole office tapped into her greatest fear: that her mother would go back to prison. Danae rarely talked about it, but she had been worried about this possibility from the moment her mother returned home from prison.

This was part of the reason she had been reluctant to get close to her; she did not want to get used to the idea of having her mother around, just in case she did not stay long. After all, Danae had already watched two uncles come home from prison, then get arrested and leave once again.

Even before this latest saga, Danae had disliked Officer Russell. She had watched many parole officers pass through her home over the years, and this one she especially loathed. One night, Officer Russell had approached Jamel, Danae, and their friends while they were hanging around outside the Wald Houses. "It's past your curfew," the officer said to Jamel. "You need to be upstairs right now."

Danae could see that Jamel was mad, but that he was powerless, too. The idea of this woman embarrassing her older brother in front of his friends upset Danae. "It's like she's his mother, instead of being his parole officer," Danae said.

Another day, Danae was the only person home when Officer Russell knocked on the apartment door. "I'm looking for Jamel Paschall," she said.

"He's not here," Danae replied.

Officer Russell headed down the narrow hall, poking her head in each bedroom.

"I'm telling you, he's not here," Danae said. "I wouldn't lie. He's not here. You can't do that. You don't have a search warrant."

Over the years, Russell had encountered many family members of parolees who were not happy to see her walking in their front door. Usually she told them all the same thing. "If you don't want me to come back to your house, have him live in a shelter," she said.

Hearing that this same woman had now almost sent her mother back to jail, Danae was furious. "That shit got me tight," she said. "If I see her in a dark alley, I'm going to beat her. Every time everything goes good for us, something goes wrong."

There were twelve days until Christmas, and Danae was looking forward to celebrating the holiday with her mother, sister, and both brothers. She had never been with all of them on Christmas before, except for her first Christmas, when she was only a year old. This year, there was talk of a six-foot tree, dozens of presents, and tables full of food. Finally, the family had some money. Elaine had just received a check from the lawsuit she had filed after her car accident. It was for $16,108.

Danae knew that her mother had to go back to the parole office the following Thursday, five days before Christmas. What if something happened and she got arrested? Danae could tell that her mother was trying to be strong for all of them, just as she had all those years in the prison visiting room. "We can't let anyone mess up our holiday," Elaine had said. Still, Danae worried all the time that she would lose her mother once again.

CHAPTER 42

Elaine did not know who had slipped the one-page flyer under the apartment door, but it promised exactly what she wanted.

STOP PAYING RENT NOW!!

At Last
We are in your Neighborhood!

Lay-A-Way Homes

LOOK HOW EASY WE MAKE IT:

1-4 family homes in the Bronx, Brooklyn,
Staten Island, and Westchester.
Good, bad or no credit. We can help!
Low down payment! *
Low to No closing cost! *

Two weeks after Christmas, Elaine called Lay-A-Way Homes. Somebody on the phone told her about a home for sale in the South Bronx, and so she and Satara went to check it out. A salesperson showed them a three-family building. After looking around the place—at the backyard, the kitchen, the bedroom—they decided it was perfect. The broker informed them that it was $299,000 but that monthly payments would only be about $2,300. Elaine figured she could rent out two of the units, then use that rental income to make her own payments.

There was one catch, however. The salesperson told Elaine that she would have to pay $5,000 up front to hold the place. To Elaine, this demand sounded reasonable. After all, she certainly did not want anyone else to get this house; she wanted to move her family in as soon as possible.

Most people planning to purchase a home would likely know other people—friends or relatives—who had already negotiated this daunting maze. Not Elaine. Except for a few coworkers, she did not know anybody who owned their own home. Brokers, down payments, mortgages, interest rates—all of this was foreign to her. She had picked up a few brochures about mortgages at her bank, but she found them very confusing.

Elaine spent the next week mulling over what to do. Jamel told her to pay the $5,000. "Ma, don't worry about it," he said. "We'll rent rooms out. We'll make it happen. We'll do what we need to." All day, every day, he lobbied her to hurry up and give the broker the money. Every time the floor creaked or the toilet gurgled, he said, "That's Grandma telling y'all it's time to go. What are you waiting for?"

Eight months after leaving prison, Jamel was still sleeping in the living room. Elaine and his girlfriend Joanna had bought him a futon so that he would no longer have to lie on the floor. Still, he had no privacy. By now, the living room was extremely messy. Jamel was so tired of being in this apartment that he had stopped cleaning. This was the same tactic he had used in prison. When he was unhappy about where he was living—when he wanted the guards to move him from one cell block to another—he had broadcast his displeasure by refusing to clean his cell.

At times, Elaine sounded ready to hand over the $5,000. "You gotta take risks," she said. "If you don't, nothing will happen." Part of her eagerness had to do with the timing: The second anniversary of her release from prison was two weeks away. By now, she thought, she should have already achieved her dream: living in her own home with all her children. The reality of her current life—residing in somebody else's apartment, sharing a bed with her older son—made her feel as if she had accomplished nothing.

Elaine called Lora for advice. "Don't jump on the first thing," Lora said. Elaine thought about Lora's words and eventually decided not to give the broker the money. By now, Elaine and Jamel were no longer on Officer Russell's caseload; for some reason that had not been explained to them, they had been moved to another officer. This meant there was one less reason they had to hurry up and move. Nonetheless, Jamel was furious when he heard the news; he thought Elaine had made a mistake. Now neither of them would ever know what might have happened if she'd handed over the money.

The longer it took Elaine to find a place to live, the less money she had in her bank account. Christmas had been costly. She had bought presents for everyone, including a red leather jacket for Tenéa, who was now two and a half years old. Lora gave Elaine her first cell phone, a Nextel, as a Christmas gift, and over the next days it rang constantly. The news about Elaine's lawsuit settlement had spread quickly, and now everybody wanted a piece of it: her sister Michelle, Michelle's children, Michelle's neighbor, Frankie's widow, Becky, Becky's sons.

These calls enraged Elaine. Becky, for one, had never visited her in Bedford Hills. "This woman didn't bring up my nephews once to come see me in the whole sixteen years, and she got the audacity to call me to pay her cable and put food in the house," Elaine said. Despite her grumbling, however, Elaine gave Becky's family almost two weeks' pay: $80 for a cable bill, $46 for food, $200 for a winter coat, and $200 for a plane ticket so one of Becky's sons could get back to Iowa, where he was attending college on a basketball scholarship.

Elaine's savings continued to shrink in February and March. For Satara and Danae's birthdays, she gave them each $200. When Apache had a fund-raiser for Exodus, his basketball club, she spent more than $100 on tickets. The event was held at Riverbank Park in Harlem, and tickets were ten dollars each. Elaine bought enough so that all her nieces and nephews could attend. At the game, Michelle complained that she was broke; Elaine grudgingly gave her $200. "Fuck that," Elaine said afterward. "Everybody can't just think they're going to live off of me."

At work, Elaine confided in her friend Felix about her money stresses. He understood. The previous summer, Felix had been released from prison after thirteen years. At first, he, too, had spoiled his son, buying him expensive new sneakers and clothes because he felt guilty about having been gone for so long. "You get all caught up in trying to please people," he told Elaine. "It was hard, but I had to cut that off." He urged her to do the same. She tried to follow his advice, but then, just as she was getting better at saying no, she got her first cell phone bill. It was nearly $500.

In the spring, Apache told his mother about Yvonne Stennett, who runs the Community League of West 159th Street, in Washington Heights. Apache had met Yvonne several months earlier, and they had become allies. She was impressed with his efforts to build a basketball club. And she fell in love with his mission: to help teenagers from poor neighborhoods win college scholarships. To help him out, she had organized his first fund-raiser.

When Apache told Yvonne about his family's housing problems, she offered to help. Her organization owns several apartment buildings in Washington Heights, which are subsidized by Section 8, the federal housing program. The guidelines are stringent, but Yvonne told Elaine that she could have an apartment if she received approval. In March, Elaine collected the requisite paperwork—birth certificates, statements of income—and delivered it all to the Community League's office. At the end of May, Elaine was still waiting for word about an opening.

Meanwhile, Star and Satara were also trying to get out of Apartment 13B and had applied to the Housing Authority for a transfer.

"The apartment has been in our family for twenty-two years and we have had some rough times," Star wrote on the application. "We no longer feel comfortable living here. Our uncle died here in 10/93 (Ronald Bartlett) next to our grandmother in 3/98 (Yvonne Bartlett) and now recently my mother in June of 2001 (Sabrina Bartlett). We are ready to move on to a new start where we won't feel so peculiar, when we are home alone."

Star and Satara's transfer application was for a three-bedroom place—enough room for them and their two children. Satara remembers telling Elaine about applying for a transfer, but Elaine insists she knew nothing about it. At any rate, in mid-May, Elaine found out that Star and Satara had been assigned a new apartment in the Polo Grounds project in Harlem. At the end of June 2002, the Bartlett family was going to lose the lease to Apartment 13B. Now Elaine, Jamel, Apache, and Danae had four weeks to find a new place to live.

CHAPTER 43

Elaine sat on the edge of a storage bin in the back bedroom, sorting through papers and photos: a snapshot from Jamel's twelfth birthday, Satara's fourth-grade class picture, a letter from Project Renewal chastising her for "failure to report to work." Plastic storage bins surrounded her, climbing almost to the ceiling. This room held everyone's possessions: Jamel's shirts, Tenéa's Easy-Bake oven, Apache's basketball trophies. Long ago, Elaine had stopped referring to this as her bedroom; instead, she called it "my storage room."

It was the last Saturday afternoon in June, and the temperature on the street was 84 degrees. In this room, it felt much hotter. Elaine wore boxer shorts and a T-shirt with a teddy bear on it. A scrunchy held her hair up in a ponytail atop her head. The room reeked of sweaty dogs. By now, she owned three: Kyra, the rottweiler, and two red-nose pit bull puppies, named Red and Mills. (Jamel had picked the name Mills, which was short for the word *millions*.) The pit bulls were in a cage and the rottweiler was chained to the radiator. To keep them cool, Elaine dropped ice cubes in their water bowls.

Soul Train played on the television atop the bureau behind her, but she did not watch. Instead, she kept sorting through her papers. She discovered a receipt from a clothing store, where she had spent $297.68 on gifts for Tenéa and for Star's son Joe. The receipt reminded her of how much money she had frittered away buying things for her family. She tore it up and dropped the pieces in a plastic bag. "I don't need to keep receipts, because they make me angry," she said.

For Elaine, this weekend marked the end of one chapter in her life and the start of another. It was the end of twenty-nine months of prayer and sweat: scanning apartment listings, leaving phone messages, visiting apartments, waiting for return calls, filling out forms, badgering various agencies. A few days ago, she had received good news: the Community League of West 159th Street had an apartment available. It was a fifth-floor walk-up, and it had four bedrooms, enough space for everybody.

Finally, Elaine was about to have a home of her own. In some ways, though, this accomplishment was bittersweet. She had dreamed of living with all her children, but now the best she could hope for was three out of four. Satara's decision to apply for her own apartment felt like a betrayal, but Elaine tried not to let her hurt show. At the moment, Satara was in her bedroom packing, too.

Elaine was confident that Apache and Jamel would join her in the new apartment. She knew Apache would not be home much, though, because he was always running around to basketball tournaments. And, finally, Jamel had started making inroads into the rap industry. His friend Littles had hooked him up with Mobb Deep, and now Jamel worked for them part time, setting up for their concerts. He had gone on the road with them to Virginia, and he even had the chance to get up onstage and perform as an opening act.

Elaine wanted Danae to live with her, too, but she knew she could not force her. Pleading with her, shouting at her, threatening her—none of that was going to work. Elaine had already given her a set of keys to the new apartment. "You're twenty," she told her. "Do what you want."

Two and a half years of effort on Elaine's part had not straightened out Danae, at least not in Elaine's opinion. A year ago, she had been arrested for taking a motor scooter from a Chinese restaurant and riding it around in the Wald project. The crime was only a misdemeanor, but Elaine thought it was a bad sign. Then, several months ago, Danae had dropped out of high school in her fifth year.

Now, as far as Elaine could tell, Danae spent every day smoking marijuana and hanging out with her girlfriend, Nena, who lived nearby. Nena was Danae's first girlfriend, and they made no secret of their affection for each other. Nena had scribbled "Nena ❤ Nay-nay" on walls all over the project. Elaine did not mind Danae having a girlfriend, as long as she was doing something productive. Danae sometimes talked about getting her GED or joining Job Corps, but she never seemed to do much more than talk.

Earlier that day, Jamel had packed his clothes and letters into two large duffel bags, and now he was off hanging out with a girl. Apache was coaching a basketball game. Elaine had no idea where Danae was. Then, at 6:00 p.m., she appeared in the doorway of the back bedroom, a red-and-white baseball hat perched sideways atop her head.

"Ma, I'm hungry," Danae said.

"There's some spaghetti in the fridge," Elaine told her.

"That shit has been there for three days."

"Oh, well."

Danae walked out.

"Good-bye," Elaine said.

She rolled her eyes. "They come here and tell me they're hungry, and I'm supposed to buy something for them when I'm trying to move?" she said. "They're crazy."

The only family member interested in helping Elaine pack was Tenéa, who had recently celebrated her third birthday. She ambled into the bedroom wearing gold earrings, a gold necklace, and no pants. Her yellow terry-cloth top had snaps along the crotch, but at the moment it was unsnapped. Tenéa leaned over and picked up a matchbook off the floor. "Here, Grandma," she said.

Elaine held open the trash bag and Tenéa dropped the matchbook in.

"Thank you for being so helpful," Elaine said.

· · ·

At the beginning of July, Elaine moved into the new apartment in Washington Heights, just north of Harlem. She should have been ecstatic, but she was not. Like much in her life, this summer was not turning out at all the way she had hoped it would. A few days after she moved, she went to the bank, slipped her card into an ATM machine, and discovered her balance was zero.

She marched over to a teller. "There's no way there could be no money in my account," she said. "That's impossible. Y'all have got to be messed up."

Elaine did not study her account summaries when they arrived in the mail each month, but she thought she had about $7,000 left over from her lawsuit settlement. The teller reviewed her account and told her that many of her checks had been cashed recently. This confused Elaine. She remembered writing only two checks, both about a year ago. Then she had tossed her checkbook in a bag and shoved the bag in the back bedroom closet at 13B.

Had somebody fished out her checkbook and stolen her checks? Standing in front of the teller, Elaine silently reviewed the possible suspects: everybody who might have been in that back bedroom. She doubted a stranger had sneaked in and found her checkbook. It had to have been a family member. Elaine did not explain this to the teller, however.

When she got back to her new apartment, she did not tell Apache or Jamel or anyone else about the missing money. She found a gold chain Jamel had given her as a gift, took it to a pawnshop, and got $300, enough to buy food and subway tokens until she got her next paycheck. She knew Jamel would be irate if he found out she had pawned the chain, so she told him she had dropped it off at the repair shop.

Elaine did not call any of her relatives and interrogate them. In some ways, she did not even want to know who had stolen her checks. Once she knew for certain, she would have to confront that person, and this time she did not think she would be able to control her fists. So much rage had built up inside her that once she unleashed it, she worried, she would be capable of just about anything. "I'm like a time bomb," she said.

Another person in her predicament might have called the cops, but Elaine did not want to involve the police in her family dramas. That would only invite extra scrutiny from her new parole officer, which she certainly did not want. Silence seemed the only solution. She tried to forget about the missing money altogether and to pretend that everything was okay. This was the only way she could think of to quiet her rage.

Several days later, Elaine got a phone call that reminded her about her empty bank account. Satara told her that Michelle had just been arrested. In fact, this was the second time Michelle had been arrested in five days. In both cases, one of Michelle's friends, who worked as a home health aide, had allegedly stolen checks from an employer. She had given some of these checks to Michelle, who was accused of depositing them in her own bank account.

The news upset Elaine so much that she started pacing the apartment, walking in circles around the living room. Satara's call made her suspect that Michelle had robbed her, too, but right now her missing money was the least of the family's problems. Now there was an apartment full of kids, with no mother to watch them.

Nobody knew what would happen with Michelle's case—whether she would get probation, do a short sentence on Rikers Island, or be sent upstate. The fact that she did not have a criminal record would work in her favor, but there were no guarantees. Under different circumstances, Elaine would have gone downtown to the courthouse for her sister's arraignment. But on this night, she stayed home.

Michelle spent the next four days in the women's jail on Rikers Island. She had been charged with grand larceny and accused of stealing more than $18,500. After her husband posted $5,000 for bail, she was released.

On the last weekend in July, while she was waiting for her cases to be resolved, she threw a huge family picnic in Rucker Park, near West 155th Street and Eighth Avenue. Elaine showed up for a few hours. She managed to get along with Michelle by barely talking to her and by never raising the subject of her missing money.

Despite her suspicions, Elaine had no evidence that Michelle was the culprit. She had never followed up with the bank and obtained copies of the checks that had been cashed. If she had, she might have been able to figure out who was to blame.

The following night, Elaine was at her apartment when someone rang the buzzer to her front door. She pressed the button on the intercom. "Who is it?" she asked.

The response was scratchy, but she could just make out the words: "Mel jumped off a bridge and he's in the hospital."

Elaine grabbed her pocketbook and sprinted down the five flights of stairs. In front of her building, she found Michelle and Satara. Elaine did not have a phone in her apartment and she had just lost her Nextel. In order to deliver the latest news, Michelle and Satara had come over on foot.

Apparently, Jamel had been unable to reach Elaine, so he had called Michelle's apartment. Michelle did not know exactly what had happened, but she did know Jamel was at Bellevue Hospital. Elaine flagged a cab, and she and Satara climbed in.

By the time they got to the hospital, Apache was already there. Danae showed up soon after. A police officer informed Elaine that she could not see Jamel. "Your son is under arrest," the officer told her. He did not say what Jamel was accused of doing, but he told her she had to go to the nearest precinct to get permission to see him.

Elaine had no intention of leaving the hospital. She searched around and found a nurse, who told her that Jamel was upstairs in the X-ray area. The nurse showed her which room to wait in. Eventually, Jamel was rolled in on a stretcher; he was wearing a neck brace and had a cast on his right leg. Elaine hurried over to him and covered his face with kisses. "Are you all right?" she asked. "What's hurting?"

She held his head up so he could talk, and Jamel told her a convoluted tale. Somebody had threatened his friend Chiquito, so he had tried to defend him. A pack of people chased both of them down Delancey Street, toward the Williamsburg Bridge. To escape the crowd, Jamel had jumped off the side of the bridge near the entrance, injuring his leg and his foot when he landed. Cops found two guns at the scene, and now here he was, lying on a hospital bed, one wrist cuffed to the bed frame.

"Ma, don't be mad at me," Jamel said. "I couldn't help it. I couldn't let them fuck up Chiquito."

"Oh, my God," Elaine said. "Here we go again."

CHAPTER 44

January 26, 2003, marked the third anniversary of Elaine's release from prison. She celebrated by taking a week off from work. On the day her vacation ended, she got up at 5:00 a.m. Seated on the edge of her bed, she peered into the mirror above the dresser. Her bedroom was dark except for a bulb above the mirror and the glow of the television. She picked up a comb and began working it through her hair. In three hours, she had to be at Project Renewal.

She had moved into this apartment seven months ago. For the last six months, Jamel had been on Rikers Island, charged with gun possession. Because this is a C-level felony, he faced up to fifteen years in prison. Michelle had pleaded guilty in her two cases, and had received five years probation. She had spent a total of thirty-nine nights in jail, and now she was back home.

So far, Elaine had only managed to scrounge together enough cash to decorate her bedroom and the bathroom. With help from Reverend Bovian of the Women's Advocate Ministry, she had bought a lacquered bedroom set, including a queen-size bed, two night tables, an armoire, and a dresser. Her mother's antique doll, which she had found in Apartment 13B—the black girl dressed in a green coat with fur trim—stood atop the armoire.

Two of her grandchildren sprawled on the bed. Tenéa hugged a pillow. Little Mel stretched diagonally across the sheets. Despite the hissing of the radiator and the voices from the television, both children were asleep.

A slender young man walked in and stretched out on the bed beside the children. He had a seductive smile, uneven facial hair, and skin the color of dark chocolate. Everyone who met him assumed he was Elaine's son or nephew. In fact, he was her boyfriend. At twenty-one, he was less than half her age, and younger than three of her four children. He was not quite as stunning as Taye Diggs in *How Stella Got Her Groove Back,* but he was pretty close.

His name was Deon, and she had met him two years earlier at Project Renewal, where he had been a resident. At first, she had treated him like one of her children, calling him "my son," but after a while their relationship became romantic. Staff members were forbidden from dating clients, so they had kept secret their feelings for each other. After she had moved uptown, he'd left Project Renewal and moved in with her.

This morning, he wore gray sweatpants and a T-shirt. He usually wore his hair in cornrows, but now it was unbraided and half its usual length. He rubbed his head and muttered something about how he did not like the way she had cut it the day before.

"It's five-thirty-five in the morning," she said. "I don't feel like debating with you what you're going to do with your hair."

She walked across the hall to the bathroom, which she had decorated with a dolphin motif. Dolphins appeared on the bath towels, the hand towels, the shower rug, the toilet seat cover, and the shower curtain holders. She washed her hands, then returned to the bedroom.

"Ain't nothing wrong with your hair," she said. "It was dead. It needed to come off. You want me to buy you a wig?"

Deon didn't answer.

"I'm going to get a few wigs," she continued. "I'm going to try being a blonde and see how they're living. They say blondes have more fun."

She sat back down on the bed, squeezed a little lotion into one palm, then rubbed it on the heels and soles of both feet. With two children asleep next to her, Elaine's life now was not so different in some ways from the one she had led twenty years ago, before she had gone to prison. Little Mel was now the same age Jamel had been when she was arrested. Tenéa was one year older than Satara had been. Some weekends, Apache's daughter, Baby Tara, came here, too, riding the train in from her mother's house on Long Island. She was now eight, two years younger than Apache had been when Elaine had left him.

At the moment, Elaine had on a tank top and a pair of skin-tight Pepe jeans that Deon had bought for her. The jeans had silver stars sewn onto the right thigh and a small U.S. flag on the left shin. They looked like the sort of pants a teenager would wear, not a forty-five-year-old woman.

She stood in front of her closet and searched for a shirt. By now, she owned so many clothes that the closet was stuffed. There was not even enough room for all her jackets, and so they hung from the closet's doors. She owned nearly thirty pairs of shoes, which she had double- and triple-stacked on the closet floor: pink Timberland boots, blue Timberland boots, several pairs of Nikes, high heels, loafers, sandals.

"My clothes are getting limited," she said. "I need a whole new wardrobe. For real."

She grabbed a white T-shirt off the closet shelf. Then she crouched down and picked out a pair of black Nikes with a red swoosh, another gift from Deon. Earlier, Tenéa had been squirting baby powder around her room, and the evidence was on Elaine's sneakers. She carried them into the kitchen, turned on the cold water, stuck the corner of a hand towel under the faucet, and then scrubbed the sneakers.

A whimpering sound came from the darkened living room. She had given away the rottweiler, but she still had the two pit bulls. She had last walked them at 2:00 a.m., and so she decided not to take them out again. "Be quiet!" she shouted.

Back in the bedroom, she found her Girbaud denim jacket and began to unbutton it. She slipped on the jacket, then put on a red leather belt Nate had sent her from prison. Although she had not been back to see him in a year, he still called her every week or two. Ever since he'd found out about Deon, however, their phone conversations had turned into shouting matches.

Elaine squirted jasmine-scented body mist on her hair, wrists, and neck. Then she turned to her closet once again and pulled out her Baby Phat parka. She searched its pockets for money, discovered a few bills, and stuffed them in her jeans pocket. In the top drawer of her dresser, she found a few Metrocards.

She put one hand in the pocket of Deon's jacket, which hung on the closet door. "I know you got some gum in here," she said. She found a pack of Big Red and took a piece. Then she leaned over and kissed him on the lips. He squeezed his arms around one of her denim-clad thighs. She kissed him once again, then giggled.

"C'mon," she said. "I gotta go." She quickly inspected his hair. "I'll fix it up when I come home," she said. "See you later."

She headed down the hall past Danae's bedroom, which had been transformed into a playroom over the last few months.

Shortly after Elaine had moved into the apartment, Danae had moved in, too, bringing her girlfriend with her. The fact that neither of them worked or went to school aggravated Elaine. To her, it seemed they spent all their time in their room with the door closed. "The only time you come out of that room is to eat or buy some weed," Elaine had said to Danae. "The only time you talk to me is when you want five dollars."

Eventually, Elaine had told Danae and Nena to leave. The next day, she spent her last thirty-eight dollars on a new lock for the front door. Danae was now staying with Nena at Michelle's house. Elaine still hoped Danae would move back, though not with her girlfriend. Elaine clung to any promising sign. The most recent had occurred a few days earlier, when Danae stopped by, gave her a hug, and told her, "I love you."

Across the hall from Danae's bedroom was Apache's room. This morning, his bed was empty; he had spent the night at his girlfriend's apartment on the Lower East Side. Lately, he had been spending many nights there, trying to help out his girlfriend's family. In an eerie coincidence, her father had been sentenced recently to 15-to-life under the Rockefeller drug laws. Like Elaine, he had not had a prior arrest record.

The hall turned left and led to Jamel's bedroom. Jamel had picked the room closest to the front door because it had the most privacy, but he had slept there only a few nights. Elaine opened the door and turned on the light. CDs covered his bed. Baseball caps lined the closet shelf, next to a box of Trojans. A crack ran up the door; it had appeared after Jamel put in a lock.

"That boy is going to have a fit if I don't fix his door," she said. She shut the door and walked out of the apartment.

Sunlight streaked the sky by the time she emerged from her building and headed north on Amsterdam Avenue. Every storefront was closed, except for the bodegas and the twenty-four-hour Laundromat. "Good morning," she said to the man behind the counter at the bodega on West 161st Street. "Can I have a light and sweet?" She handed him a dollar through a bulletproof window. He gave her a cup of coffee.

At 6:20 a.m., she crossed the street and descended the steps to the subway. Since it was a Sunday morning, it was impossible to predict how long her commute would take. Usually she tried to leave the apartment by 6:00 a.m. on Sundays.

She stopped in front of the token booth and pulled seven Metrocards out of her pocket. She slid each one through the machine. None had any money left on them.

"Can I have a three-dollar Metrocard?" she asked the clerk in the token booth.

Usually, she bought a $17 card, which entitled her to seven days of unlimited rides, but this morning, she wanted to hold on to her dollars. Little Mel had just moved in and started first grade at a school around the corner. She didn't know yet what he would need, so she wanted to make sure she kept a few dollars in her pocket.

She needed to travel south, but a pink ribbon stretched across the three turnstiles leading to the downtown trains. She had no choice but to go uptown. This was not surprising; the downtown train often did not run early on Sunday mornings.

Some days, Deon walked her here and waited with her for the subway to come. She stood on one side of the turnstile and he stood on the other. They hugged and kissed and joked with each other until they heard a train approach.

"All right," she would say. "You can go see your other girls now."

"Why are you saying that?" he would ask.

She liked to make these sorts of jokes, the ones that minimized his affection for her. The opposite was actually true. It seemed he would do just about anything for her: baby-sit her grandchildren, carry a washing machine up five flights of stairs, pick her up at the train at 1:30 a.m. when she had to work late, cook dinner, mop the floor, go to court for Jamel, take Little Mel to school, walk the pit bulls. Deon did not have a full-time job, but he occasionally did construction work. The rest of his time he spent trying to help Elaine.

She waited for an uptown train on a deserted platform, leaning against a steel column with peeling gray paint. Eventually, a subway appeared. She stepped onto it and got off at the next stop in order to transfer. As she neared the staircase leading to the downtown train, she heard a familiar rumble. She sprinted down the stairs, spilling a few drops of coffee along the way. She got on the downtown A train just before the doors closed.

This morning, she had forty dollars in her pocket. Payday had fallen on the previous Thursday, while she had been on vacation. She had gone to work anyway to pick up her paycheck. The check had put meat in her freezer, but she still had a $130 electric bill to pay.

She had set aside money for this bill, but then Michelle had called, complaining that her children were hungry. Elaine gave Satara $150 to deliver to Michelle. A few days later, she told Satara, "Tell Michelle to call me, because I have to pay my electric bill." Deon overheard her and rolled his eyes, as if to say, You're a fool. Elaine knew he was right; she would not get her money back anytime soon.

By now, she had been working at Project Renewal for two years and eight months. She could hardly believe she had lasted this long. Searching lockers. Breaking up fights. Feeling like a prison guard. She still had an entry-level job as a residential aide. She still earned only $18,000 a year, which was less than she had made when she was twenty-five and working at a beauty parlor.

At the West Fourth Street station, Elaine stepped off the subway and walked to the platform for the F train. She had made this trip on enough mornings to know she should walk to the far end of this platform. That way, when she got off the F train, she would be near the Second Avenue exit, the one closest to her job.

She rode the train to her stop, then walked up the stairs to the exit. There, she discovered that the turnstiles and the revolving doors were locked. She could not get out. She headed back down the stairs and walked all the way to the opposite end of the platform, toward the First Avenue exit.

"You gotta laugh to keep from going insane, or getting mad," she said. "Who wants to get mad first thing in the morning? I had too many of those days."

She tried not to think about prison anymore, but the concrete floor of subway platforms always reminded her of the tunnels at Bedford Hills. Whenever she saw somebody painting a station or mopping its floors, she thought of her own days working in prison on the construction crew.

She left the station, walked down Houston Street, then turned right on Second Avenue, into a strong, freezing wind. The sidewalk was empty except for five pigeons and a few pages of *The Village Voice*, which swirled in the wind. She tugged up the zipper on her parka, then stuck one hand in her pocket and pulled out a Newport. She had only one more cigarette left. Ever since the mayor had increased the tax on cigarettes—raising the price of some brands to seven dollars a pack—she had stopped bringing a whole pack to work. If she did, she knew she would give all her cigarettes away by the end of her shift.

Walking to work early on a Sunday morning did not feel like much of an accomplishment to Elaine, but in many ways it was. Getting up early every day, going to work at a full-time job, and staying out of jail constituted a triumph for any former prisoner.

Nevertheless, this was not the future Elaine had imagined during all her years in Bedford Hills. Nobody in prison fantasizes about returning home to a low-wage job, a three-train commute, a pile of unpaid bills, an angry daughter, a son in jail, a 9:00 p.m. curfew, an empty refrigerator.

Three years after leaving prison, she still had plenty of unmet goals. She wanted to quit smoking, furnish her apartment, start her own business, get Jamel home. And, of course, she was still waiting to go to Jamaica.

She turned left on East Third Street, took one last drag on her cigarette, and dropped it on the sidewalk. It was 7:29 a.m., a half hour before her shift started. She pulled open the door to her job and headed up the stairs.

EPILOGUE

The Rockefeller drug laws turned thirty years old on May 8, 2003. Despite Governor Pataki's promises to rewrite the laws, they remained intact. That spring, Russell Simmons, the hip-hop entrepreneur, joined the battle against them. He teamed up with Randy Credico's group and organized a rally for June 4, to be held on a portable concert stage just south of City Hall. He recruited rap stars to record radio ads and got them aired on the city's hip-hop stations. The list of rally speakers was to include a slew of famous rappers, as well as Elaine Bartlett.

When the rally began, there she was, standing on the stage, next to Satara. Her turn to speak came near the beginning of the rally, right after Fat Joe, but before the Beastie Boys. From the stage, she could see a crowd of thousands. Maybe ten or twenty thousand people, maybe more. It was, of course, the largest audience she had ever had. She looked out at the sea of faces, most of them brown and black— young people who had come to see their favorite rappers, plus a smattering of activists. She knew that her friend Lora Tucker was out there somewhere. And so were two of her "children" from Bedford Hills— women now in their thirties who had recently come home.

Elaine gripped the podium with both hands and leaned toward the microphone.

"For sixteen years, I was known as 84-G-0068," she said in a strong, confident voice. "That's not the person who stands before you today. I'm a mother of four, a grandmother of three. When I went to jail, my daughter Satara Bartlett was two, who stands right here by my side today. I spent sixteen years in Bedford Hills Correctional Facility, under the Rockefeller drug laws. I was a first-time offender, never been arrested a day in my life.

"When I speak today, I'm not only speaking for me; I'm speaking for everybody that is locked up and cannot speak. I'm speaking for everybody's kids that has went through the pain, the agony, and the suffering. When you lock us up, you lock up our whole families. You destroy lives."

Three JumboTron screens projected her image up Broadway, past City Hall. Her words echoed through the streets, amplified by an elaborate sound system. "I'm here to tell you these laws need to be repealed," she continued, her voice angry and insistent. "Clemency is a Band-Aid. Governor Pataki, you gave me clemency, and that was the happiest day of my life. But today is an even happier day of my life. Because today my people know that they can come together. They know they can stand up, and they can fight for their loved ones. And their loved ones know that we're out here fighting for them."

The longer Elaine spoke, the more passionate she became. Soon she was nearly shouting. "We want to tell you that we want these laws changed! We want you to take this money, and instead of wasting it on housing us in prison, put it back into our communities. I don't want to have to go to jail and see my kids! I don't want to have to go to jail and see my grandchildren!

"I'm here to tell you we are sick and tired of the politicians playing with our lives, because that's what you are doing. You tell me that the war on drugs works? I'm telling you the war on drugs does not work! And I'm telling you that we need you to change these laws and help us rebuild our lives for us and our children. Thank you."

Applause and cheers rose from the crowd. Elaine could see people raising their arms and punching the air with their fists. It was the sort of response that so far had greeted only the rap stars. The next day, a columnist for the *Daily News* reported that her speech had "brought many in the crowd to tears."

Reporters from Russia, Germany, and England lined up backstage to interview Elaine. Meanwhile, a steady stream of performers and hip-hop moguls filed past: P. Diddy, 50 Cent, Damon Dash, Mariah Carey, Busta Rhymes. They took turns at the microphone, denouncing the drug laws, then posed for photos backstage. Standing a few feet away, Elaine felt a little like a celebrity, too.

This afternoon was a rare high point in the midst of yet more personal catastrophes. Two months earlier, she had been fired from her job at Project Renewal because she had not been showing up for work. Despite receiving a written warning from her supervisor, she had continued to take days off without permission. After she was fired, she signed up for unemployment. She started receiving $173 a week, which was almost as much as she had earned when she was working.

Now that she had more free time, she devoted much of it to helping Jamel, who was still in jail. She showed up for his court dates, gave him pep talks on the phone, met with his lawyer, and trekked to Rikers Island. At the moment, Jamel was trying to decide whether to accept a prosecutor's offer of 5-to-life or to go to trial and risk getting 15-to-life. Elaine told him to plead guilty. "I can do five years with you, but I can't do fifteen," she said. A week after the rally, Jamel followed her advice. In early July, he was sent to Franklin prison in the northeastern corner of New York state, near the Canadian border.

Nathan was still in prison, too, although he was hoping he would be set free before the end of 2003. The state legislature had not reformed the Rockefeller drug laws during its most recent session, but it did pass a "merit time" provision, allowing certain longtime drug prisoners to be released early if they have a clean prison record. Nate thought he would qualify. But then, in the late summer, he heard there was a catch: only inmates who had completed a certain six-month drug rehab program would be eligible for early release. He signed up for the program and hopes to be set free in 2004.

Meanwhile, Elaine finally managed to get discharged from parole.

Now she no longer has to report to a parole officer. No more drug tests, no more travel passes, no more curfew. Getting off parole was a significant accomplishment, albeit one that did not attract any cameras or news stories. Finally, almost twenty years after her arrest, she was completely free of the criminal-justice system. She celebrated by going over to the apartment of a former coworker and smoking weed.

While there had been countless changes in her life since she'd been released from prison, there was one aspect of it that had not changed: She was still having the same dream. It came to her at night when she slept, and it came during the daytime, too. She never talked about the dream with anyone. Nobody would really understand it, she thought. They would probably think she was crazy. After all, in her dream, she returned to Bedford Hills.

She did not want to go back as a prisoner, of course. And she did not want to return as a visitor, able only to go into the visiting room. She wanted to be whisked through the prison to the gym and then brought up onto the stage, where everyone would be able to see her. She would wear a brand-new outfit, something colorful and stylish. Her hair would be freshly dyed. Her nails would be perfect.

There would be a banquet held in her honor and everybody would be invited—the inmates, the guards, the civilian workers, the administrators, even Superintendent Lord. She knew all her friends would come—the long-termers she had known for years. And she thought all the other prisoners would come, too. By now, she figured, most of them knew her name, even if she did not know theirs.

She could not imagine a sweeter revenge than standing onstage in the prison gym, looking out over this crowd, and delivering a speech. No longer would anybody be able to dismiss her as just another poor, uneducated felon. She would dazzle them with her speaking skills the way she had done on that stage next to City Hall, decrying the Rockefeller drug laws. And she would send a message to every prison official who had ever doubted her. "Remember when you used to look down your nose at me?" she would say. "Well, look at me now."

AUTHOR'S NOTE

SELECTED
BIBLIOGRAPHY

ACKNOWLEDGMENTS

I first met Elaine Bartlett on April 30, 1998. At the time, I was working on a story for *The Village Voice* about the twenty-fifth anniversary of the Rockefeller drug laws, and I traveled to Bedford Hills to interview her and two other prisoners. A photographer came with me; the first two women I interviewed appeared to have dressed up for him. One wore a sleeveless knit top and had her hair pulled up in the back. The other had put on fresh lipstick, eyeliner, and two gold necklaces.

Elaine's was the last interview of the afternoon. When a guard escorted her into the conference room, my first thought was that she looked absolutely awful. Tangled hair. Gray roots. No makeup. No jewelry. She could have worn a blouse or sweater with her green state-issued pants, but instead she had stuck with the complete inmate uniform. Later, I would learn that her friends had told her to dress up, but she had refused. She didn't want to look any better than she felt.

Elaine had never spoken to a reporter before. She was nervous; sweat droplets covered her brow. Yet she spoke with what seemed unusual frankness. For two hours, she spoke to me, a white stranger, about the emotional toll of her imprisonment—her guilt, failures, disappointments, frustrations. Just as she had refused to dress up for this interview, she also refused to pretty up her words. This was, I would come to learn, the way she was nearly all the time: blunt, unpolished, painfully honest.

Only those who have been imprisoned can ever truly know what life in captivity is like, but I was determined to try to learn as much as I could about the experience, and Elaine, it turned out, was more than willing to teach me. When the *Voice* article about the Rockefeller laws appeared, I had already been reporting on New York's prison system for more than a year, visiting prisons across the state. Over the next months, while continuing on that beat, I interviewed Elaine several more times. And on the morning she was released, twenty-one months after our first meeting, I joined the small crowd of reporters waiting across the road from the prison.

At the time, I assumed that her release from Bedford Hills was the happy ending to her story—that her long struggle was over when the governor gave her clemency and she walked out of prison. But when I spoke to her over the next few days, I realized that I was dead wrong. In many ways, it seemed, her struggle had just begun; she had traded one set of hurdles for another.

I asked Elaine if I could spend time in her company in order to write a story about her first year on the outside. She agreed. Over the next months, we spent hundreds of hours together. Sometimes, I asked questions. More often, I just tagged along, watching and taking notes, while she went about her day-to-day life. In her first months home, she had few friends, and I became a sort of confidante. After a while, her family started to refer to me as "Elaine's friend," even though everyone knew I was a reporter.

The Village Voice published a story about Elaine's first year out of prison at the end of 2000. Not long afterward, I began to think that perhaps the story should be expanded into a book. Elaine's experience was becoming increasingly common; more than 600,000 people were leaving prison every year. And I thought that people who had never been to prison would be able to relate to some of her struggles—her efforts to find a job and a place to live, her desire to be a good mother, her determination to stop herself from descending into bitterness.

Elaine, too, had been thinking that she wanted a book to be written about her. She hoped a book might erase her feeling that she had lost so much of her life to prison. "I've got to make those sixteen years count for something," she said.

Over the next two and a half years, from early 2001 to the middle of 2003, I continued to spend many days and months with Elaine while also researching her and her family's past. With the help of an assistant, I tracked down police, court, housing, orphanage, prison, and parole records. I also interviewed close to a hundred people. In order to write about Elaine's arrest, trial, and incarceration, I relied upon these documents as well as memories relayed by her, her family, and other participants. This book contains no pseudonyms; every person is referred to by his or her real name.

In writing about events that occurred after Elaine's release from prison, I relied largely upon my own observations. I witnessed first-hand most of these scenes; for those at which I wasn't present, I conducted interviews with the participants. Virtually everybody I approached for an interview agreed to speak with me. Descriptions of Elaine's inner life—her thoughts and feelings at various moments—are based on in-depth conversations with her. For the most part, these interviews were conducted during or immediately after each event.

Many former inmates try to keep their prison time a secret, never telling anyone but their closest friends that they were once locked up. This is perfectly understandable. After all, prisoners are one of the most despised classes of people in the United States, perhaps second only to terrorists. In many people's eyes, they will be defined forever by their mug shots, their rap sheets, their inmate numbers.

All of this makes Elaine's willingness to cooperate in the writing of this book especially remarkable. It is not easy to trust your life story to a reporter, but for an ex-prisoner it must take tremendous courage, since it requires opening yourself up to the judgments of a society that has already condemned you once. Elaine's hope, and mine, was to challenge some of these assumptions by putting a human face—her face—on a phenomenon that has been largely ignored, and in this way to expose the hidden consequences of our nation's punishment policies.

SELECTED
BIBLIOGRAPHY

Selected Sources

This book is based on the expertise of a great many people, some of whom are mentioned in the preceding chapters. However, there are many other people whose assistance was invaluable. These include: Jeremy Travis, Angela Browne, Robert Gangi, Jennifer Wynn, Marc Mauer, Todd Clear, Michael Jacobson, Elizabeth Gaynes, Jonathan Chasan, David Werber, Heather Barr, Richard Wolf, Cathy Potler, Alice Green, Debbie Mukamal, Craig Haney, Thomas LeBel, Edmond Taylor, Robert Sanchez, Julio Medina, Terrence Stevens, Tyrone Coleman, Hakim Hasan, Thomas Chaskley, District Attorney Paul Clyne, Sheriff James Campbell, Bill Gray, Judge Philip Caponera, Douglas Rutnik, Special Agent Fred Marano, Investigator Robert Sears, Lieutenant Laurie Wagner, Pamela Clickner, Dawn Hurd, Jennifer Duncan, Barbara Martinsons, Benay Rubenstein, Ann Jacobs, John Rakis, Carol Shapiro, Fred Weinberg, Murray Edwards, Richard Levy, John Meehan, Thomas Grant, Martin Cirincione, Joseph Lima, Robert Martinez, Barbara Thompson, Marge Cohen, Linda Foglia, Martin Horn, Thomas Antenen, Stephen Rynn, Barry Apfelbaum, Herbert Fischman, Judith Goldiner, William Cook, Howard Marder, and Christopher Uggen.

In addition, this book benefited from the insights and information contained in the following books, articles, and reports:

Abadinsky, Howard. *Probation and Parole: Theory and Practice.* 7th ed. Upper Saddle River, NJ: Prentice-Hall, 2000.

Abbott, Jack Henry. *In the Belly of the Beast: Letters from Prison*. New York: Random House, 1981; reprint ed., New York: Vintage Books, 1991.

bandele, asha. *The Prisoner's Wife: A Memoir*. New York: Scribner, 1999.

Brown, Claude. *Manchild in the Promised Land*. New York: Macmillan, 1965.

———. "Manchild in Harlem." *The New York Times Magazine*, September 16, 1984.

Butterfield, Fox. *All God's Children: The Bosket Family and the American Tradition of Violence*. New York: Knopf, 1995.

Christianson, Scott. "The Battle Over Punishment." *Empire State Report*, March 1999.

———. *With Liberty for Some: 500 Years of Imprisonment in America*. Boston: Northeastern University Press, 1998.

Cleaver, Eldridge. *Soul on Ice*. New York: McGraw-Hill, 1968; reprint ed., New York: Dell, 1999.

Dash, Leon. *Rosa Lee: A Mother and Her Family in Urban America*. New York: Plume, 1996.

Enos, Sandra. *Mothering from the Inside: Parenting in a Women's Prison*. Albany: State University of New York Press, 2001.

Erickson, Rosemary J., et al. *Paroled But Not Free*. New York: Human Sciences Press, 1973.

Fellner, Jamie. *Collateral Casualties: Children of Drug Offenders*. New York: Human Rights Watch, 2002.

———. *Cruel and Usual: Disproportionate Sentences for New York Drug Offenders*. New York: Human Rights Watch, 1997.

Freedman, Estelle B. *Their Sisters' Keepers: Women's Prison Reform in America, 1830–1930*. Ann Arbor: University of Michigan Press, 1981.

Gabel, Katherine, and Denise Johnston, M.D., eds. *Children of Incarcerated Parents*. New York: Lexington Books, 1995.

Grodin, Charles. *I Like It Better When You're Funny: Working in Television and Other Precarious Adventures*. New York: Random House, 2002.

Haney, Craig. "The Psychological Impact of Incarceration: Implications for Post-Prison Adjustment." Working paper for From Prison to Home conference. Washington, D.C.: U.S. Department of Health and Human Services and the Urban Institute, 2002.

Harris, Jean. *Stranger in Two Worlds*. New York: Macmillan, 1986.

———. *They Always Calls Us Ladies: Stories from Prison*. New York: Macmillan, 1988.

Irwin, John. *The Felon*. Englewood Cliffs, NJ: Prentice-Hall, 1970; reprint ed., Berkeley: University of California Press, 1987.

Jackson, Michael B. *How to Do Good After Prison: A Handbook for the "Committed Man."* Willingboro, NJ: Joint FX Press, 2001.

Kramer, Michael, and Sam Roberts. *"I Never Wanted to Be Vice-President of Any-*

thing!" An Investigative Biography of Nelson Rockefeller. New York: Basic Books, 1976.

Lynch, James P. and William J. Sabol. _Prisoner Reentry in Perspective_. Washington, D.C.: Urban Institute, 2001.

Maruna, Shadd. _Making Good: How Ex-Convicts Reform and Rebuild Their Lives_. Washington, D.C.: American Psychological Association, 2001.

Massing, Michael. _The Fix_. New York: Simon and Schuster, 1998.

Mauer, Marc, and Meda Chesney-Lind, eds. _Invisible Punishment: The Collateral Consequences of Mass Imprisonment_. New York: New Press, 2002.

Mauer, Marc, and the Sentencing Project. _Race to Incarcerate_. New York: New Press, 1999.

McCleary, Richard. _Dangerous Men: The Sociology of Parole_. 2nd ed. Albany, NY: Harrow and Heston, 1992.

Moore, Y. Blak. _Triple Take_. New York: Villard, 2003.

Musto, David F. _The American Disease: Origins of Narcotic Control_. 3rd ed. New York: Oxford University Press, 1999.

Nelson, Marta, Perry Deess, and Charlotte Allen. _The First Month Out: Post-Incarceration Experiences in New York City_. New York: Vera Institute of Justice, 1999.

New York. Department of Correctional Services. _Standards of Inmate Behavior, All Institutions (Inmate Rules, Penalties and Outline of Procedures)_. Albany: Department of Correctional Services, 1998.

New York. Department of Labor. _The Prime Objective: A Guide to Preparing the Job Seeking Ex-Offender_. Albany: Department of Labor, 2001.

New York. Division of Parole. _Manual for Parole Officers_. Albany: Division of Parole, 1953.

O'Brien, Patricia. _Making It in the "Free World": Women in Transition from Prison_. Albany: State University of New York Press, 2001.

Persico, Joseph E. _The Imperial Rockefeller: A Biography of Nelson A. Rockefeller_. New York: Simon and Schuster, 1982.

Petersilia, Joan. _When Prisoners Come Home: Parole and Prisoner Reentry_. New York: Oxford University Press, 2003.

Petersilia, Joan, and Jeremy Travis, eds. _From Prison to Society: Managing the Challenges of Prisoner Reentry, Crime & Delinquency_. Vol. 47. Thousand Oaks, CA: Sage Publications, 2001.

Porter, Bruce. _Blow: How a Small-Town Boy Made $100 Million with the Medellín Cocaine Cartel and Lost It All_. New York: HarperCollins, 1993; reprint ed., New York: St. Martins Press, 2001.

Rafter, Nicole Hahn. _Partial Justice: Women, Prisons, and Social Control_. 2nd ed. New Brunswick, NJ: Transaction Publishers, 1990.

Rideau Wilbert, and Ron Wikberg, eds. _Life Sentences: Rage and Survival Behind Bars_. New York: Times Books, 1992.

Rose, Dina R., and Todd R. Clear. "Incarceration, Reentry and Social Capital: Social Networks in the Balance." Working paper for From Prison to Home conference. Washington, D.C.: U.S. Department of Health and Human Services and the Urban Institute, 2002.

Ross, Jeffrey Ian, and Stephen C. Richards, eds. *Convict Criminology.* Belmont, CA: Wadsworth/Thomson Learning, 2003.

Rothman, David J. *Conscience and Convenience: The Asylum and Its Alternatives in Progressive America.* Boston: Little, Brown, 1980.

Schlosser, Eric. "The Prison-Industrial Complex." *The Atlantic Monthly,* December 1998.

Shapiro, Carol, and Meryl Schwartz. "Coming Home: Building on Family Connections." *Corrections Management Quarterly* (Summer 2001): 52–61.

Sheehan, Susan. *A Prison and a Prisoner.* Boston: Houghton-Mifflin, 1978.

Simon, Jonathan. *Poor Discipline: Parole and the Social Control of the Underclass, 1890–1990.* Chicago: University of Chicago Press, 1993.

Sull, Errol Craig. *Makin' It: A Parole & Probation Survival Guide.* Buffalo, NY: Aardvark Publishing, 1999.

Thomas, Piri. *Down These Mean Streets.* New York: Knopf, 1967; reprint ed., New York: Vintage, 1997.

Tonry, Michael, and Joan Petersilia, eds. *Prisons: Crime and Justice.* Vol. 26. Chicago: University of Chicago Press, 1999.

Travis, Jeremy, and Sarah Lawrence. *Beyond the Prison Gates: The State of Parole in America.* Washington, D.C.: Urban Institute, 2002.

Travis, Jeremy, Amy Solomon, and Michelle Waul. *From Prison to Home: The Dimensions and Consequences of Prisoner Reentry.* Washington, D.C.: Urban Institute, 2001.

Watterson, Kathryn. *Women in Prison: Inside the Concrete Womb.* Revised ed. Boston: Northeastern University Press, 1996.

Wengerd, Al. *Life After Prison.* Scottdale, PA: Herald Press, 1984.

Wynn, Jennifer. *Inside Rikers: Stories from the World's Largest Penal Colony.* New York: St. Martin's Press, 2001.

Zimmer, L. *Operation Pressure Point: The Disruption of the Street-Level Drug Trade on New York's Lower East Side.* New York: Center for Research in Crime and Justice at New York University School of Law, 1987.

ACKNOWLEDGMENTS

This book grew out of many years of reporting on the criminal justice system for *The Village Voice*. Editor-in-chief Don Forst played a crucial role by permitting me to spend nearly all of 2000 reporting on Elaine's daily life, by publishing a lengthy story about her first year out of prison, and then by granting me a generous leave of absence. Karen Cook, then executive editor, encouraged and skillfully edited all the stories that became the background material for this book. Without their support I could not have begun this book, much less finished it.

Many other current and former *Voice* employees offered encouragement and/or assistance over the years: David Schneiderman, Judy Miszner, Doug Simmons, Guy Trebay, Mark Schoofs, Alex Press, Ed Park, Lynn Yaeger, Meg Handler, Mike Tomasky, Lenora Todaro, Frank Ruscitti, Jessica Bellucci, Joseph Jesselli, Julie Lobbia, Nat Hentoff, Nita Rao, Barbara Cohen, and Adamma Ince. In particular, I am indebted to Wayne Barrett and Bill Bastone for their investigative reporting lessons, and to Tom Robbins for his guidance on how best to tackle the book's trickier reporting tasks.

Thank you to editors Colin Harrison, then of *Harper's*, and Paul Tough, of *The New York Times Magazine*, for assigning stories that enabled me to delve deeply into New York City's criminal justice system. I am also grateful to photographer Andrew Lichtenstein for teaching me a great deal about the prison system.

In reporting this book, I benefited from the help of two talented research assistants, Katie Worth and Solana Pyne, as well as a top-notch fact-checker,

Darren Reidy. Many friends read drafts of the book and offered smart criticisms: Andrew Goldberg, Katherine Eban Finkelstein, Motoko Rich, Julie Fraize, Karen Cook, Tom Robbins, and Jane Isay. Anthony C. Thompson and Scott Christianson also read the manuscript and provided crucial expert advice. Special thanks to Julie Fraize and Andrew Goldberg for help with setting up the book's website.

Thank you to my agent, David Black, for believing in this book from the moment he heard about it, and then aggressively championing it over the years. And thank you to my editor, Paul Elie, for his enthusiasm and his editing prowess. I owe him an enormous debt, as this book was his idea long before it was mine. Also, thanks to Carol Edwards for her expert copy editing.

Many friends offered much-needed encouragement: Annabel Hobley, Sue Johnson, Tanya Selvaratnam, Farai Chideya, Kimani Paul-Emile, Sontine Kalba, Elizabeth Allan, Lenora Todaro, Amy Tobey, and Greg Beals. I am indebted to the Wang family—Harvey, Sophia, and Sakira—for two-plus years of meals and morale boosts. Thank you to my own family for all their support: Betsy, Mike, Pete, Tobey, and Becky. And thanks to Dave Isay for his vigorous cheerleading down the homestretch.

My greatest debt, of course, is to all the Bartlett family members who shared their memories and insights: Michelle Marcus, Sabrina Bartlett, Donjuan Bartlett, Shyan Bartlett, Rebecca Bartlett, Nathan Brooks, Ronald Jones, Pastor Robert Paschall, Arletha Bogeé, Barbara Reed-Pearson, Sherry Renée Reed, Sonja Reed, Apache Paschall, Jamel Paschall, Satara Bartlett, and Danae Bartlett. And lastly, thank you to Elaine Bartlett for spending many hundreds of hours with me, for inviting me into her life, and for trusting me with her story.